Writing

and the

Holocaust

Writing

and the

Holocaust

Edited by Berel Lang

HM

HOLMES & MEIER New York London

Published in the United States of America 1988 by

Holmes & Meier Publishers, Inc.
30 Irving Place
New York, N.Y. 10003

Book Design by Dale Cotton

The paper used in this publication meets the requirements
of the American National Standard for Permanence of Paper
for printed Library Materials, Z39.48-1984.

Library of Congress Cataloging-in-Publication Data

Writing and the Holocaust.

    Includes index.
    1. Holocaust, Jewish (1939–1945)—Personal narratives
—History and criticism.   2. Holocaust, Jewish (1939–
1945)—Historiography.   3. Holocaust, Jewish (1939–1945),
in literature.   I. Lang, Berel.
D804.3.W75   1988   940.53'15'03924   88-11249
ISBN 0-8419-1184-3 (alk. paper)
ISBN 0-8419-1185-1 (alk. paper: pbk.)

Manufactured in the United States of America

Contents

PART II   *The Representation of Evil*

PART III   *Fiction as Truth*

Acknowledgments

The essays collected in this volume, with the exceptions noted below, were originally presented as papers at a conference, "Writing and the Holocaust," which was held at the State University of New York at Albany, April 5–7, 1987. The conference was organized and sponsored by the Center for the Humanities and the Office of General Studies at the State University of New York at Albany and by the New York State Writers Institute. The committee that planned the conference included Kathryn Gibson, Director of the Office for General Studies at SUNYA; Tom Smith, Assistant Professor of English at SUNYA and Associate Director of the New York State Writers Institute; Sarah Blacher Cohen, Professor of English at SUNYA; and Berel Lang, Professor of Philosophy and Humanistic Studies and Director of the Center for the Humanities at SUNYA. Ruth Ellenbogen, Jeanne Finley, Nancy Ross, and Nancy Warmzer helped greatly with the organizational work of the conference.

Support for the conference was generously provided by grants from the Lucius N. Littauer Foundation, Mr. Morris Masry, the New York State Writers Institute, the Office of the Vice-President for Research and Graduate Studies at SUNYA, and the New York State Legislature.

"Writing and the Holocaust," by Irving Howe, appeared in *The New Republic* (October 27, 1986) and is reprinted by permission of THE NEW REPUBLIC © 1986, The New Republic, Inc. "The Long Life of Meta-

ix

phor: An Approach to the 'Shoah,'" by George Steiner, appeared in *Encounter* (February 1987), © George Steiner, and is reprinted here by permission of the author. "Writing the Holocaust: Jabès and the Measure of History," by Berel Lang, appeared in Eric Gould, ed., *The Sin of the Book: Edmond Jabès*, published by the University of Nebraska Press, 1985, and is reprinted here by permission of the University of Nebraska Press. "Considering the Apocalypse," by Sidra DeKoven Ezrahi, is published here for the first time.

Writing

and the

Holocaust

PART · I

The Memory of History

Introduction

by Berel Lang

*I*t is almost a half-century since the beginning of the events collectively referred to now as the Holocaust. Writings *about* the Holocaust began to appear almost simultaneously with the occurrence of the events themselves, and these writings—if we include scholarly work (history, philosophy, literary studies, social science) as well as "imaginative" literature (poetry, drama, the novel)— now number in the tens of thousands. That number, moreover, has increased in the past decade more rapidly than before, and there is no reason to believe that this increase has yet reached a turning point.

In certain respects, little distinguishes this group of writings from others of the same period that have quite different subjects. Here, too, we find a variety of literary forms or genres meant for diverse audiences—from technical historical studies in scholarly journals to popular fiction and television adaptations that presuppose no special knowledge or even interest in the Holocaust. These writings, furthermore, cover the spectrum of moral and political commitment, and manifest no less wide a range in quality; they include work that is serious and honest but also writing that can only be described as exploitative and meretricious.

Notwithstanding these points of resemblance to writing on other topics, it is clear that the Holocaust is not a conventional or "normal" subject at all, that the evidence of its moral enormity could not fail to affect the act of writing and the process of its literary representation. The latter notion, in any event, constitutes the main premise on which the essays collected in this volume turn: that there is a significant relation between the moral implications of the Holocaust and the means

1

of its literary expression. The essays included here, diverse as they are in other ways, thus reflect a common set of questions: What constraints, whether in the use of fact or in the reach of the imagination, are imposed on authors or readers by the subject of the Holocaust? How does that subject shape the perspectives from which it is viewed—the stance, for example, of the "disinterested" scholar, or the assumption of aesthetic distance or "negative capability" in the poet or novelist? Is the enormity of the Holocaust at all capable of literary representation? And what would be the justification for attempting such representation even if it were possible? In his much-quoted statement condemning the "barbarism" of writing poetry after Auschwitz, Theodor Adorno suggests a larger boundary-question for *any* writing that takes the Holocaust as its subject: Placed in the balance with the artifice that inevitably enters the work of even the most scrupulous author, what warrant—moral or theoretical or aesthetic—is there for writing about the Holocaust at all?

This last question, however, is not beyond question itself; it is, in any event, anticipated by the authors included in the present volume who appear here not only as writing about Holocaust writing, but as having written, before that, about the Holocaust itself. Whatever they might concede to arguments against writing about the Holocaust, then, has evidently been outweighed for them by other evidence. It could well be objected, for example, that any blanket criticism of writing about the Holocaust will be tendentious, insofar as it presupposes a definition of the historical or moral uniqueness of the Holocaust when that definition itself remains very much at issue. This issue, in fact, as Saul Friedländer points out in his essay, is closely tied in certain "revisionist" accounts to the reconceptualization of roles within the Holocaust—to the extent that such accounts lead even to the renaming of its victims and its perpetrators. Indeed, more graphically than in the more usual views of the Holocaust, such revisionist accounts suggest a connection between the "facts of the matter" and the means of their written representation. This becomes clear, furthermore, even without reference to the most extreme versions in writings that deny that the Holocaust occurred at all; in them the means of writing are used to blot facts out of existence. (This position passes almost unmentioned in the essays here, presumably on the grounds that the view is either beyond argument or unlikely to have any general influence.)

A second objection directed in general against writings about the Holocaust has been that those writings often do little more than echo traditional artistic or critical or ethical themes; this dependence, it is objected, may obscure or diminish the moral significance of the Holocaust by generalizing, and thus moving away from, its *particular* character. But this variant formulation of the claim of uniqueness can, it seems, be addressed in much the same terms as the first one. It is obvious that certain questions with broader historical reference stand in the background of Holocaust writing. The moral consequences of artistic representation, the relationship between facts and values, the ethical responsibilities of artists and scholars to their subjects and to their audiences—these are issues with long histories that could not be avoided by writers addressing a topic as complex as the Holocaust. To admit this, however, hardly detracts from the *specific* representations in which those general themes appear. The former may in fact compel changes in the traditional concepts: if *any* literary or scholarly subject could challenge the role conventionally assumed by authors, it is the radical evil exemplified by, and then to be represented in, the events of the Holocaust. Even when such evil is viewed as not fully capable of representation (for Raul Hilberg as historian and for George Steiner as critic, this means that there seems to be no sufficient empirical explanation; for Aharon Appelfeld, it results in the novelistic representation of evil as an absence or privation), the general principles thus brought to bear do not diminish the force of the specific accounts they provide.

More generally still, it may be objected that to call attention to the *writing* in writing about the Holocaust must have the effect of distancing readers and writers from the subject of the Holocaust itself. Surely, this objection goes, what ought to be central are the issues raised by the events of the Holocaust, not the manners of its representation. But the most compelling response to this objection is the one required by Adorno's boundary-question, as it might doubt the adequacy of *all* writing about the Holocaust, history no less than poetry, philosophy as well as the novel. One could concede the possibility of this failure and *still* hold that such writing is justified—because of the menace of the alternative; that is, the silence into which the Holocaust would otherwise disappear. To avoid the latter, it could be argued, the risk of barbarism, or even worse, would be warranted. And analogously: as writing about the Holocaust, like all other writing, takes on the features of its writer's individual style, the reader, in order to gain access to what that writing is *about,* must be able to find a way through the one of these to the other. The configurations of literary means may in the end be less important than the subjects that are written "about"—and if this is true generally, it would hold with special force for the subject of the Holocaust. But without an understanding of the means by which a subject is "written," access to the subject itself is unavoidably impeded.

The questions underlying the essays of this volume thus point to a common assertion that writing which takes the Holocaust as its subject requires moral as well as aesthetic justification—more generally, that these two aspects of writing are closely related. To be sure, the thesis that literature has moral presuppositions and consequences is not startling. But moral accountability has rarely been pressed against the writer for the very *act* of writing—a condition that now comes to be added to the writer's responsibility for the effects of his writing on the lives of his audience and for respecting the integrity of his subject. Again, these demands on writing about the Holocaust reflect larger literary issues and broader aspects of the relation between moral and aesthetic judgment. But this fact does not diminish the significance of the subject itself. Quite the contrary: the importance of writing about the Holocaust for the understanding of writing *and* of the Holocaust would be further evidence, if any were required, of the extraordinary dimensions of that subject.

The common issues that thus figure in writing about the Holocaust are never far from the consciousness of the writers whose essays appear in this volume. So, for example, Saul Friedländer reflects on the tension between the "facts" of the Holocaust and the varieties of narrative form by which historians have represented those facts; those diverse representations suggest, by the different roles they assign to the principal characters of the Holocaust, the use of the devices of literary emplotment in history as well as in "imaginative" writing. Even historical facts that may seem to "speak for themselves," we understand here, will not do so unless the facts have first been "spoken." That certain historians or literary theorists have inferred from this conclusion a view of historiography as consisting of quasi-fictional narratives is not incompatible, in Friedländer's view, with the literalness of the facts of the Holocaust itself (although how to demonstrate this consistency remains an issue).

Or again, George Steiner, pressing the search for a means in language of adequately representing the Holocaust (and along the way disputing the adequacy of *that* term, which he would replace by the Hebrew "Shoah"), settles—improbably, it may seem—on German or at least the German of Paul Celan as such a means. In reaching this conclusion, Steiner also indicates a more inclusive standard by which representations of the Holocaust are to be judged: they have to account for that event in the context of Jewish history, if they are to account for the event itself.

The links among the essays assembled here are substantive as well as formal. (This obviously does not imply a consensus among the authors on any particular issue—a point demonstrated, for example, by the differences between Terrence Des Pres and Leslie Epstein on the status of "literary realism" in fictional writing about the Holocaust.) But various lines of emphasis distinguish the essays, and these are reflected in the divisions among the three sections of the present volume. The essays in Part I, "The Memory of History," bear on the question of how the past enters or shapes representations in the present; these essays reflect a common premise that historical discourse (in scholarship as well as in fiction), however intent it is on recapturing the past "truthfully," nonetheless imposes on the past conditions defined by the present. A problem for any writer who takes the past as a subject, then, is how to mediate between the often conflicting requirements of past fact and present understanding—and it is this issue that Raul Hilberg articulates in considering the limitation, for an historian of the Holocaust, that "I Was Not There." This limitation, Hilberg suggests, forces him (and historians generally) into the domain of the imagination, however deeply rooted their concern with the literal record. To be sure, such constraints apply not only to writers of the Holocaust: few historians write about events they have witnessed themselves (even if they were there, of course, they would not have been "everywhere" there). But this, too, it seems, adds weight to Hilberg's proposal of a role for the imagination in historical writing.

Lawrence Langer, in "Interpreting Survivor Testimony," which is based on a series of videotaped interviews with survivors of the Holocaust, argues for the distinctiveness of such oral accounts. These narratives are not, he suggests, preliminary to written history, but independent; they are, moreover, informative in ways that distinguish them from their corresponding written forms, such as memoirs or autobiographies. This difference, on Langer's view, is due to the unmediated character of oral narrative and the spontaneity in it of the narrative voice in which expression merges with memory itself. Such a claim may seem to be overstated (oral discourse, too, after all, depends on literary conventions). But even if one understood here only the more limited view that the structures of oral discourse *differ* from those of written accounts, the importance attached to first-person narratives would be justified on the basis of their unusual access to the events narrated and perhaps to the understanding of memory itself.

Ellen Fine's essay, "The Absent Memory: The Act of Writing in Post-Holocaust French Literature," describes the development of that literature in the hands of a number of authors who were born after the Holocaust and who thus *could* not remember it; these writers felt an obligation (morally, but also intellectually) to establish their *right* to address that event as a subject. The challenge to the imagination here—how to represent history truthfully in the absence of memory—results in a variety of responses that Fine details; all of them in common, however, were tested by the standard they set for themselves of historical and moral authenticity (with little distinction drawn between *these*).

In "Memory: The Problem of Imagining the Past," Lore Segal discusses a possibility related to Langer's position, but in terms that bear on memory as such, whether reported orally or as written. (We find here the echo of a question in recent literary theory: as between oral or written discourse, which is the *natural* medium of memory or expression?) In considering the origins of her novels in her own memory—the accrued impressions in the mind of a child in Vienna just before the Holocaust—Segal comes close to describing the transformations of items of memory as the basis of a general theory of fiction. Here, as often elsewhere, writing about the Holocaust discloses an unexpected foundation beneath familiar structures; Segal's account also underscores the difficulty of locating the point at which imaginative or fictional "memory" diverges from the "factual" images of history. For Segal, this difficulty is not accidental, since the difference between those two, she implies, is always indefinite.

Even events less complex than the Holocaust lead to widely different representations—and Saul Friedländer outlines a number of sharply divergent emplotments constructed in recent historiography from the facts of the Holocaust. In his response to Friedländer, Emmanuel Le Roy Ladurie places the events of the Holocaust in a context that reaches back to seventeenth-century France—and this, too, in Friedländer's terms, could be considered a narrative version within which the Holocaust is to be viewed. Certain contemporary historians have concluded from this conception of historiography that history *as such* is a form of narration, that there are no independent means of assessing alternative narratives. But neither Friedländer nor Ladurie accepts this conclusion, and the reasons for this dissent are evident in their discussions. The view of historical representation as an explicit "choice" among alternative emplotments entails a conception of the historian as himself situated outside history. For the historian of the Holocaust who recognizes that this is not an option but who finds nonetheless that alternative writings and readings of particular historical events are possible, there must nonetheless be a ground for the one narrative to which he commits himself. That alternative narratives are *possible* does not determine the historian's judgment for him; if the "choice" among those alternatives is not to be simply arbitrary, then, the facts that do not quite speak for themselves may still resist being "spoken for" by certain voices. Falsification, in other words, is also possible: the alternative would be to deny the historicity of any particular event—a challenge of extraordinary consequence where the Holocaust is concerned.

The essays in Part II, "The Representation of Evil," address the question of how evil can be conceptualized or, in the case of the artist, concretely embodied—one or the other of those issues faced by virtually everyone who writes about the Holocaust. In this connection, Kenneth Seeskin calls attention to the claim of an important philosophical tradition for the basic unintelligibility of evil, and to the implication of this view that evil can never be adequately described or represented. So, for example, since on Plato's account evil as an absence or privation is not "real" (and is never chosen for itself), there can be neither an adequate understanding nor representation of it; when Augustine or Kant posit a will to evil in order to show that evil *can* be chosen knowingly, moreover, they only defer the question of what it is that is posited. This general perplexity, Seeskin suggests, applies to attempts to understand the specific enormity of the Holocaust, attempts that invariably seem inadequate, underdetermined; the latter fact, too, in his view supports the conception of evil as unintelligible and thus as requiring, even in writing, a different, nontheoretical form of address to which he gives the title "practice."

Seeskin's conclusion does not imply that the Holocaust was *not* evil, although the objection might be made in any event that if philosophers (even including Plato) find evil inconceivable, the problem here is with philosophy: at least to this extent, the facts *do* speak for themselves. It should be noted, however, that the view described by Seeskin is by no means peculiar to philosophy. It figures also in historical reflection on the Holocaust (for example, in Hilberg's assessment that the Holocaust is historically incomprehensible) and in "imaginative" writing where the inability of the *imagination* to devise an adequate representation might be viewed as more telling still. Aharon Appelfeld, responding once in conversation to a comment on the obliqueness of his novels' representations of the horrors of the Holocaust, commented that "one does not look directly at the sun." This recommendation of indirectness is in part also the subject of Appelfeld's essay here, as it describes how the practice of writing and of the arts more generally revived "After the Holocaust"—mainly, as it happened, among the children-survivors for whom the "culture" of the Holocaust, which was the only culture they knew, served as an eerie but productive means. There is no sense in Appelfeld's account of this revival as redemptive. Indeed his description, heartening in itself, attests still more strongly to the harshness of the conditions which *required* that new beginning; certainly it is no less compelling in this representation than those accounts which depict the events of the Holocaust more directly.

A quite different aspect of the representation of evil motivates Philip Hallie's essay, "Writing about Ethical Ambivalence during the Holocaust." One consequence of the view of evil as unintelligible is that also the good becomes less comprehensible. (If it is impossible to will evil knowingly, how is it possible to will the good?) This problem, as Hallie encounters it in his study of Major Julius Schmahling—head of the German occupation forces in the Haute-Loire *and* protector of the Huguenot villagers of Le Chambon and of the Jews whom they sheltered—is in part psychological: how can one, whether as philosopher or Jew, write in defense of a man who, notwithstanding the one side of him that resisted, was nonetheless part of the structure responsible for the Holocaust? But a more basic issue goes beyond psychology, and this is the question of how to understand in *any* terms the decision of a conscience, made at great personal risk, to resist an engulfing evil. Schmahling's own rather embarrassed explanation ("What's right is obvious, obvious") seems to reiterate the question rather than to answer it. Yet not to be able to explain his decision affects our understanding not only of Schmahling's response, but also of the countless decisions of whether to resist or not that were forced on everyone involved in the Holocaust: on other Germans, on the "bystanders" of the Nazi genocide in other countries, and, of course, on the victims themselves. In his own conclusion, Hallie anticipates what he takes to be the likely uncertainty of all such explanations, citing a combination of "passion and compassion" that he finds the most plausible characterization of Schmahling himself.

In "Unwilled 'Chaos': In Poem We Trust," William Heyen points to a formal division in his own poetry that runs parallel to the moral ambivalence cited by Hallie—between those of his Holocaust poems which are willed and "controlled," and others which "rave or hallucinate . . . or speak in tongues." The latter, Heyen claims, come closer to reflecting the "opacity" of the Holocaust itself. And so a strange reverberation is set up for the poet: he finds himself obliged to resist the impulse to try to understand fully the working of a poem insofar as its *subject* first requires that limitation.

Sidra Ezrahi, in "Considering the Apocalypse," proposes that the issue of the representation of the Holocaust can be usefully formulated in terms of two opposed views of Jewish historiography and religious interpretation. In the anti-Apocalyptic view, catastrophe is seen as part of a recurrent pattern of "suffering and redemption" that, if it does not quite explain Jewish survival, provides a means of characterizing the history itself; the Apocalyptic view in which catastrophe is not only a possible but even a necessary and quite genuine *end* is linked in an opposing tradition to various historical expressions of Messianism. One way of integrating what has been written about the Holocaust into historiography more generally, then, is by judging it by this distinction—and indeed, Ezrahi finds that those writings tend to align themselves with one or the other of the alternatives.

The twofold challenge—of the moral intractability of the Holocaust and of the role it assumes in the overall structure of Jewish history—also, it seems, leads George Steiner to look for what can be made intelligible of the Holocaust in the German language itself. Even that possibility, however, is precarious. Since, on Steiner's view, all empirical explanations of the Holocaust have failed, it must be by way of "metaphoric constructs" that any more adequate explanation will be discovered. This is, we infer, also the status of Steiner's own view of the Shoah as the culmination of the long tradition of anti-Semitism and of the interpretation he attaches to *that*. On this view, the Jews were attacked by the Nazis not because they were "God killers," but—quite the contrary—because they were the "inventor[s] of God," persistently recalling God's existence when much of the world would prefer, to the extent now of committing genocide, to remain oblivious. The evil involved here is thus more radical than it would be it if were "only" deliberate: it is, beyond that, a commitment.

The persona of an author is never far removed from his work, and nowhere is the moral presence of the author more insistently asserted than in the "imaginative" writing that takes the Holocaust as its subject. This is due, it seems, to a constraint on such writing even beyond those which affect writing about the Holocaust in general. Writers of fiction about the Holocaust almost without exception give evidence of being apprehensive that their turn to the imagination seem to cast doubt on the facts or "reality" of the Holocaust; for many writers, even the possibility of this interpretation exerts a continuing pressure. Some such explanation, at any rate, seems necessary to explain two distinctive features of Holocaust fiction: the frequent attempts to revise traditional literary forms and genre—as if acceptance of traditional conventions would deny the unusual nature of the Holocaust as a literary subject— and the recurrence, accompanying such "fictions," of statements attesting to an essential truthfulness in them. The numerous "Introductions" to works of Holocaust fiction that emphasize its verisimilitude (for example, in Jean-François Steiner's *Treblinka* or Thomas Keneally's *Schindler's List*); the embedding in such fiction of historical documentation (as in D. M. Thomas's *The White Hotel*)—such devices suggest that historical discourse is viewed even by writers of the *imaginative* literature of the Holocaust as a condition to which they aspire.

The essays in Part III, "Fiction as Truth," call attention to a number of works and writers that engage the latter theme. Thus, Irving Howe, in his conspectus of imaginative writing about the Holocaust, identifies in that writing a range of literary representation that extends from the diary written within the events themselves—and which is thus quite literally "true" or self-verifying—to the representations of surrealism or of the hallucinatory (as in the work of Piotr Rawicz) that move as far as imagination can from immediate experience. Howe suggests that, beyond the differences between these extremes, they are bound together by the intent to represent the events of the Holocaust at once imaginatively and truthfully—a joining of often divergent impulses that results in an unusual assembly of literary means.

The essays that follow Howe's in Part III discuss those means as they appear in a number of specific works and writers. So James Young examines the unusual relation between D. M. Thomas's *The White Hotel* and its documentary base in Anatoly Kuznetsov's *Babi Yar.* (That the latter is a novel which draws on still other documentation complicates, but does not alter, the emphasis in both works on the value of authenticity.) Terrence Des Pres, reiterating the need for a justification of Holocaust writing, poses an unusual question about that justification in "Holocaust *Laughter?*"—the possibility in such writing of comic forms. In Tadeusz Borowski's *This Way for the Gas, Ladies and Gentlemen,* Leslie Epstein's *King of the Jews,* and Art Spiegelman's *Maus,* Des Pres finds a variety of comic motivation that, in his view, far from inhibiting recognition of the enormity of the Holocaust, affords both writer and reader a powerful means of indictment. The comic fosters the "liberty to take heart" against the more compliant terms of the Holocaust's "normal" appearance in other representations.

Whether such moral resistance is, as Des Pres claims, a more likely consequence of the comic than of other literary modes is no doubt open to argument; in any event, the remaining essays in this section point to other literary means to which the same intention is ascribed. Repeatedly, we find reference here to the goal of truthfulness on the part of the writer—and recognition of the constant challenge of this ideal to both the writer's integrity and his craft. Again, Howard Needler finds in the Hebrew of K. Tsetnik's novels the occasion of an unusual literary genre shaped by the events of the Holocaust. Not only does K. Tsetnik's use of Hebrew constantly disclose traditional echoes (for example, the evocation of the Haggadah in the death camp's "spires of smoke") ("timrot ashan"), but his books, viewed together, comprise a "revisionist scripture"—a grotesque reversal of the biblical source. In the Holocaust, it is darkness that is created rather than light, the deformation of man rather than his appearance in the "image of God"—this allegorical pattern itself being presented by K. Tsetnik as historical narrative. Berel Lang cites Edmond Jabès's *The Book of Questions* as an example of the break initiated in much Holocaust writing from conventional literary forms. Jabès, he suggests, attempts by techniques of textual dislocation to efface the role of the author—in effect, to represent the Holocaust as "writing itself." To the extent that Jabès succeeds in this, he would preempt criticism of the "imaginative" re-creation of the Holocaust—since it *would* then be the facts that were speaking for themselves.

Admittedly, it might be objected to this persistent emphasis on historical authenticity that the writers of fiction committed to that ideal could after all have turned—or at least *now* turn—to the writing of history: why not simply forgo the writing of fiction? In her comments in the "Roundtable Discussion," Cynthia Ozick expresses regret at not having done just this, and Leslie Epstein, in "Writing about the Holocaust," quotes an earlier statement of his own that points in the same direction. But both Ozick and Epstein move quickly to qualify these reservations, and in doing this, Epstein expresses a view that in some form seems to be a necessary premise for all imaginative writing about the Holocaust (in this sense, it serves also as a response to Adorno's objection). Imaginative literature, Epstein suggests, provides for the reader a means that is unavailable in historical or other discursive representation, no matter how faithful to the facts. That means, he argues, is the sense conveyed by the imagination of individual agency and intersubjectivity—a sense that enables the reader to associate himself with a past event (even one like the Holocaust) and to shape the emergence of that past in the consciousness of the present; the "facts" themselves, Epstein implies, could not provide this mediation, even if agreement could be reached about what they are. Such a claim, admittedly, would be a large one to make for writing of any sort. Quite aside from its particular defense of imaginative writing in respect to the Holocaust, however, it has the special value of showing why such a defense is needed: in writings about the Holocaust, not even their own possibility can be taken for granted.

It will be evident that a number of important questions relevant to the topic of "Writing and the Holocaust" are not addressed in the essays collected here, and certain of these ought at least to be mentioned.

Although the issue has received attention elsewhere (and by some of the authors included here), much remains to be said about the status of language in relation of the events of the Holocaust. In addition to the explicit codes and "language rules" stipulated for official use by the Nazis, symptomatic changes occur in colloquial German and in public and private writing immediately before and during the period of the Holocaust. Such writing is not exactly "about" the Holocaust, but it is nonetheless an expressive means—as are the views of the Holocaust evident in the writings of post-Holocaust German writers. The latter do not figure largely in the essays of the present volume, and although many other writers and works about the Holocaust are also omitted, the Holocaust as it appears in German literature obviously will have special pertinence to many of the questions that bear on writing about the Holocaust. The definition of authorial—and social—"point of view" is only the most immediate of the topics that would arise in this connection.

A second question that might be addressed on related grounds concerns the *history* of writing about the Holocaust. That there have been substantial shifts of form and perspective in this writing during the half-century of its history is evident. These shifts undoubtedly reflect corresponding changes in the identities and circumstances of the authors and of their reasons for writing—and also these correlations between history and the "institution" of writing warrant more attention than they have received. Then, too, the sheer number of writings about the Holocaust is a social "fact" within the more general process of the institutionalization of the Holocaust; both of these require understanding not only as part of contemporary social history, but as an indication of the workings of social memory more generally.

A third issue relevant to the present volume is the relation between writing about the Holocaust and other representational forms—for example, in film and painting as these have addressed the Holocaust. Film especially is closely related to the representations of writing, although with large enough differences to warrant consideration in its own right. Here again, it is clear that the general problems of meaning or truth in the visual arts (and in their relation to literature) have recurred in the history of aesthetics; but *also* again, this underscores rather than diminishes their relevance to the specific analysis of representations of the Holocaust. A version of this same issue concerns the relationship among the genres of *writing* about the Holocaust, since it is not self-evident that certain features are shared by all such forms (by historiography, for example, as well as by poetry). Such characteristics, accordingly, have to be demonstrated, and even beyond this, the differences among the genres of writing about a common subject would still remain to be explained. Thus, the question persists as to how a subject—and not least, *this* subject—affects the means of its representation.

Such issues are no less relevant to the topic of "Writing and the Holocaust" than the ones addressed in these pages, and although to acknowledge this hardly compensates for their omission, it adds their weight to the purpose of the volume as a whole. It has become increasingly evident that for anyone who reflects now on the events of the Holocaust, the principal access to the Holocaust is by way of the writings about it which are now available. (Strangely, but unavoidably, this has become true to some extent even for the survivors of the Holocaust.) As we add to this condition the truism that writing does not write itself, that it is never transparent or self-interpreting and thus that the medium of writing constantly obtrudes on its subject, the need to consider writing about the Holocaust *as writing* becomes clear. Without the understanding that such analysis may provide, we can hardly recognize what or how much we know of the Holocaust itself or even what we are entitled to imagine of it.

To the issues that bear in this way on the topic of "Writing and the Holocaust," one last consideration may be added—to the extent, that is, that an absence can be said to be "added." The writers whose work appears in this volume, and other authors who have written on the Holocaust, some referred to here, others not—these together have shaped a collective literary representation that, although obviously not redeeming the terrible events which are their subject, have nonetheless brought to those events an unusual power of human vision and understanding. Without these efforts (and as proof of this, to an extent even with them), the events of the Holocaust, their causes and means, would be inchoate and incomprehensible. It is thus impossible to deny that such writings have "succeeded"—the term itself is thankless in this context—in at least breaching the wall that otherwise separates the enormity of the Holocaust and the moral and intellectual understanding of the peoples among whom—and to whom—that enormity occurred.

Such writings, then, in history and critical theory, in poetry and the novel, have justly won the regard of their readers. But any such recognition would be incomplete if it did not also leave a place for another group of writings that does not appear among them *because* of the Holocaust. We do not know, of course, what writings there might now be before us—written from Vilna or Prague, from Warsaw or Vienna—if the Holocaust had not occurred. But we know enough, as we imagine reading those unwritten texts, to speculate about them—and to understand that they would also have been significant and life-giving. To be sure, if they existed, the work included in this volume would not—and that fact itself remains an aspect of the volume's content. It is no substitute, however, for those writings which are not present now, but should be, and which in this sense are also to be counted among the writings of the Holocaust—a larger instance of what Isaac Babel had earlier founded as the "genre of silence." Their absence remains in fact the most closely literal representation of the Holocaust.

1 · Raul Hilberg

I Was Not There

"*I*f you were not there, you cannot imagine what it was like." These words were said to me in Düsseldorf some years ago by a one-legged veteran of the German army who had been trapped in the Demyansk pocket on the Russian front at the end of 1941. The man had been wounded six times. One cannot deny that he had a valid point.

I recall another occasion when one of the earliest Holocaust conferences was held in San Jose, California. It was a gathering called on a grand scale with hundreds of guests. One visitor, an elderly person, perhaps nearing eighty years of age, sat there quietly for the three days. I wondered who he was. Since he had a name tag, and since there was also a book display, I could search for a book he might have written. I found one. It was an autobiographical work about the battle of Verdun, which had taken place in the First World War, and the book was titled *Holocaust*. It may not be said that he was not entitled to the use of this word.

Yet among man-made disasters, such as purges, massacres, and wars, the Holocaust is a novel event and a new marker in history. Contrast it for a minute with warfare. When a soldier speaks of chance, he is usually assessing the possibilities of being killed. A Holocaust survivor who refers to chance is talking about the good fortune of having been left alive. Nor do the comparative casualty rates constitute the only difference. The Holocaust is unique in structure. It is a process, wilfully shaped by perpetrators, suffered by victims, and observed by bystanders. Unlike a battle, which is the same or a similar experience for participants on both sides, the encounter with the Holocaust is one story coming from German bureaucrats, quite another from the Jewish victims, and still another, or others, from numerous, distinct onlookers.

Furthermore, there is no commonality in the form of these accounts. The Germans left a mass of records. The United States alone captured 40,000 linear feet of these documents, that is to say, folders in boxes lining that many feet of shelf. Included in this material are a few orders, some letters, and a great many reports, including official war diaries and the like. Voluminous as these reports may be, they are often extraordinarily terse in content. Thus a single line in a report of the local military headquarters in the Black Sea port of Mariupol, dated October 29, 1941, stated: "8,000 Jews were executed by the Security Service."

In German documents one may discover the Holocaust in all of its bureaucratic complexity, but records of this kind tend to deal with people in the aggregate. They are filled with references to jurisdictions, procedures, regulations, numbers, places, and dates. Yet if we look for personal accounts of the perpetrators, we will find ourselves largely stymied. The Germans left few private diaries, and their memoirs for the most part are heavily self-censored.

The situation is the reverse in the case of Jewish sources. Jewish documents, in the main the correspondence of Jewish councils, are relatively sparse in number. On the other hand, there are multitudinous statements of survivors recording their recollections. Sometime during the second half of the late 1950s, the historian and bibliographer Philip Friedman, a survivor himself, told me that survivors' accounts were getting out of hand, that they were too numerous to list. At last count there were 18,000. That was thirty years ago.

A more pointed statement about survivors' testimonies came from Theodore Ziolkowski of Princeton University, writing in the Fall 1979 issue of the *Sewanee Review.* Ziolkowski said that these accounts all resembled one another. Whereas each survivor may have thought that he had a special tale to tell, a reader stepping back to examine the whole lot would conclude that all these people were speaking in unison about virtually identical experiences: what it was like during the last moments of peace, what happened when the Nazis came, how rapidly the Jewish community was engulfed, how family and friends vanished in gas chambers, and how finally the survivor, all alone, was liberated just in time to start a new life.

There *is* a sameness in these statements, not only in terms of what is written but also in regard to what is left out. Survivors by and large are special kinds of people who share personality characteristics, an outlook on life, and a way of describing the world. If we want something else from them—for instance the "before" and "after" enclosing the Holocaust years, or the nature of their crucial relations with parents or others who were very close to them—then we would have to reduce the tens of thousands of their accounts to a handful. Let me tell you about one of these more unusual testimonies.

The story, which I discovered during a late evening hour in March 1987 while watching television in Germany, begins with a "Catholic author" who died several decades ago and who was almost forgotten after her death, Elisabeth Langgässer. I must confess that this opening on the show almost made me turn the dial, but soon I learned that although Elizabeth's mother was a Catholic, her father had been a Jew who converted to Catholicism. In other words, this author was "non-Aryan." During her youth, Elisabeth became a school teacher and writer. She had an affair with a Jew whom she could not marry, because he was already married and the father of children. In 1929, Elisabeth had a daughter with this man and she named the girl Cordelia. By 1933, Elisabeth was isolated. Unable to teach school after she had born a child out of wedlock, unable to publish anything because she was non-Aryan, she married a German. Cordelia grew up in this household and long afterward, in 1984, she wrote her own story in Swedish, translated into German two years later, and published in Munich as a novel, *Gebranntes Kind sucht das Feuer* (Burned Child Seeks the Fire). By the time I bought the book, a day after the television broadcast, it had gone through eight printings.

Cordelia is Cordelia Edvardson now, but she does not live in Sweden. Her childhood in Germany was peaceful enough—she remembers having attended an SS wedding as a nine-year-old and having danced with an SS officer who was unaware of her background. Gradually, however, the situation became more ominous. In September 1941 the Jewish Star was introduced and before long the first transports moved to the East. Cordelia's mother was protected by virtue of having been half-German, Catholic, and married to a German, but Cordelia herself, three-quarters Jewish by descent, was considered a Jewish person under the Nuremberg law, without regard to her adherence to a Christian religion. The frantic mother attempted to arrange a marriage with a Spanish officer who had volunteered to serve on the Russian front, but Cordelia was too young. She then attempted to place her with an older Spanish couple for adoption, so that the youngster might have the protection of the Spanish flag. The strategem was discovered by the Gestapo, which confronted not the mother but the daughter with the following proposition: first, that evading the anti-Jewish decrees was a crime for which the mother might be sent to a concentration camp, but second, that if Cordelia signed a piece of paper accepting her status under German law, her mother would be excused. Cordelia recoiled, then signed.

The daughter had protected her mother and now she was unprotected herself. She was dropped from her Catholic club, the motto of which was "One for all and all for one." Adopted by a Jew who was deported, she was lodged in Berlin's Jewish hospital for a while. Then she was sent to Theresienstadt, a ghetto in Czechoslovakia, from which most inmates were deported to Auschwitz. Cordelia herself was sent on to this camp. She was number A 3709 there. Since she was young and alert, she had a chance to survive. At the end of the war, the emaciated girl was brought to Sweden for recovery. Her mother wanted to know all about Auschwitz so she could write a novel about it. Cordelia stayed in Sweden, married there, and had a Christian family of her own. During the October War of 1973, she rebelled. Drawn to Israel, she dropped her Catholicism and stayed in Jerusalem, while her daughter, in Germany, went on to edit Elizabeth's manuscripts.

The survivor knows isolation. Survival is a solitary experience in any case, but Cordelia was doubly alone because she had suffered a Jewish fate as a Christian. She did not know her Jewish father and she could not go back to her half-Jewish Catholic mother. She was becoming middle-aged before she liberated herself to settle in Israel. At long last, she stands before us, not with a fragment of her life, but with her entire exceptional existence and that of her mother.

These then are our primary sources. There is incompleteness in them, and taking them as a whole, there are imbalances within imbalances. Nor can this state of affairs be corrected. Even if we keep searching for more documents in archives—and we will—or generate more testimony in oral history projects—and we do—the resulting picture will surely be more detailed, but it will not contain a sharply new perspective.

And that is only half of the problem, because the question is not confined to *what* we should describe; it is also a matter of *how* we should write. Are there any rules? Friends of mine who write novels tell me that there are no commandments to the creator of imaginative liter- ature, that the imagination cannot be hemmed in, that the page facing the writer is as blank as the canvas of the artist. Yet one hears about rules governing the exploration of *this* subject almost all of the time. We may label them political or even religious, but these concerns are secondary or subsidiary when the main issue is art. Once we speak of writing as an art form, we raise the question whether Holocaust writing is fraught with risks not encountered in the treatment of other topics. To be sure, the Holocaust has caught us unprepared. Its un- precedentedness and, above all, unexpectedness, necessitates the use of words or materials that were never designed for depictions of what happened here. This is a problem that affects everyone, including those who had seen these occurrences first-hand.

Let me cite two examples from the plastic arts. I recall visiting Auschwitz and Treblinka in 1979. The trip was organized by President Carter's Commission on the Holocaust and our purpose in traveling to these sites was a hope of finding some guidance in the planning of our own Holocaust museum in Washington. Treblinka, the death camp, does not exist anymore. It was torn down by the Germans, and after the war Polish sculptors created a stark symbolic camp of stone in its place. When we went on to Israel, our chairman, Elie Wiesel, said something startling. Everywhere we had gone, he said, the places we had seen were beautiful. Indeed, Treblinka, where bodies were once lying around unburied and clothes were heaped high, is now a serene memo- rial.

Another story, told by the late poet and survivor, Abba Kovner of Israel, also refers to Treblinka. In a kibbutz near Haifa there is a scale model of the camp, built by one of the few Treblinka survivors who happened to have been a carpenter. When the model was finished, its maker called in Kovner for an opinion. Something was missing, said Kovner. But what, asked the survivor. After all, the fence was in place, and so were the reception barracks, the S-shaped curve to the gas chambers, and the gas-building itself. What could have been missing? And Kovner replied: the horror was missing.

I am told that when the memorial authority Yad Vashem was founded in Israel during the early 1950s, it was imbued with a philosophy that there should not be analytical writing about the Holocaust. The activities of Yad Vashem staff were to be concentrated on collecting the data: the ingathering of the documents. Soon enough this self-confining impulse vanished, but that it should have existed in the first place is not without significance.

Among the early researchers were the editors and compilers, notably H. C. Adler, who worked on Theresienstadt, and Lucjan Dobroszycki, the elegantly sophisticated specialist on Lodz. Both Adler and Dobroszycki made extensive use of texts, replicating documents with brief explanations that did not obliterate the records in their pristine form.

The step beyond compilation is reportage, a kind of writing that hews close to the primary sources to portray an event, but which submerges these sources in the story that is told. Some of these works are biographical. John K. Dickerson interviewed 172 persons to write a pathbreaking book about an obscure Jewish victim, *German and Jew* (Chicago, 1967). Gitta Sereny talked to witnesses on three continents for her study of Treblinka commander Franz Stangl, *Into That Darkness* (New York, 1974). Reportage are also those books, based partially or significantly on comments solicited by the author from participants, and describing what happened to an entire community, such as Robert Katz's work on the first transport from Rome, *Black Sabbath* (New York, 1969).

The authors of such works espouse actuality, but that is not to say that they have replicated it. They may have dipped into document collections that, despite their size, are incomplete, and they may have seen something relevant in the material, overlooking or discarding the rest. If they were going to rely on oral testimony, they could not—to borrow a phrase from Pablo Boder—interview the dead. Even among the living, they may have engaged in—if one may use the term—a selection. Claude Lanzmann's massive film *Shoah* (Paris, 1985) encompasses the testimony of perpetrators, victims, and bystanders. It includes Germany, Corfu, Auschwitz, Treblinka, Sobibor, Chelmno, and it is 9½ hours long. Yet in its raw, unedited state, questions and answers take up something like 350 hours.

How much more removed from the actuality of reportage are those works whose authors have introduced a theory or theme or just a visible thought to which the evidence has been subordinated? These recreators of the Holocaust, be they historians, sculptors, architects, designers, novelists, playwrights, or poets, are molding something new. They may be shrewd, insightful, or masterful, but they take a larger risk, and all the more so, if they take poetic license to subtract something from the crude reality for the sake of a heightened effect.

It is at this point that we must become specific about rules. One of them is, paradoxically, silence. Of course, there cannot be silence without speech. Silence can only be introduced between words, sometimes with words. We become aware of silence in Lanzmann's *Shoah*. There is a long painful lapse when Lanzmann interviews the barber Abraham Bomba who is admonished to speak of the days when he had to practice his craft in Treblinka on Jewish women about to be gassed. There is a scene with the Polish station master Jan Piwonski at Sobibor who explains that after the first trainload was delivered to the death camp, it was the silence that alerted him to something ominous. And at the end of the film, a veteran of the Warsaw ghetto battle, Simha Rottem, tells Lanzmann how he returned to the rubble immediately after the fighting. In the dark night Rottem heard the voice of a woman but could not find her. He was all alone then and thought of himself as the last Jew.

Another rule is aimed at a kind of minimalism. Elie Wiesel once said about the museum to be built in Washington that it must be spare like a cathedral. Minimalism is not to be confused with length or size. It is the art of using a minimum of words to say the maximum. Wiesel himself is a practiced minimalist. Few readers are familiar with his first book in its first version, published in Yiddish in Argentina under the accusatory title *And the World was Silent*. Everyone knows the condensation of this work in French, or in the English translation from the French with the brief title *Night* (New York, 1960). Wiesel made his work spare. Sometimes he speaks elliptically in order to voice ultimate thoughts. A half-crazed woman spots a flame as the cattle car enters Auschwitz, but no one else can see the fire. Describing what had happened in the camp, he draws his famous apotheosis of a young boy being hanged, next to or flanked by two hanging adults. Where is God? asks one voice. It is the boy, answers another.

If it is a novel, it is not about Auschwitz, says Wiesel, and if it is about Auschwitz, it is not a novel. The statement is not an observation, but a law. It prohibits trivialization, above all, the deliberate bending of known facts to cajole the reader. In regard to Holocaust literature, we often hear the word "genuine." Perhaps we should add the obvious conclusion that the opposite of genuine is "forgery."

Examples of counterfactuality in Holocaust novels and plays are legion. It may, therefore, suffice to cite the most extreme illustration, Rolf Hochhuth's play, *The Deputy* (New York, 1963). Hochhuth, a Protestant German writer, condemns a Pope and praises a Protestant SS-officer, Kurt Gerstein. The names in the play are real, but many invented words are put into their mouths, and situations are created that did not occur and could not have occurred. Not mentioned by Hochhuth is the sheer fact that as late as 1944 Gerstein delivered gas to Auschwitz.

The rules, whatever their contents, have evolved with the literature, sometimes *after* offending literary works appeared, but forty years ago, when I began my work, I was not aware of any restrictions save those that I imposed on myself. As far as I knew, I was the only one addressing this subject analytically, at least the only one dealing with it as a whole. In my quest, I also *felt* alone, a reaction faintly similar to that of survivors whose preoccupation with their experiences was not welcomed or understood. I worked at first on the dimly lit fourteenth floor of the Columbia University Library, where I read the transcript of a trial, *U.S.* vs. *Altstötter.* It was one of the so-called Nuremberg subsequent trials, and the defendants, just below the uppermost tier, had been officials in the German Justice Ministry or they had been judges themselves. As I paged through this material day after day, I hardly grasped what I was reading. At one point I saw references to a mysterious "Night and Fog" decree, and it took me some time to discover that this measure, imposed on the occupied Western countries in December 1941, provided for the arrest of suspected members of the resistance, who were to disappear in a concentration camp as if in night and fog. Some of the defendants were tried for a trial they had held in which the crime of the Jewish victim had been "race pollution," and in which the Jew, an older man who had been a leader of the Jewish Community of Nuremberg, had been condemned to death for allegedly touching a young German woman who had been his ward.

I sat there all by myself with this eery transcript. One day, a young friend of mine who specialized in political theory and German affairs, dropped in. I said to him that the case I was reading was so different from anything I had ever come across, that so much was reflected there from the Nazi depths, that I should really write a play about the Altstötter trial. Of course, I dismissed the thought as soon as I had uttered it. Many years later I saw a film. As I watched the first few reels it was immediately evident to me that someone had examined the case and written a screenplay based on the testimony. The writer's name was Abby Mann and the film, made by Stanley Kramer, was *Judgment at Nuremberg* (1961).

You all remember Adorno's dictum that it is barbaric to write poetry after Auschwitz. I am no poet, but the thought occurred to me that if the statement is true, then is it not equally barbaric to write footnotes after Auschwitz? I have had to reconstruct the process of destruction in my mind, combining the documents into paragraphs, the paragraphs into chapters, the chapters into a book. I always considered that I stood on solid ground; I had no anxieties about artistic failure. Now I have been told that I have indeed succeeded. And that *is* a cause for some worry, for we historians usurp history precisely when we are successful in our work, and that is to say that nowadays some people might read what I have written in the mistaken belief that here, on my printed pages, they will find the true ultimate Holocaust as it really happened.

2 · *Lawrence Langer*

Interpreting Survivor Testimony

To whom shall we entrust the custody of the public memory of the Holocaust? To the historian? To the survivor? To the critic? To the poet, novelist, dramatist? All of them re-create the details and images of the event through written texts, and in so doing remind us that we are dealing with *represented* rather than unmediated reality. For the critic and imaginative writer, this is obvious; for the historian and survivor, perhaps less so. My concern here is with the survivor account, which in the very process of forming a narrative by describing events with words, adopts a procedure that makes it impossible to avoid some kind of teleology, a view of experience invested with meaning and purpose. Indeed, as we shall see, some of the most self-conscious survivor accounts include a commentary on this process as part of the substance of their narrative. Some years ago, in the preface to *Versions of Survival*, I wrote that an "axiom of the narrative mode, from which survivor memoirs are not exempt, is that all telling modifies what is being told."[1] This led me to an inquiry into whether an unmediated text about the Holocaust experience is ever achievable. And this in turn roused my curiosity about the nature of the difference between written memoirs and oral testimony, particularly videotaped testimony, which in addition to language includes physical gesture, a kind of eloquent silence that is impossible to render on the printed page, and above all a freedom from the heritage of literary form and literary precedent to which anyone who attempts a written narrative is indebted.

The content of a written survivor memoir may be more harrowing and more gruesome than most autobiographies, but such a memoir still abides (some more consciously than others) by certain literary conventions: chronology, description, characterization, dialogue, and above all, perhaps, the invention of a "narrative voice" to impose on apparently chaotic events a perceived sequence, *whether or not that sequence was perceived in an identical way* during the period that is being rescued from oblivion by memory and its companion, language. The most persuasive example of this dilemma that I know comes from Charlotte Delbo's Auschwitz memoir, *None of Us Will Return:*

> I stand in the midst of my comrades and I think that if I return one day and want to explain this inexplicable thing, I will say: "I used to say to myself: you must stand, you must stand for the entire roll call. You must stand again today. It is because you will have stood again today that you will return, if you do return one day." And this will be false. I did not say anything to myself. I did not think anything. The will to resist no doubt lay in a much deeper and more secret mechanism which has since broken; I shall never know.[2]

The teleological imagination of the present narrative voice emerges in the conclusion that "it is because you will have stood again today that you will return," while the voice of the skeptical commentator exposes the limitations of trying to clarify *now* what was shadowy *then*. Of course, *both* voices belong to Charlotte Delbo, who impersonates herself as a split observer in search of a point of view, simultaneously looking ahead from Auschwitz (as a victim) to time future when she will try to represent the truth of her ordeal ("je dirai"), and looking backward from the present (as a writer) in an attempt to re-create a moment that has been victimized by time ("je me disais"). Every survivor who writes about his or her experience, though few are as sophisticated as Delbo, adopts some such strategy to provide access for the reader's imagination into that distant world. Delbo herself elucidated the paradox when she said in commenting on her work, "Today, I am no longer sure that what I have written is true, but I am sure that it happened" ("Aujourd'hui, je ne suis pas sûre que ce que j'ai écrit soit vrai. Je suis sûre que c'est véridique").[3] In distinguishing between "vrai" and "véridique," Delbo illuminates the difference between the abstractness of truth and the concreteness of experience. She also exposes the rift that separates words from the events they seek to animate.

The organic metaphor, with its evolutionary corollary, which dominated much of nineteenth-century thought, bequeathed us a vocabulary of purpose, and a mental stance to accompany it, that infiltrates survivor literature with perplexing results. Such infiltration reminds us that even memoirs ostensibly concerned with nothing more ambitious than recording horrible facts cannot escape from traditional literary associations. Some draw consciously on such associations in order to impose a layer of continuity over the discontinuous interval of the death-camp universe; others exploit the literary use of language to clarify and emphasize the permanence of the discontinuity. For example, when the young Eliezer, in Wiesel's *Night*, protests, "I did not deny God's existence but I doubted His absolute justice,"[4] the words may be his at that moment, but the voice and the idea belong to Ivan Karamazov, who exclaims to his brother Alyosha, "It's not that I don't accept God, you must understand, it's the world created by Him I don't and cannot accept." The question of Ivan's sincerity is not relevant here; but it is worth mentioning that the narrator of Wiesel's second novel, *The Accident*, is struck by an automobile while on his way to see the movie *The Brothers Karamazov*. The uniqueness of Auschwitz is thus briefly qualified by a literary precedent.

Dostoevsky intrudes on another account of Auschwitz, Victor Frankl's *Man's Search for Meaning* (perhaps more widely read than any other book on the concentration camp experience). Indeed, Frankl fills his volume with a system of allusion and analogy, chiefly to nineteenth-century figures, in a way that provides a literary subtext for the naked events he purports to describe. It is as if Frankl approached the crumbling edifice of twentieth-century humanism in Auschwitz armed with intellectual props from an earlier era, determined to shore up the ruins and reassure his readers that in fact there has been no irreparable damage to the architecture of thought about the human spirit from Spinoza and Lessing to Nietzsche and Rilke, and up to the present. Frankl cites all of these, in addition to Dostoevsky, Tolstoy, Schopenhauer, Bismarck, and Thomas Mann (together with Ecclesiastes and the Gospel of John). And they *do* reassure. It is comforting to hear from Frankl that Dostoevsky once said, "There is only one thing that I dread: not to be worthy of my sufferings." It is even more consoling to hear Nietzsche's aphorism: "Was mich nicht umbringt, macht mich stärker" ("That which does not kill me, makes me stronger").[5] But such a system of allusion and analogy causes the experience of Auschwitz to be filtered through the purifying vocabulary of an earlier time; the wary reader, though perhaps comforted and consoled by such a system, will understand that verbal assertion has been imposed on a chaotic reality in order to weld an apparently broken connection between Auschwitz and the literary-philosophical traditions that nurtured Frankl's vision.

Locked in the middle of Primo Levi's *Survival in Auschwitz* is a brief chapter called "The Canto of Ulysses," in which Levi accompanies an inmate named Jean on the daily ritual known as *Essenholen* or *chercher la soupe*. Jean is multilingual, showing equal facility in French and German, a facility he demonstrates by alluding to an SS *Blockführer* as *sale brûte* or *ein ganz gemeiner Hund*. One of Levi's subtexts here is that language in Auschwitz not only sometimes determines survival (since *not* understanding an order has led to the gas chamber), but that words interpreted through what he calls free-world associations lead to a misconstrual of the Auschwitz experience. Levi recites from Dante's *Inferno* for Jean, then slowly tries to offer a rendering in French. Can it be coincidence that in the expression "Then of that ancient fire" Levi has difficulty finding an appropriate translation for the Italian *antica*? What indeed do "ancient fires" have to do with the flames in whose proximity Levi carries on his daily tasks in Auschwitz? How, after Auschwitz, shall we connect the "ancient" with the "new" that happened there? No wonder Levi's memory stumbles, suffering, as he says, lacunae. But it is not Auschwitz that he is forgetting; it is literature, Dante, poetry, the *Commedia*. These have been replaced by an historical event that the traditional term "tragedy" will never adequately describe. Levi then quotes lines from Dante that some have taken as an affirmation of hope in the desert of the death camp:

> Think of your breed; for brutish ignorance
> Your mettle was not made; you were made men,
> To follow after knowledge and excellence.

Or, more literally:

> Take thought of the seed from which you spring.
> You were not born to live as brutes,
> But to follow virtue and knowledge.

But I think the irony of this passage, whose content contrasts so visibly with the setting and the scene, is unavoidable. For a moment, both Levi and Jean forget who and where they are. And this is precisely the point: when literary form, literary allusion, literary style intrude on the survivor account, we forget where we are and imagine deceptive continuities. It is a dramatic interval in Levi's own text, as Dante's lines seize him with a kind of fervor and transform him for an instant into the literary reality of the poem. He becomes, for only a few seconds, a Viktor Frankl, seeing in Dante, as he admits, "in a flash of intuition, perhaps the reason for our fate, for our being here today. . . ."[6]

Among the babel of tongues that infiltrates Auschwitz is the literary voice, but it fades from the text here, never to reappear. Levi's brief parable has dramatized its seductive powers, for anyone seeking a form and a language for recording the Auschwitz experience. But when we return from Dante's world to Auschwitz, we learn that the babel of tongues is more concerned here with eating than with speaking: the question behind *Essenholen* or *chercher la soupe* is, "What's *in* it?" (not the language, but the *soup*), and Levi's multilingual answer rudely replaces Dante's definition of man as an adventurous spirit subject to God's will with the equivalent of Elie Wiesel's definition of man in Auschwitz as a "starved stomach." The verbal repast for today, according to Levi's menu of words, feeds the body, not the literary imagination: *Kraut und Rüben, choux et navets, kaposzta es repak*—cabbage and turnips. Four versions of survival, without literary echo: language as the thing itself. The counterpoint between the literary and the historical realities continues to chapter's end, which quotes the final line from "The Canto of Ulysses": "And over our head the hollow seas closed up"[7] (literally, "Until the sea closed over us again"). Ulysses' fate is sealed, Dante tells us, "as pleased Another"—that is, by the will of God. But this is hardly a gloss on man's fate in Auschwitz. The Inferno is followed by a Purgatorio, as we know, and a Paradiso. The *Commedia* records a journey of the human spirit to a divinely conceived, if not predetermined, goal. The chapter following "The Canto of Ulysses" in Levi begins, "Throughout the spring, convoys arrived from Hungary," dismissing the literary subtext and reasserting the primacy of the unwilled voyage to an unchosen destination.

The following excerpt from an oral survivor testimony also alludes to a boxcar journey, this time *from* Auschwitz, but it is totally devoid of literary context, imposing on us a vision of the reality it represents which is strictly controlled by the speaker's own limited perspective:

One morning, I think it was morning or early afternoon, we arrived. The train stopped for an hour; why, we don't know. And a friend of mine said, "Why don't you stand up?" There was just a little window, with bars. And I said, "I can't, I don't have enough energy to climb up." And she said, "I'm going to sit down and you're going to stand on my shoulders." And I did; and I looked out. And I saw Paradise! The sun was bright and vivid. There was cleanliness all over. It was a station somewhere in Germany. There were three or four people there. One woman had a child, nicely dressed up; the child was crying. People were people, not animals. And I thought: "Paradise must look like this!" I forgot already how normal people look like, how they act, how they speak, how they dress. I saw the sun in Auschwitz, I saw the sun come up, because we had to get up at four in the morning. But it was never beautiful to me. I never saw it shine. It was just the beginning of a horrible day. And in evening, the end—of what? But here there was life, and I had such yearning, I still feel it in my bones, I had such yearning to live, to run, to just run away and never come back—to run to the end where there is no way back. And I told the girls, I said "Girls, you have no idea how beautiful the sun is," and I saw a baby was crying and a woman was kissing that baby—is there such a thing as love?[8]

"Film," writes Carlos Fuentes, "invites us to exercise choice through sight in a world full of material objects. The way we see is the way we choose, and the way we choose is the way we are free."[9] But testimony is not "film," which is a cultural phenomenon from the normal world, exploiting, as Fuentes argues, a "repertory of possibilities" that in the scenario we have just heard shrinks and diminishes and finally vanishes. What I call the cattle-car point of view astounds the imagination because it inverts traditional expectations: everything Edith P. sees from her confined space mocks the impulse to choice and the will to freedom. "I had such yearning," she says, "to just run away and never come back"; but she knows, and her visual representation confirms this, that she draws such yearning from her repertory of *im*possibilities, facing not the quandary of freedom, of unlimited choice, but its opposite—the quandary of the Auschwitz inmate who was "free" to watch the sun rise every morning, but never to see it shine.

This narrative moment evokes for us the challenge of interpreting not only survivor testimony, but the Holocaust experience itself, dramatizing the audience dilemma as few other texts do. Imagine the scene in terms of a painter's vision: a station, the sun gleaming on the platform, and that archetypal human configuration, the mother and child, occupying the center of the canvas. Above the platform, however, hangs a mirror, and in it we see reflected (rendered faithfully by the artist) a boxcar resting on the tracks and, peering through a barred opening in an upper corner of the boxcar, a woman's face. She gazes at the woman on the platform—who gazes back. Or does she? And we gaze at both, searching for the "real meaning" at the heart of the visual representation, wondering which is the primary world, which the reflected one: the woman in the boxcar or the mother on the station. The one indeed faces a repertory of possibilities; the other, none. In exercising her "choice through sight," Edith P. reminds herself and us that she "cannot" do what she seems to be doing: *her* choice of sight is only an illusion, insofar as it confirms the constraints, not the flexibility, of her perspective.

Suppose we were to read Edith P.'s testimony in a printed text, instead of seeing it and hearing it from her own lips. I am convinced that the effect would be different, chiefly because the text would be different. Writing invites reflection, commentary, interpretation, by the author as well as the reader. Edith P.'s allusions to mother, child, sun, and love are unmediated by literary subtexts to enrich their resonance, and we are invited by her testimony to appreciate the poverty of such vocabulary when shorn of such associations. Oral testimony is distinguished by the absence of such literary mediation: it avoids the interference of art. (The mediating role of memory, unassisted by the structural aids of a written text, remains to be explored.) But the material and emotional substance that we traditionally identify with "sun," "love," "mother," and "child" have lost their contours. To ask "Is there such a thing as love?" questions the physical and the metaphysical basis of the universe we presume to know—and the one Edith P. knows she has lost.

Edith P. narrates a pause in her journey, an unfinished voyage that ends with the word but not the experience of liberation. Numerous survivors, perhaps a majority, refuse to conclude their narrative with an account of their liberation, although encouraged to do so by their interviewers. The narrators' imaginations are chained to memories that have little to do with sequence or chronology. Most written survivor narratives, on the other hand, end where they have been leading—the arrival of the Allies, and the corresponding "freedom" of the victims. Oral survivor testimony violates our own need for conclusions, and thereby imposes on us an angle of vision that wrenches us from the traditional assumptions that govern our responses to "normal" narrative. Written survivor texts run the risk of letting their "reality" be framed by cultural assumptions alien to the experience they are seeking to capture. For example, one of the most unusual perspectives we possess in a written survivor narrative is Filip Müller's *Eyewitness Auschwitz: Three Years in the Gas Chambers*. The title of the American edition itself invokes the importance of point of view. Yet even Müller's text cannot escape the temptations of teleology, or the patterns of self-conscious literary thought. Speaking of his fear as a member of a work detail engaged in piling corpses in a mass grave, Müller says: "I tried to recall exemplary men and women down the centuries who were put to death. I remembered that we must all die. Death, I told myself, was, after all, part of our lives and we would have to face it sooner or later."[10] With a verbal flourish, he seeks to transform individual doom in Auschwitz into an exemplary expression of universal history and human fate in time, thereby affirming a continuum that the death camp is determined to sever. We must establish the authenticity of the voice before we can respond to the reliability of the text.

Oral survivor narrative unfolds before our eyes and ears; we are present at the invention of what, when we speak of written texts, we call "style." What is style, as Jonathan Swift reminded us, but the search for proper words in proper places? The following excerpt invites us to the birth of a "style," but takes us back to the difficulty of conception, as the speaker struggles to develop an idiom consonant with her dark vision of a permanently divided existence that has nothing to do with the integrated strength implied in her interviewer's question:

INTERVIEWER: How do you get the strength? Look, you've been talking and you've been with it for the last two hours or so. Where is your strength? How did you get the strength then? How do you get the strength now? . . .

Mrs. W.: To function?. . .

INTERVIEWER: Well, it's not only . . . it's more than functioning.

Mrs. W.: To . . . well . . . I often think about it, of course, how there is a sort of division, a sort of schizophrenic division, you know, a compartmentalization of what happened, and it's kept tightly separated, and yet as I said, it isn't. There is this past of daily living that one has to attend to and adhere to, and family and children and their needs and everyday needs and work and so on, and that must not interfere, the other must not become so overwhelming that it will make so-called normal life unable to function. It's always there; it's more a view of the world, a total worldview . . . of extreme pessimism [*sudden sharp breath-intake by interviewer*] of sort of what feels . . . of really knowing the truth about people, human nature, about death, of really knowing the truth in a way that other people don't know it. And all of the truth is harsh and impossible to really accept, and yet you have to go on and function; so it's a complete lack of faith in human beings, in all areas you know, whether it's politics or whatever: you hear one thing and you believe something else. I mean you say, "Oh well, I know the truth." And . . .

INTERVIEWER [*interrupting*]: Mrs. W., you are one of the greatest optimists I've ever met.

MRS. W. [*laughing deferentially*]: How do you . . . how do you come to that conclusion [*smiling, but not retreating from her position*]?[11]

If we listen carefully, we hear how this interviewer's response is framed by the vocabulary of purpose I mentioned earlier, caught between assumptions about strength and optimism that determine our conception of the heroic spirit. Almost every interpretation of the Holocaust experience requires some acknowledgment of how "normal life" and "the other," as Mrs. W. refers to them, interact. The interview itself, or this moment in the narrative, is a dramatic reenactment of such interaction, as two verbal motifs and their accompanying points of view vie for priority. "A total worldview of extreme pessimism" encounters "you are one of the greatest optimists I've ever met," and the interview ends a few moments later in a stalemate, the two perspectives unreconciled. The credibility of the experience is not in question, at least not explicitly. But implicitly, how can we separate the challenge of representing it with an uncontaminated vocabulary from the authenticity of the narration? The audience's resistant imagination is at odds with the receptivity demanded by the evolving text.

Readers do not talk back to a written text, whatever they may be thinking or feeling during the experience. But in oral survivor testimonies, interviewers sometimes play the role of reader, revealing through their responses how the reader's silent imagination contends with the reality of the page. The following brief excerpt gives us a glimpse of such an interaction, which I hesitate to call a stalemate because it seems to end with the "defeat" of the survivor, or at least the survivor's vocabulary. Here words literally contend with each other for supremacy, offering a stunning instance of the near impossibility of achieving a purely objective text. The narrator has survived *two* deportations to Auschwitz, with stops at Majdanek and Plaszow in between, and the discussion is about how she survived:

> INTERVIEWER: You survived because you were so plucky. When you stepped back . . .
>
> HANNA F.: No, dear, no dear, no . . . no, I had no . . . *[meanwhile, the two interviewers are whispering with each other audibly offscreen about this exchange, ignoring the survivor, who wants to reply]*—how shall I explain to you? I knew that I had to survive; I had to survive, even running away, even being with the people constantly, especially the second part, the second time, being back in Auschwitz. That time I had determined already to survive—and you know what? It wasn't luck, it was stupidity. *[At this moment, the two interviewers laugh deprecatingly, disbelievingly, overriding her voice with their own "explanation," as one calls out, "You had a lot of guts!"]*
>
> HANNA F. *[simultaneously]:* No, no, no, no, there were no guts, there was just sheer stupidity. No . . . *[More laughter from the interviewers, one of whom now stands up between camera and survivor, blocking our vision, silencing her voice, terminating the interview. Why?]*[12]

Nothing has been concluded; in fact, the desired conclusion, that Hanna F. survived through pluck and guts, has been undermined by her insistence that she has survived through luck and stupidity. Words of denial and affirmation leap from the screen, signifying far more than a conflict between skeptical interviewers and determined survivor. No one bothers to ask her how one survives through "stupidity," as if she has made some senile remark too obviously irrelevant to warrant investigation.

We are faced here with a confusion of tongues, a dispute of wills, the audience's need to preserve preconceived interpretations by searching through the thesaurus of heroic terms for words like "pluck" and "guts" to confirm such interpretations, while the narrator—helplessly, as it turns out—ventures her own version of survival with a word deleted from that thesaurus: "stupidity." Here is an encounter that is no encounter, since her use of words, as anyone who watches her expression throughout the testimony can recognize, is memory-specific, while their response is identified with a long tradition of historical behavior and expectations. *Her* use of language interprets her narrative for her and them; *their* use of language interprets her narrative for them and her. And never the twain do meet.

This conflict between preconceived, culturally nourished moral expectations and the violation of that expectation is internalized in a less humorous and more intricate way in the following narrative moment from the videotaped testimony of a single survivor, Alex H. It is as if we are in the presence of two narrative voices, each seeking expression: the first, time- and place-bound by what we might call the chronicle mode; the other, struggling like Charlotte Delbo to detach "the way it was" from how we think it was and to see it from the vantage point of today. The recording imagination intersects with the will to interpretation; the memory of atrocity meets traditional moral authority, and they vie for control of the narrative:

> December 1944, when the war started coming to an end, although we didn't know that, or we did not know to what extent—we were taken out of camp and started off to march—the Russians came near and the Germans took us out from camp and they marched us to other camps. It was terrible cold; we had no clothes. Whoever could not walk they shot. We had no food. It was . . . the real horror story of my camp started in December of 1944. At night they herded us in some farm . . . a barn. In the morning very early they took us out and we had to march again; we marched for days. And that march, my brother . . . he could not walk anymore and he was taken from me and shot on the road. It is difficult to say, talk about feelings. First of all we were reduced to such a animal level that actually now that I remember those things, I feel more horrible than I felt at the time. We were in such a state, that all that mattered is to remain alive. Even about your own brother or the closest, one did not think. I don't know how other people felt. . . . It bothers me very much if I was the only one that felt that way, or is that normal in such circumstances to be that way? I feel now sometimes, did I do my best or didn't I do something that I should have done? But at that time I wanted to survive myself, and maybe I did not give my greatest efforts to do certain things, or I missed to do certain things. . . .[13]

Ostensibly, the passage begins as part of a chronological sequence, assuming a past, present, and future—in short, temporal continuity ("we marched for days"). It even assumes continuity in space—we left this camp, and went to that one. But suddenly, another voice intrudes on the idea that this is merely a dramatic moment in time embedded in a larger temporal pattern. When Alex H. breaks off his narrative to announce that "the real horror story of my camp *started* in December of 1944," he introduces a *discontinuity* into his account that detaches it from his previous efforts at chronology. He shifts from the mode of *in medias res*—which views the Holocaust as an event sandwiched between the prewar and postwar periods—to what we might call the mode of *in principio*, where, according to most oral survivor testimony, the Holocaust has a different beginning for each witness and provides closure for none. Both modes afflict his imagination, as is evident when he explains: "actually now that I remember those things, I feel more horrible than I felt at the time." Both the history of morality and the so-called morality of history educate us about "normal" and desirable behavior in most circumstances. But Alex H. is speaking of what he calls "such circumstances," specifically his inability to help his weakened brother and prevent the Germans from shooting him. He seeks continuity retrospectively between his repertory of possibilities "now" and the repertory of impossibilities "at that time." Finding no connection, he remains in a condition of permanent distress. In other words, the interviewer-in-him is dissatisfied with the interviewee-in-him.

Why is this so? His brother's death is a random moment that surfaces in his narrative not as a culmination of logically preceding events or the inspiration for subsequent ones, but as a creation of anguished memory, born of Alex H.'s efforts to reconstruct his experience of the Holocaust. History demands accuracy, chronology, significance, interpretation, which provokes this survivor's question: "did I do my best or didn't I do something that I should have done?" Remorse and recrimination are part of the moral authority that supposedly governs our lives as social beings. To the question of why moral consciousness seems such an issue now, when it apparently was less so then, we might reply that the nature of the interview situation (to say nothing of the written survivor narrative) provokes it. Almost all of the more than one hundred videotaped interviews that I have seen begin in the same way: tell us something about your childhood, family, school, community, friends—that is, about the world of pre-Holocaust "normalcy." And most of them end in the same way, too, insofar as the Holocaust experience is concerned: tell us about your liberation. The reluctance of so many survivors to see "liberation" as a form of closure only confirms the need to understand the unorthodox implications of the narrative mode of *in principio* when responding to survivor testimony. Asked to describe how he felt at the moment of liberation, one survivor declared: "Then I knew my troubles were *really* about to begin," inverting the familiar sequence of conflict and resolution that we have learned to expect of traditional historical narrative.

During this last narrative moment, we observe consciousness inviting itself to transform a random event into a pattern of sequenced meaning, a process more difficult to detect, and perhaps impossible to detect, on the printed page of a written text. It is as if Alex H. were asking, "How can I tell you, how can I tell *myself,* what I 'know' about that moment now that I'm back in human culture, where fraternal solicitude is a major measure of acceptable conduct?" The search for value contends with the absence of value, giving us a glimpse into the evolution of historical consciousness at its most elementary level, consciousness constructing history out of reality by exposing the illogic of atrocity and trying to replace it with some form of moral continuity. What student of history, inquiring why Alex H.'s brother was shot, would be content with the reply, "Because he was too weak to walk"? Far more satisfactory to the imagination is Alex H.'s own hesitant, vaguely guilty response: "maybe I did not give my greatest efforts to do certain things. . . ." This voice from the cultural present, where traditional moral explanations of conduct presumably prevail, speaks from *in medias res,* a world of continuity. His *other* voice, from what I call *in principio,* is detached from past and present, emerging in what he calls "the real horror story of my camp." But as Alex H. tells this story, as he re-perceives the reality on which it is based, he instinctively realizes how uncongenial is the principle of being that he himself has formulated: "all that mattered is to remain alive." This is too primitive a behavioral foundation for the society he now inhabits.

But is it accurate? And even if it is *part* of the truth, how do we clear our minds of verbal cant in order to represent it accurately? When Irene W. speaks of knowing the truth as others do not know it; when Hanna F. tries to explain that she survived through "stupidity"; when Alex H. wonders about definitions of "normal" under the circumstances of the death march he endured; and when Edith P., in a desperate appeal, asks, "Is there such a thing as love?"—they raise an issue that Western civilization has yet to confront in our post-Holocaust era. Have we moved beyond the tragic dimensions of history into a new kind of cultural atmosphere where the redeeming power of love approaches bankruptcy and the more solitary goal of the Socratic quest, "Know thyself," has exhausted its charm and its value? Edith P.'s question, "Is there such a thing as love?", betrays the misery of her own condition; but it also threatens the integrity of the social and religious fabric that supports our civilization. I have found in these oral testimonies, when they escape the restrictions imposed on them by the interview situation and the importunate prodding of the interviewers to achieve closure, refreshingly new texts that, precisely because of their indifference to "conclusions," free the imagination to explore implications that more traditional narratives are less inclined to inspire. Although a negative reply to the question "Is there such a thing as love?" is of course inadmissible, that is precisely why, when telling the story of the Holocaust, we must entertain the possibility that for this period of time, at least, for unnumbered potential victims, it might nonetheless have seemed true.

Notes

1 · Lawrence L. Langer, *Versions of Survival: The Holocaust and the Human Spirit* (Albany, N.Y.: SUNY Press, 1982), p. xii.

2 · Charlotte Delbo, *None of Us Will Return*, trans. John Githens (New York: Grove Press, 1968), p. 72.

3 · Ibid., p. 128.

4 · Elie Wiesel, *Night*, trans. Stella Rodway (New York: Bantam, 1982), p. 42.

5 · Victor Frankel, *Man's Search for Meaning* (New York: Pocket Books [revised and updated ed.], 1984), pp. 87, 103.

6 · Primo Levi, *Survival in Auschwitz: The Nazi Assault on Humanity*, trans. Stuart Woolf (New York: Collier Books, 1961), pp. 103, 105.

7 · Ibid., p. 105.

8 · Video Archive for Holocaust Testimonies at Yale: T-107 (Interview with Edith P.).

9 · Carlos Fuentes, "Velázquez, Plato's Cave, and Bette Davis," *New York Times*, March 15, 1987.

10 · Filip Müller, *Eyewitness Auschwitz: Three Years in the Gas Chambers*, trans. and ed. Susanne Flatauer (New York: Stein & Day, 1979), p. 24. Complicating our response to Müller's written text—we have an opportunity to compare it with his oral testimony in Claude Lanzmann's film *Shoah*—is the detail on the title page that Helmut Freitag was his literary collaborator, and Susanne Flatauer his translator *and* editor. Beyond dispute in oral testimony is that every word spoken falls directly from the lips of the witness. Not as much can be said of

written survivor testimony that is openly or silently edited. Whether or not this seriously limits the "authenticity" of some written memoirs is a question that still needs to be investigated.

11 · Video Archive for Holocaust Testimonies at Yale: T-65 (Interview with Irene W.).

12 · Ibid.: T-18 (Interview with Hanna F.).

13 · Ibid.: T-210 (Interview with Alex H.).

3 · *Ellen S. Fine*

The Absent Memory: The Act of Writing in Post-Holocaust French Literature

*I*n Elie Wiesel's novel, *The Fifth Son*, the protagonist, a son of survivors, states: "Born after the war, I endure its effects. I suffer from an Event I did not even experience. Feeling of void: from a past that has made History tremble, I have retained only words."[1] Here Wiesel points to the dilemma of post-Holocaust generations: how to live with Auschwitz after Auschwitz. Afflicted by the unhealed wounds of memory, those born in the aftermath of genocide continue to bear its burden. They have inherited the anguish, yet at the same time feel excluded from a universe they can never know. This sense of being shut out of a momentous era compels writers of the second generation to fill the void created by the Holocaust. They are confronted with a difficult task: to imagine an event they have not lived through, and to reconstitute and integrate it into their writing—to create a story out of History.

An exploration of the literary responses to the Nazi genocide in France, from writers who did not themselves directly experience the oppression, reveals an obsessive need to return to the past. Born in France during the 1940s, of immigrant parents or grandparents, these writers grew up immersed in the stories and silence surrounding the Nazi Occupation and the collaboration of the Vichy government that resulted in the persecution and deportation of nearly 30 percent of France's Jewish population (approximately 75,000), including French native- and foreign-born Jews. The history of France during the Nazi Holocaust established its grip upon the literary imagination of those who came after. By means of the creative process, they attempt to project themselves back into that epoch, to recover the past by inventing it. Like their predecessors—survivors of *l'univers concentrationnaire* who chose to testify to their encounter with death through the written word—they, too, are faced with the impossibility of communication.

The Holocaust (or "Shoah," meaning "Catastrophe," as it is now called in France) caused a shattering of world order, a crisis of values and of language. How to speak, how to find the words, witnesses of the genocide often ask. In the introduction to his eyewitness account, *L'Espèce humaine*, Robert Antelme describes the disproportion between what he endured in Buchenwald and what, subsequently, he related to others:

> From the first days on, it seemed impossible for us to bridge the gap that we discovered between the language available to us and this experience which was still continuing in our bodies. . . . Hardly did we begin to tell the tale than we choked. What we had to say began to appear unimaginable, even to ourselves. [2]

In her book entitled *Paroles suffoquées*, the French psychoanalyst Sara Kofman, whose father died in Auschwitz, studies this double bind: the necessity to tell all and the almost physical impossibility of speaking without suffocating. Robert Antelme's self-imposed moral code, she says, is to be obliged to speak without being able to, to speak while choking on words that stick in the throat and strangle. These words are at the same time necessary ("exigé") and forbidden. [3] *L'Espèce humaine*, which she calls "sublime," is in effect a testimony to this contradiction inherent in Holocaust literature. For despite the impenetrability of this dark realm, modes of literary expression, however inadequate they may be, have been found to depict conditions of extremity. Yet, for the survivor-writer, an abyss will always exist between the reality of the event and the telling of the tale.

Survivors of the Holocaust are torn between the mission to bear witness and an equally compelling fear of betraying the sanctity of the subject. Faced with the tensions of this struggle, some chose silence as an alternative, burying their memories in the recesses of their scarred psyches; others wrote *témoignages*, forcing themselves to gaze once again into the Holocaust flames as they tried to convey to the outside world the memories they carried within. Still others, after more than fifteen years had passed, decided to translate their personal recollections into fiction. Such survivors as Anna Langfus, Piotr Rawicz, and Elie Wiesel, who came to France after the war from countries in Eastern Europe, adopted French as their literary language and opted to write novels. The technique of this genre allowed them the distance to reenter a domain otherwise inaccessible. Transforming events into a fictional mode was a means of detaching oneself from the pain, a way of becoming an "other." For the generation of Auschwitz, the act of writing—narrating, composing, choosing, interpreting—seemed to bestow an order on a reality that had none. As Robert Jay Lifton observes, "Artistic re-creation of an overwhelming historical experience has much to do with the question of mastery."[4]

The notion of mastery is significant for survivor-writers, as well as for those removed from the circumstances. Both generations are faced with what Lifton calls "creative guilt," a fear of hubris associated with imaginatively reconstructing an historically sacred event.[5] If writers of the first generation feel guilty for transgressing boundaries in their representation (or misrepresentation) of the dead, their question, *how to speak* of the unimaginable, becomes for the second generation, *do I have the right to speak?* Henri Raczymow, born in the France of 1948, and one of the most articulate spokesmen of the new group of post-Holocaust Jewish-French writers, asks, "What right does one have to speak if, as in my case, one has been neither victim, nor survivor, nor witness of the event?" His question contains its own answer: "I do not have the right to speak."[6] Nevertheless, Raczymow reveals that he is possessed by an urgent need to speak that conflicts with the interdiction of the word, a tension that shapes his later works.

For those born in the shadow of genocide, apprehensions about the right to speak are often linked to the guilt of nonparticipation, a kind of regret for having been born too late. They are haunted by the world that has vanished; a large gap exists in their history, and they desire to bridge this gap, to be informed about what occurred, to know something about members of their family who perished. However, they feel frustrated by the impotence of incomprehension; the past eludes and excludes them. Repeatedly met with the silence of their parents and relatives—who transmit the wounds of genocide, and not the memory—they grow up in "the compact void of the unspeakable," as Nadine Fresco affirms in her "Remembering the Unknown," an analysis of how young Jews born after World War II relate to a traumatic event they have not experienced. These Jews, she says, are like "people who have had a hand amputated that they never had": they inherit the pain, but it is "a phantom pain in which amnesia takes the place of memory. . . . One remembers only that one remembers nothing."[7]

This sense of nothingness caused by the deprivation of memory, or by memory that is concealed, refused, or forbidden, is intensified by the survivors themselves. Elie Wiesel has frequently made the observation, "Who has not lived through the event, will never know it."[8] Yet the message is contradictory, and therein lies the predicament. "*At the same time one can never know, one must know, and one must not forget,*" Maurice Blanchot notes in *L'Ecriture du désastre.*[9] "Les enfants de l'après-genocide" ("the post-genocide children")[10] are thus obliged to fill in the blank spaces with their own words and imagination, to find their own way back to the past that has been denied them—to remember what they did not know.

Absence, particularly the absence of memory, is a principal theme in the literary texts, autobiographical narratives, and psychological and social commentaries of those writing in the aftermath. Linked to the notion of absence are the repeated words—void, lack ("manqué"), blank, gap, hole, and nothingness—pointing to a general sense of loss and emptiness. Erika Apfelbaum, a sociologist, observes that the generation born after the genocide grew up with years of imposed silence, and are thus "deprived of collective historical landmarks." Their knowledge of the Holocaust, based on the fragments of personal memories of their immediate families, is circumscribed. It was not until the 1970s that an explosion of publications brought the Holocaust from private into public consciousness. Apfelbaum became acutely aware of her own lack of knowledge when confronted with a need to communicate the history of the Holocaust to her young daughter. Because her memory was limited and her ignorance vast, she could transmit only what she calls "un héritage en forme d'absences" ("a legacy in the form of absences").[11]

"All began by absence. . . . I knew a lot about the Holocaust, but I was not deported," Claude Lanzmann explains.[12] For the author and director of the nine-and-a-half-hour film *Shoah,* that absence became the basis of his work. Although born in 1925, he and his family were saved by French peasants during the war and, therefore, he never entered the death-camp universe. "I had to start from nothing, from nothingness," Lanzmann states.[13] The task of organizing this nothingness into images ("donner à voir les images du néant") gave him the same kind of vertigo that the writer experiences in front of the blank page.[14] Lanzmann's objective was to find traces of the extermination that the Nazis themselves had abolished. Without using any documents of the era, he plunged into a reality that had been obliterated and made this reality come alive. This was accomplished through words and images. By allowing the audience to hear the words of eyewitnesses— survivors, bystanders, and oppressors—juxtaposed against the seemingly peaceful landscapes in which the scars of annihilation lie deeply embedded, Lanzmann succeeded in resurrecting the past as present, and in re-creating a presence out of the absence.

The theme of absence is also the driving force behind the novels of Henri Raczymow, both in his theoretical commentaries about his own writing and throughout the texts themselves. Like Claude Lanzmann, he is perturbed by the white page or, as one of his narrators puts it, "whitened pages whose letters were suddenly, angrily erased in the monstrous Catastrophe that preceded his birth."[15] Unlike the familiar anguish of the writer facing the unknown, Raczymow's narrator explains that he experiences "the disarray of an archeologist, disarmed and virtually without landmarks. Alongside the 'site' without vestiges, the site that has returned to its original desertlike state, he reconstitutes— the fruit of his imagination rather than of his knowledge—a dotted line of hypotheses, bits of fantasy rather than of memory."[16]

Raczymow recognizes the absence of memory and, thus, the necessity for reconstructing the past through the imaginary. In an article clarifying why he writes, Raczymow states that his books do not try to fill the memory gap, but only "to present it as absent . . . to restitute a nonmemory that, by definition, is unable to be filled."[17] "La mémoire absente," the absent memory, is "la mémoire trouée," a memory filled with holes or gaps, both symbolic and real. Raczymow characterizes the different kinds of real gaps that exist for an Ashkenazic Jew born after the war in the Diaspora: a gap in the memory of a Poland unknown to him, for it has completely disappeared; a gap in the memory of the

Shoah, which was before his time; a gap in his genealogy. He can trace his family lineage to his grandparents, but after that all records have been burned: there are no tombs to mark time or space. The genocide has therefore deprived Henri Raczymow of his roots and, most important, of the knowledge of his roots. Writing alone provides the means by which he can "remember" his past.

In search of his lost genealogy, Raczymow projects himself imaginatively into three main period motifs in his works: (1) the *shtetl* of Jewish prewar Poland (or what he calls "prehistory"); (2) the Warsaw ghetto; (3) the Jewish community of Belleville in Paris during the 1950s. Writing to find out about his origins, and to establish his identity as a Jew growing up in a post-Holocaust era, he pieces together scraps of information acquired through the tales told to him by his maternal grandparents, who raised him until age five. At one point, before commencing his book on Poland, *Contes d'exil et d'oubli* [Tales of Exile and Forgetfulness], he considered publishing a document based on research and personal testimony. However, he eventually rejected that mode of expression: "What is dead seems to me to be able to be restored only through the imagination, and not through history and bibliographic research, even though they have their own interest."[18]

With filtered fragments of other people's memories, Raczymow shapes a mythic, imaginary vision of the vanished Jewish community. He returns to the source by inventing it. The creative process enables him to achieve a certain mastery over the void. Yet, if words can militate against the feeling of being exiled from one's past, the writer acknowledges their limitation: the reality of the *shtetl* and of *l'univers concentrationnaire* is irretrievable. Raczymow knows that his words cannot fill the vacuum left by the Shoah. Unlike a survivor, he cannot keep the memory alive, but can only evoke the *absence* of memory, and this is precisely what he does in his writing. By focusing his novels on the recurrent theme of absence, and by using the narrative device of telling a story within a story, the author renders his own version of the painful legacy he has inherited.

Before examining the representation of the theme of absence in two of Raczymow's novels, *Contes d'exil et d'oubli* (1979), a return to an imaginary prewar Poland, and *Un Cri sans voix* (1985), a fictitious portrayal of life in the Warsaw ghetto, it may be useful to look briefly at the author's literary background. There are two main stages in Henri

Raczymow's development, marked by the year 1978. His early novels, *La Saisie* (1973), *Scènes* (1975), and *Bluette* (1977), were influenced by the *nouveau roman*. Like Alain Robbe-Grillet, he had "rien à dire," nothing to say, no message to deliver; and, like Flaubert, he wanted to compose "a book about nothing, with no exterior attachment, that relies only upon the strength of its internal structure."[19] Raczymow was clearly more interested in the negation of the narrative than in the traditional linear plot.

La Saisie (The Seizure), Raczymow's first novel, is in effect a Kafkaesque story of a man whose belongings have been confiscated from his apartment for some unknown reason; he is left "naked as a worm."[20] Ashamed of his passivity and impotence, all the narrator can do is set down on paper the record of his dispossession. The novel is essentially a detailed account of a man's obsessive struggle to write a book about the emptiness that pervades his room and himself. The narrative technique is the *mise en abyme*, a story within a story, or a book within a book. The reader enters the narrator's consciousness and is exposed to his endless groping for nouns, verbs, and images as the writing process reveals itself. *La Saisie* centers on the nothingness—the *tabula rasa*—experienced by a writer who must be rid of all attachments before setting forth his creation upon the white page.

At the core of Raczymow's following novels, *Scènes* and *Bluette*—which explore different aspects of the question, why write?—also lies a blank space that writing itself tries to fill. However, after 1978 the author changed his focus from the void he suffered as a writer to a more personal sense of void—the immense gap in his own memory. He suddenly realized that the emptiness he felt within came from a lack of knowledge due to the nontransmission of collective and family memory. He was possessed with a need to explore the origins of his ancestors, a need to learn about the names that were erased from history. With the publication of *Contes d'exil et d'oubli*, Raczymow entered a new stage in his literary itinerary. Called by critics *le nouveau roman juif,* his fiction began to integrate the self-reflective mode of the *nouveau roman* with the telling of Jewish tales and legends.[21]

The son of parents born in France who sought to assimilate, and of immigrant Polish grandparents, Raczymow is in quest of his Jewish identity and his dispersed Jewish roots. In *Contes d'exil et d'oubli*, he embarks upon an imaginary voyage to Konsk and Kaloush, small villages in Poland, supposedly where his grandparents came from. Like Claude Lanzmann in his endeavor to resurrect a reality that was destroyed, Henri Raczymow returns to a landscape that has disappeared and brings it back to life. His book, composed of picturesque portraits of characters from the *shtetl*, recounts their hardships and humor as they cope with a life that was not always easy. Filled with anecdotes, stories, and songs, the text is written in a style that reproduces the accent, rhythms, and intonations of Yiddish. The narrative device is a story within a story; that is to say, the reader listens to tales, at times told by the uncle Noïoch Oksenberg to his nephew, but primarily by the grandfather Simon Gorbatch to his grandson, Mathieu Schriftlich, the narrator-protagonist, who (like the author himself) was born in Paris after the war.

The grandfather tries to recall souvenirs of his Polish relatives—his own paternal grandfather, the peddler Simon Davidowicz; his maternal grandfather, Rabbi Schlomo Grunenflamm; his mother, Rywka; his young wife, Matl Oksenberg—and other members of the family and Jewish community. Like Mathieu, the reader does not know if the scenes from these little towns are real or invented. The grandfather's memory is tired and unsure, "une mémoire trouée,"[22] groping for names and faces that will lead the old man back to a place that no longer exists. The result is an impressionistic series of unordered sketches in which figures appear and disappear as if in a dream. This is the memory process at work.

Despite the fragmented narrative structure, which seems to reflect the world it is portraying—and the unfolding of its destruction—the text is unified by recurrent motifs and images, threads that weave together the pieces of torn fabric. For example, the motif of names is repeated throughout the book. The narrator often recites litanies of names, of Jewish towns and of people chased from those towns (pp. 60, 69, 74, 97, 105). He is in search of the names that have perished in the smoke of the crematorium: "beloved names, a nebula of dead stars wandering above the lake of Kamenetz" (p. 74).

The lake of Kamenetz, situated at the center of Konsk (or Konski as the villagers affectionately called their town), also plays a central role in the telling of the tales. Simon tells his grandson that reality, like the water of the lake of Kamenetz, renews itself, shifts, and is transformed to the extent that it is unrecognizable (p. 84). The water of the lake is inexhaustible, but the source has run dry. Once a shining lake, the transparent waters become muddied, then turn into a swamp, and finally an arid pond. Toward the end of the text, the lake, depicted as frozen and impenetrable, opens up like the Red Sea and, like a marble tomb, engulfs the villagers (pp. 105–6). The lake as tombstone can be seen as a metaphor for the Jewish town, a vast cemetery that is now dead, or for the memory of the town.

Hovering above the lake in dense fog is the figure of Matl Oksenberg, "the living image of death" (p. 104), whose tomb is the sky. The image of Matl Oksenberg increases in importance throughout the text. As Mathieu listens to Simon's words, he is haunted by this shadowy form whose name "turns around in his brain as in a cage, rendering him mute and hesitant" (p. 59); her name evokes all those who have been assassinated and whom he never knew. Burdened by the weight of this woman whose blurred face he finds impossible to envisage, Mathieu drags her heavy body along the lake of Kamenetz, trying to pull her from the East to the West, to take her out of exile. The muted sounds of the lake mingle with the noises of trains rolling along the plains of Europe with cries coming from afar (p. 89). Mathieu wants to call out to Matl, but knows she cannot hear him: "His love for his grandmother comes back to himself, coils around *absence*. *Perhaps this distance, this absence are necessary for Mathieu*" (p. 92, emphasis added). Matl's presence is significant precisely because of her absence, and while the void obsesses Mathieu, it allows him the necessary distance to restitute Matl through his imagination, to invent the words she would say to him if she could speak. "It is time I disappeared for good," he hears her murmur. "Stop pursuing me, and pulling me along the Kamenetz. . . . I have lost the memory of the future. I have disowned my offspring. The best part was murdered. The other was stillborn. I have forgotten all of them" (p. 107).

"What do you want from me?" Matl asks Mathieu (p. 103). "Where does this usurped right to weave me into the midst of your fictive memory come from? What am I doing in this rumbling, this confusion that are yours and yours alone, and which I neither hear nor want to hear?" Matl's admonition to the narrator raises the issue of whether one has the right to disturb the dead, revealing the author's fear of trespassing upon sacred grounds. Reiterated in different modes at various intervals throughout *Contes d'exil et d'oubli*, the question is: do I have the right to dig up buried remnants of the past, and do I have the right to write?

As the surname chosen for the narrator, Mathieu *Schriftlich* ("written, in writing") indicates, Henri Raczymow has indeed opted to gather living memories of his people through the written word. Mathieu listens attentively to Simon's sometimes true, sometimes fabricated, always unfinished legends about his youth in Poland. The grandson presses his grandfather to continue speaking because of his own "dark obsession with stirring up the Polish mud in order to find a golden nugget" (p. 49). Mathieu preciously holds on to the few phrases and images transmitted to him like pieces of a broken mirror, as he advances precariously and uneasily into the Polish landscape, trying to take possession of it, that is to say, "to touch reality." Elusive, this reality "opens like a shell, and closes up immediately like death closing on a dead thing" (p. 54).

If, on the one hand, Mathieu desires to stir up the mud and bring to the surface things long forgotten, on the other hand, he constantly expresses misgivings about his pilgrimage to the dead town. "What good is it to stir up the past? What is dead is dead," he says, and this refrain is repeated throughout the narrative by Noïoch Oksenberg, Matl's brother, and by Simon as well. What is dead is dead, they say, and cannot be resurrected; it can only be invented (pp. 21, 46, 54, 66).

By integrating these comments into the text itself, Raczymow is sharing with the reader his own doubts as he traces his way back to what for him is now a mythic land. He is exposing the reader to the problems of reconstructing a memory that is not one's own. The grandfather's manner of recalling the past does not conform to chronological storytelling. The interruptions and discontinuities in his narrative, the bits of detail, the names and faces that surge and then vanish—these are evidence of the holes in his memory. It is Mathieu who sews together the torn fabrics with his own interventions and inventions. However, as Raczymow has stated, it is not his intention to fill the memory gaps, but to present memory as absent.

This is precisely what he does in *Contes d'exil et d'oubli*, first, by Mathieu's continual questioning as to what Simon does not remember, what he himself does not know because he has no memory, and where this voyage into the imaginary past is leading him. The act of remembering—or of recovering memory—is conscious of itself. Second, the

theme of absence is reinforced by Mathieu's obsession with his ancestors who have disappeared without a trace into the night and fog of
the "concentrationary universe." The absence of Matl Oksenberg, and
the importance it assumes in the text, is representative of all the others
whose annihilation hangs over the village of Konsk. Described, in what
seems to be a contradiction of terms, as "a *white shadow* in the memory
of Mathieu Schriftlich" (p. 74, emphasis added), this black-white image
of Matl is both a reminder of the darkness into which the grandmother
plunged, and a remembrance of the void left in her place. The transformation of Matl's absence into a presence and the composition of a book
that sets her at its center, is, in effect, Henri Raczymow's way of
bringing his lost ancestor out of exile and "touching" a forgotten reality.

If in *Contes d'exil et d'oubli* the author is preoccupied with the recollection of memory (asking essentially what right he has to remember), six
years later, following the publication of two other novels, *Rivières d'exile*
(1982) and *On ne part pas* (1983), Raczymow asks in *Un Cri sans voix*
(1985) whether he has the right to write? In an interview in 1979, he
talks about the impossibility of thinking about the past, and the silence
that reigned for thirty years. "It was, in my opinion," he notes, "silence
in the face of the reality of Auschwitz, a kind of muteness from which
we are barely emerging: now one can speak."[23] Yet, in his 1986 article,
as we have seen, Raczymow inquires: "What right does one have to
speak if, as in my case, one has been neither victim, nor survivor, nor
witness of the event?" He acknowledges that he is in a double bind: he
does not have the right to speak, but he must. This struggle between
language and silence forms the basis of *Un Cri sans voix* [A Cry without a
Voice] and raises a fundamental question for those born in the aftermath
of the Shoah, as well as for those who did not participate directly in the
Catastrophe: who has the right to speak?

In *Un Cri sans voix*, written forty years after the war's end, Raczymow
dares to approach the abyss in Jewish memory, separating the prewar
from the postwar epoch. Nevertheless, he does so with trepidation, as
evidenced by the expressions of guilt and impotence of his narrator,
once again named Mathieu and once again a writer. Mathieu feels
impotent for not being able to find words that can gather together the
absent and the exiled or, as he put it, the milligrams of ashes from
Auschwitz scattered "like invisible stars in the night of the world, which

is the night when the writer writes";[24] his guilt stems from even venturing to do so.

As a writer composing the book that he thinks his dead sister, Esther, wanted to write about the Warsaw ghetto, and placing her in it (repeating the narrative device of the *mise en abyme,* or the book within the book), Mathieu puts himself in the skin of his dead sister and the ghetto inhabitants, and feels guilty for usurping their role. He imagines the voice of Esther accusing him: "Only the surviving victims have the right to words. The others, and especially those born after the war, should be silent, silent. Their words are obscene, impudent" (p. 129). If Esther's harsh reproach echoes Matl's warning to the narrator in *Contes d'exil et d'oubli* ("Where does this usurped right to weave me into the midst of your fictive memory come from?"), it is because the author is ultimately critical of himself for writing in the aftermath.

In effect, *Un Cri sans voix* is an in-depth exploration of the different responses to the genocide by those who did not experience the event—remembering, forgetting, and/or writing about the unimaginable—and of the guilt that this entails. As with *Contes d'exil et d'oubli,* the novel revolves around an absent figure, also a woman, and the reconstitution of her presence through the narrator-writer's imagination. Like Matl Oksenberg, a victim of history, Esther Litvak is also a victim—but by choice. Born in France on August 2, 1943, the day of the revolt at the Treblinka concentration camp, the narrator's older sister, Esther, a teacher and aspiring writer, commits suicide by gas in 1975 at age thirty-two. Although she has no personal memories of the Shoah, she has inherited its unhealed wounds. She is representative of those traumatized young people who, as Nadine Fresco observed, suffer from the amputation of a hand they never had.

Obsessed with the genocide, Esther is burdened by the guilt of nonparticipation; she feels guilty for being alive and for having "missed the train" that would have deported her to Treblinka (p. 109). She blames herself for not having been a fighter or a victim. In fact, she is the victim of her own fantasies, and clearly identifies with the Holocaust victims. She has internalized the ghetto, desperately holding on to vestiges of an era she never knew. On the wall of her room in Belleville, the Jewish community of Paris where she lives with her parents and two younger brothers, hangs a photo of young women fighters from the Warsaw ghetto lined up in front of an SS execution squad; Esther often walks round Paris wearing an oversized cap similar to those worn by the women in the picture. At a certain point, she even dons a pair of striped pajamas, shaves her head, and stops eating. Her family considers her to be incurably ill, "malade du passé" (p. 119); for them, she is a living testament to a past that is dead but not buried.

Unlike Esther, who gazes so intensely into the Holocaust flames that she finishes by being burned, her younger brother Mathieu, born after the war, looks away; thus, two contrasting reactions to the event are illustrated. After Esther's suicide, her brother and the rest of the family try to erase her from their memory: the story of Esther is a prohibited subject, submerged in silence. However, in 1982, seven years after her death, when Israel invades Lebanon and the newspapers compare Beirut to the Warsaw ghetto and Israel to the Nazis, Mathieu, now working in a government office as a civil servant and married with a son of his own, is suddenly possessed with a desire to reclaim his dead sister. He, who once closed his ears to tales about the Nazi atrocities, embarks upon a quest for knowledge in order to fill the blank spaces in his memory and to confront his own silence.

Un Cri sans voix is divided into two distinct parts, corresponding to two periods in history, that of the Warsaw ghetto and that of postwar France. The first is a fictitious chronicle of everyday life in the Warsaw ghetto as seen from the point of view of Esther Litvak, as imagined by her brother, Mathieu. Esther keeps a journal in which she records her personal feelings, weaving them into the events taking place in the ghetto: the building of the wall; the roundups; the actions of the Jewish police; the activities of the *Judenrat*, the Jewish collaborators, and the resistance fighters; the suicide of Adam Czerniakow; the liquidation of Janusz Korczak's orphanage. In the journal Esther reveals her anxieties and her dreams, her obsessions with becoming a writer and with having a child, and her doubts about ever achieving either. Part one concludes with the supposition that Esther was killed in Treblinka along with most of the Jewish community of Warsaw.

The narrator—also the author—has ventured into the ghetto through his literary imagination, yet he stops at the gates of the death camps. By refusing to go any further, Henri Raczymow clearly recognizes that he, as a writer, cannot enter the forbidden zone that constitutes a black hole in his "absent memory." As his narrator confirms later on in the novel, with regard to Birkenau: "I see nothing. I cannot see anything. I do not wish to see anything. I should not see anything. To want to see would place me next to the SS in charge of looking through the peephole in order to see the condition of the gassed" (p. 186). For Raczymow, writing about *l'univers concentrationnaire* makes the author a voyeur, peering at the victims as did the Nazi oppressors.

If the first section of the novel is a fictional narrative of life in the Warsaw ghetto, the second is a realistic account of the Jewish experience in postwar France, as well as a commentary on what it means to write about the Holocaust, for *Un Cri sans voix* is essentially a novel that reflects upon the act of writing after the genocide. Many of the characters who appeared in the ghetto with Polish names are now French men and women situated in Belleville, Paris. The imaginary Esther of the ghetto is portrayed as a real person growing up in post-Holocaust France. Mathieu, who has blackened Esther out of his memory, pieces together the mosaic of his family history in order to put the story of Esther into perspective. To fill the gaps in his memory, he conducts his own investigation, integrating into the text itself eyewitness testimonies of surviving members of the family—his mother, father, aunts, uncles, and Esther's husband, Simon—who relate how they were persecuted both in Poland and in France under the Nazi Occupation. Mathieu begins to understand more about the sister he never really knew, as he learns how Esther was named after—and thus felt she had taken the place of—"the other Esther," their aunt, their mother's older sister, deported to Auschwitz at age twenty along with their grandmother, Rywka, when the police came to look for their mother, who was on the Gestapo's list and who had gone upstairs to hide in a neighbor's apartment during the notorious Paris roundup of July 1942.

The transmission of the name and of the trauma associated with the name is linked to the theme of absence and identity. If, on the one hand, the conferral of a dead person's name upon a living being is a means of perpetuating that person's memory, it is, on the other hand, an acknowledgment of the death of that person. Rather than replace her aunt, who has vanished without a trace, Esther represents "by her name alone the very *presence*, obvious, visible, loud, of *absence*" (p. 195, emphasis added). Indeed, Esther becomes a permanent reminder of the void that lies at the center of the family circle or, as the author puts it, of "this hole, this sea of ashes . . . from which an entire generation of Jews has been born" (p. 196). Esther so strongly identifies with "the other

Esther'' that she absents herself from life in the present. The Shoah has devoured her; she lives it and finally dies, as her brother supposes, so that the family not forget what was, and still is, "a hole in its center" (p. 195).

Esther Litvak has served as a monument to absence both in her life and in her death. Nonetheless, Mathieu discovers in speaking to Esther's husband that his sister had nightmares about usurping the place of another: she realized that she was the "false" Esther—the true one had died at Auschwitz (p. 211). This knowledge intensified her feelings of guilt; not only did she blame herself for having "missed the train" but, in trying to catch up with the train, she appropriated someone else's identity. The notion of appropriation and substitution applies to the writer as well. Mathieu grows aware of his own guilt as he slips into the universe of his dead sister, as he "uses" her to face his own obsession with the Nazi extermination of the Jews that he had previously avoided. The book of Esther becomes the book of guilt: the guilt of the second generation, for having been excluded, and the guilt of the writer for putting himself in someone else's skin.

Through his narrator, Henri Raczymow raises fundamental issues about the writer who, by projecting himself imaginatively into the world of the dead, usurps the role of the victim. The writer is compared to the "necrophore," an insect that lays its eggs inside the cadaver of another animal. Esther represents for Mathieu the dead part of himself that he wants to eliminate; yet, paradoxically, her death nourishes his writing, "faisant de cette pourriture sa nourriture ("Making of this rottenness his nourishment"). His words "dance on the decaying belly of his sister. . . . he lays his eggs on her entrails" (p. 145)—and a book is created. Mathieu writes in Esther's place; he steals her life, steals her death and, above all, steals her book.

If he dares to speak in the name of the dead, the post-Holocaust writer must bear the burden of guilt for inventing memories that are not his own. By writing—or rewriting—the story of Esther, the narrator has brought his forgotten sister back to life, transforming absence into presence, and giving a voice to silence. However, the novel terminates with the absence of memory carried to the extreme. At the conclusion of *Un Cri sans voix*, Mathieu admits that his book is an attempt to break his ties with his dead sister in the hope that he will not transmit the guilt of the Shoah to his child about to be born—to the third generation.

The past will be eradicated in order to protect the future. Mathieu intends to erase traces of Esther's memory by telling his child that he never had a sister, or that his sister died in a car accident.

This excessive, almost desperate, need to deny the past reflects the inability to come to terms with it. Clearly, certain memories, such as Esther's suicide and the genocide of the Jewish people, are too painful to bear. Yet, the author seems to be asking whether, by refusing memory, one can truly rid oneself of its wounds. Raczymow recognizes the impossibility of healing wounds that only deepen with the passage of time. For those who have inherited the trauma of the Shoah without the memory, the void cannot be filled. However, by openly revealing the apprehensions and guilt linked to the act of writing after Auschwitz, the author incorporates into the fiction itself, for the first time perhaps, the blank spaces that writers of the post-Holocaust generation must face when they confront the past. Henri Raczymow's words and imagination have enabled him to represent a new kind of memory, *the absent memory:* his way of saying that he will never know and, at the same time, must not forget.

Notes

1 · Elie Wiesel, *The Fifth Son*, trans. Marion Wiesel (New York: Warner Books, 1985), p. 180.

2 · Robert Antelme, *L'Espèce humaine* (Paris: Gallimard, 1957), p. 9. All quotations from French books and articles throughout this essay are my own translations.

3 · Sarah Kofman, *Paroles suffoquées* (Paris: Editions Galilée, 1987), pp. 45–46.

4 · Robert Jay Lifton, *Death-in-Life: Survivors of Hiroshima* (New York: Vintage Books, Random House, 1969), p. 397.

5 · Ibid., p. 473.

6 · Henri Raczymow, "La Mémoire trouée," *Pardès* 3 (1986): 180.

7 · Nadine Fresco, "Remembering the Unknown," *International Journal/Review of Psycho-Analysis* 11 (1984): 419, 421. This article was originally published as "Diaspora des cendres" in *Nouvelle Revue de Psychanalyse*, no. 24 (1981).

8 · Elie Wiesel, from his deposition at the Klaus Barbie trial in Lyon, France, *Libération*, June 3, 1987, p. 28. See also "Dialogue with Elie Wiesel," *Centerpoint* 4 (Fall 1980): 25: "The Holocaust is a sacred realm. One cannot enter this realm without realizing that only those who were there can know. . . . One can never know and yet one must try."

9 · Maurice Blanchot, *L'Ecriture du désastre* (Paris: Gallimard, 1980), p. 131, emphasis added.

10 · Alain Finkielkraut, *Le Juif imaginaire* (Paris: Editions du Seuil, Collection "Points," 1980), p. 13.

11 · Erika Apfelbaum, "La Mémoire à éclipses et la mémoire volée," *Traces* 9 (1984): 286.

12 · Claude Lanzmann, quoted in Sylvie Cohen, "Claude Lanzmann: Forcer la mémoire à la réalité du comment," *Le Droit de vivre*, no. 511 (May 1985): 19.

13 · "Intervention de Claude Lanzmann," *Mémoire et histoire: Actes du XXVᵉ Colloque des intellectuels juifs de langue française* (Paris: Editions Denoël, 1986), p. 72.

14 · Lanzmann, quoted in "Le Non-lieu de la mémoire" (interview by Edgar Reichhmann), *L'Arche* 338 (May 1985): 52.

15 · Henri Raczymow, *Rivières d'exil* (Paris: Gallimard, 1982), p. 10. All of Raczymow's novels have been published by Editions Gallimard.

16 · Ibid.

17 · Raczymow, "La Mémoire trouée," p. 181.

18 · Raczymow, quoted in "Dialogue entre Regine Robin et Henri Raczymow," comp. Jean Liberman, *La Presse Nouvelle Hebdomadaire*, September 7, 1979, p. 3.

19 · Raczymow aspires to follow Flaubert's concept of the absence of subject, quoting this well-known phrase from Flaubert's correspondence in "Henri Raczymow: L'Apprenti romancier." (interview with Pascal Bonafoux), *Canal*, no. 55 (May 1984): 29. For clarification of Flaubert's ideas, see Jean Rousset, "Madame Bovary; or, The Book about Nothing," in *Flaubert: A Collection of Critical Essays*, ed. Raymond Giraud (Englewood Cliffs, N.J.: Prentice-Hall, 1964), pp. 112–131.

20 · Raczymow, *La Saisie* (Paris: Gallimard, 1973), p. 11.

21 · Gilles Pudlowski, "Henri Raczymow et le 'nouveau roman juif': Le bon vieux temps du ghetto," *Les Nouvelles Littéraires*, May 13, 1982, p. 54.

22 · Raczymow, *Contes d'exil et d'oubli* (Paris: Gallimard, 1979), p. 61. All further references to this work will be noted in the text.

23 · Raczymow, quoted in "Dialogue entre Regine Robin et Henri Raczymow," p.5.

24 · Raczymow, *Un Cri sans voix* (Paris: Gallimard, 1985), p. 146. All further references to this work will be noted in the text.

4 · *Lore Segal*

Memory: The Problems of Imagining the Past

*T*he theme of my essay is the writing of story—more particularly, the writing of story whose theme is memory; yet more particularly, the writing of story whose theme is the memory of the Holocaust. I do not intend to talk about the theory of fiction, or the nature of memory, or the idea of holocaust; my essay, therefore, may not look to you much like an essay. What an essay does is to formulate a problem and argue it to a conclusion. I would like to do what a story does: to show you something. I want to show how fiction works when memory is its subject.

Fiction does what theater does, except that it does it in the privacy of your mind. Whereas the essay sets out to discuss its idea with you, fiction wants to stage the idea in your imagination. Essay wants to explain its thought; fiction wants the thought to happen to you—to happen in your experience—and experience may not be able to reach a conclusion.

All I want is to take you with me through my experience of writing about the Holocaust, and to leave with you some of the problems I have encountered along the way. Let me attempt a demonstration: I am walking down 100th Street toward my building on the corner of Riverside Drive. The garbage bags are piled on the sidewalk. Someone has thrown out a brass standing lamp with a fluted post—a gooseneck, with a shredded pink-silk shade, its fringe unkempt. No light bulb. If there were a bulb, you would light it by pulling the chain made out of little metal balls; it is like the lamp that stood next to my father's leather couch in the living room of our Vienna flat, which the Nazis requisitioned in the spring of 1938.

But the garbage I am talking about is in New York. The time is 1987 P.B. (Post Bauhaus). We tend toward a new homesickness for old things—things with detail and decoration, even things of the undistinguished sort exemplified by my garbage lamp. I climb over the bloated green giant vinyl bags with their unexplained bellies and elbows, and I capture this object—this lamp. I translate it, etymologically speaking—that is to say, I "carry" it "across" the threshold into my lobby and up the elevator, and I put it in my American living room. It has become *my* lamp.

It is a queer and a perfectly everyday thing that I, the writer, and you the reader have just accomplished together: I have translated a lamp in-the-world into words on-the-page, and you have translated the words into a lamp in your mind. Now it is your lamp, too.

Look at the lamp standing in your imagination—I told you it was a standing lamp. Does it look like any particular standing lamp in your past? Upon your remembered lamp my words have grafted certain details—oldness, brass, fluting, pink silk—creating an imaginary object of some visual complexity. Look again. My lamp in your head is made of such stuff as dreams are made on—an immaterial material. It is semitransparent. You see it and, through it, you see your own lamp, your picture on your wall.

You have lamps and you have garbage bags in your experience, to which my words have added my details. There are other things in my little story that I have merely named for you—lobby, elevator, living room—relying entirely on your experience of such things to fill in what I mean. In all cases, I need you to put your experience of the world at the service of what I am telling you.

And it is not only objects that we have translated together. There was a small joke about fashions in design, a protagonist (myself), and an action (my carrying the lamp). And there is yet another act that you have performed with me: my act of remembering another lamp in that expropriated living room in another past and place.

Notice that I gave my little story a locale—a street on the West Side of Manhattan—without giving you any detail with which to imagine it. Suppose you have never been to New York and have no relevant experience to help you imagine it? In this instance, I do not need you—

in fact, I need you *not* to see and feel my street in New York, in America. In this instance, my street in New York is not a seen-and-felt place but an ideal one, whose rhetorical purpose is to be at vast remove from my street in Nazi Vienna. Your experience, on which I am relying, is distance and difference.

We come home, at last, to the subject of the Albany conference and to my particular theme: the translating of the remembered past—the Holocaust past—into the reader's present experience. Our first problem is the complexity of the distance and difference between what we remember and what is in front of our eyes.

Two brief passages in my novel *Her First American* concern themselves with the problems of remembering. In one, my heroine, Ilka, has come to America with documentation that her father was killed in the last weeks of the Nazi war. Her mother was missing, but she has been found alive in a kibbutz and is about to materialize in New York:

> They went to the wharf and stood in the cold drizzle watching the people walk down the gangplank. Ilka was afraid of not recognizing her mother. She kept saying, "I haven't seen her in eleven years. I was ten years old," and saw her mother in a wheelchair being wheeled down the gangplank, but it was not her mother. Ilka ran forward, and it was her mother.
>
> In the taxi Ilka looked sideways at the woman who sat next to her, who was her mother. It wasn't the added years only: events accrued to her that Ilka did not know anything about that made her a stranger. And it wasn't only that. Her actual person coincided with Ilka's memory of her person; the memory hung about like a ghost, competing for the space filled by its incarnation. Ilka looked out the car window and Riverside Drive was real and her mother returned into that transparent, unstable stuff our memories of the dead are made of. Ilka looked at her mother. Here she was.

Later, the two return to Austria to look for the spot where Ilka's father had last been seen, on the road outside a small market town:

> The stewardess spoke German with an Austrian voice and Ilka's childhood address came intact into her head. "Mutti, hey listen: "AchterBezirk-JosephstädterStrasse81ZweiterStockTür9."
>
> They burst into the streets of Vienna. "The J Wagen!" cried her mother. "It goes—it used to go to Vati's shop. You were too small to remember. . . ."
>
> But it turned out that Ilka remembered what she did not remember, as if

she had reentered a childhood tale: she might not recall how it came out but knew what the next sentence was going to say. "JosephstädterStrasse will be the next left. It is! Cobbles! And nothing over four stories! There was a bank that had a door that cut the corner off the building that was closed when I went down with Vati, the morning after Hitler. Here it is! Mutti! You see! The corner door!" To be proved correct had that odd little importance one feels in presenting certification—a driver's license, a library card: this proves that this is me. The person standing before you is the person standing before you. It is I who lived here. "Mutti! Schmutzki's sweet shop. They had a mongoloid son. He used to peck his head forward like a pigeon, with every step. Like this."

"Oh, Ilka!" Ilka's mother laughed.

"I used to practice walking like that."

"Ilka!"

Remembering is a complicated act. The often-documented alteration of the size of the object because of the viewer's altered size is its simplest aspect. There is, besides, the coincidence of the ghostly, transparent, unstable stuff memory is made of, with the hard-edged material object, which, as often as not, is, in fact, altered: "The Schmutzkis' sweet shop selling shoes!" Ilka's mother peered through the display window and said, "The counter is the same counter but they have it on the other side. The cash register is in the same place but this is a modern cash register." And there is the degree of history the viewer shares with the view, whether it's the fact, merely, of having passed, or of having been at home here, where his neighbor hated him to death.

Ilka said, "The Schmutzkis 'put their heads in the gas oven,' as the grownups put it."

"Frau Schmutzki said to me, 'What country is going to give us a visa, with the boy?' Walter was his name. They put their heads in the gas oven, the father, mother, and the boy."

"I used to lie in bed trying to picture them kneeling side by side. I'd fall asleep trying to imagine three heads into one oven."

Ilka's mother said, "The next time, I can see that one might rather put one's head in the gas oven." "One might survive again," said Ilka.

"One might survive all over again," said her mother. "I can see how one might rather put one's head in the gas oven. Here it is. Number eighty-one. The court has got shabby."

The second problem I want to illustrate is the problem not of remembering, but of misremembering. In 1968 my husband David determined, rightly as it turned out, that I needed to face my Austrian past. I did not think I needed to do any such thing, since the past was not, I thought, giving me any sort of trouble. (It was on this trip, incidentally, that we visited the actual street fictionalized above.)

Our goal was my grandparents' old house and haberdasher's shop in the village of Fischamend. It was there that my father and mother and I had lived after the Nazis took away our Vienna flat—until the autumn, when the Nazis took away the Fischamend house as well, and turned it into party headquarters. The village was some ten minutes by rented car from the Vienna airport at Schwechat, not far from the Czech border. I used to think it was called Fischamend because there is a weather vane in the shape of a fish at the top end of the medieval tower. Childhood reminiscences require a miscomprehension or two.

I looked for the bakery where my grandmother used to take her newly-risen black bread—I remember it was the size of a small cart-wheel—to be baked in the great brick oven. The bakery was gone. In its place, like a cheap false tooth, stood a new three-story building. There was a plaque. I translated it for David:

DESTROYED BY ENEMY ACTION
REBUILT WITH MUNICIPAL LOAN, 1947

My grandparents' house—a big old place with walls three feet thick—had been restituted to our ownership after the war. I remember a letter from a lawyer representing my grandfather's young assistant, Mitzi. Mitzi had made us an offer for house and shop, with the stipulation that we pay for fixing the war damage to the west wing and for restoring the burned-out central portion.

The fish moves out of sight as the car approaches the sturdy tower straddling the road. I said, "Drive through the arch and we'll come out on the village square. The Stern house and shop will be diagonally across on the far right."

"There!" I said to David, "You see that wall with the mural of the father, mother, boy, and girl? That's new. My grandparents' house is behind there."

David said, "It says *Polizei*." "That's a new police station!" I said.

I remember walking at a running speed and sensing my husband like a dream person just out of sight behind my left shoulder. "Ask them in the police station," David kept saying. I kept walking. "There must be an opening in this new block here, somewhere where you can get to our house. We must have missed the opening, because this is already where the old police station used to be, where they kept my grandfather and my father overnight and broke my father's glasses." I turned and walked back.

David said, "Ask them at the police station." The police station had two steps up to the door, where there used not to be any steps, and this made it hard to imagine where our old floor used to be. The typewriter that the young policeman was using must have been standing just to the left of where my grandmother's iron, wood-burning kitchen stove used to stand: history had done away with my childhood floor plan.

"*Ask*," said David. The young policeman had a dimple in his chin, and his hair was tidily side-parted. He had never heard of any Stern house or shop. He placed both blond hands over his heart. He was born in 1950. There was always this police station right here.

Back in New York I told my mother, "There's a new wall with a mural." My mother said, "Of a father, mother, boy, and girl." "How did you know?" I rather squealed. "Because Cousin Rudi brought us the snapshot last year. Don't you remember? You have it here somewhere." "So where is our house?" I shouted. "They gave it back to us after the war," my mother said, "Mitzi was going to buy it. I think the Americans had bombed it, and the Russians had set it on fire the night before they left, so I think in the end it just had to be torn down."

What past was there now for me to face?

Not the dismantled stones, whose substance must exist, somewhere—as gravel, perhaps, and the dust that the people of Fischamend walk on. What baffles the imagination is the loss of the definition of the space that once contained my grandparents and my father and my mother and me. This inability to imagine where the floor must have been, and the wall, and the window at which I used to stand and watch Mitzi parading in her Hitler Youth uniform, matters not at all—it is hardly more than a conceit to which I nevertheless find myself returning, as to the absence of a place to stand and look at loss.

Finally, I shall relate an event only recently told to friends, and never before written down.

My experiences are not the extreme Holocaust experiences. My father had put me on a transport that carried five hundred children out of Vienna and brought us to England on December 10, 1938. What I want to relate is the mildest sort of event; it turns out, also, to be an indigestible one.

My tenth birthday came four days before Hitler's takeover of Vienna and I cannot say whether the following occurred in the weeks just after or just before. In any event, there was something in the air—in the remembered air—compared with which the most monstrous horror in any horror movie seems a mere cuteness, except for the anxiety, the waiting for whatever it is that is about to happen. Memory tells me that it was warm, that I was wearing no coat, that it was toward evening. My father and I walked home through one of Vienna's noble parks, with perfect lawns and great beds of massed roses. In an open area not far from our exit, by a magnificent wrought-iron gate, there were people feeding the pigeons. An old man was selling little packets of pigeon feed, and I said to my father, "I want some pigeon feed." My father said, "Let's get home."

I said, "I want some pigeon feed." I vividly remember looking down at the mass of moving pigeons. These pigeons have got into a novel of mine in an utterly different circumstance:

> On the expanse of pavement milled a crowd of pigeons in a perpetual exchange of place, dipping anxious, greedy heads with each advance of each leg. Here and here, and over there, one or another raised and shook an agitated wing. Now one, now two, now all rose off the ground and settled a few yards to the right.

The pigeons revolved around my feet—I was walking in pigeons, saying, "I *want* some *pigeon* feed."

When I turned around my father had one of those little packets in his hand, but he didn't give it to me.

I said, "Give it to me!" and reached for it but he raised it out of my reach. I said, "Give it to me give it to me give it to me!" and pulled his sleeves. He raised his hands higher. I jumped and caught his wrists. I seem to remember depending on his two arms the way a child might hang swinging a moment from two branches of a tree, and I looked into his face and it wasn't my father. It was a rather large young man with a fat, fair, round, smooth, bland face. He looked embarrassed and raised his feed packet higher in the air. And then I first became aware of my father's voice calling me from a perfectly unexpected direction, saying, "Lore! Over here! Lore!," and I ran and buried my face in the stuff of his suit and refused to talk about the matter for the next thirty years.

In what way is this a Holocaust memory? Nothing happened to me except an experience of that excruciating shame to which children and young people are unreasonably prone. The worst that can be said of the young man is that he lacked imagination: most of us, in such a situation, would say to the little girl, "Hold out your hand," and give her a palmful of feed. Maybe he was too young to imagine children. He wore a business suit like my father's—not a uniform. He had the face not of a sadistic monster, but of a silly young man. Why is he the Nazi of my memory?

A friend, a psychiatrist, theorizes a screen memory here. There was no young man, he says. It was really my father incapacitated and never again able to give me so much as pigeon feed. But memory insists on that young man. If I imagined him then, I cannot *un*imagine him now; nor can I not think of him as a Nazi. But, yes, it was my father. It was my father, who suddenly was not there. It was my father, as well as every comfortable, familiar, dependable, ordinary thing which, during that childish thirty-second mistake, had been switched on me.

Let me corral some of the problems I have wanted to demonstrate. Some pertain to writing, some to remembering, some to the Holocaust: Recollection is a double experience like a double exposure, the time frame in which we remember superimposes itself on the remembered time and the two images fail to match perfectly at any point.

The rememberer has changed, and so, in all probability, has the thing or the place remembered.

There is, to move to a different metaphor, a collision between two images—I mean the sort of collision you experience when a dream remnant overlaps into the waking mode. Memory is made of a different material from the material of the real.

I remember, as a child, standing at the corner of Josephstädterstrasse and testing out the whole business of remembering—saying to myself, "I will always remember that person, there, the one who is just stepping up onto the sidewalk." But, by the time I went to bed that same evening, I had forgotten to remember. And yet, fifty years later I remember performing that experiment with memory, and its proof! We cannot will ourselves a madeleine; nor can we rid ourselves of those memories which never cease their demands that we bear witness, that we write them into stories.

5 · *Saul Friedländer*

Historical Writing and the Memory of the Holocaust

On receiving the Scholl Prize in November 1985, the German philosopher Jürgen Habermas mentioned that the memory of the Nazi epoch had somehow remained untouched by the passage of time. For him, forty years after the war, this past still appeared as present, whereas for the adolescent he had been in 1945, the events of four decades earlier seemed to be distant history. A few months later, in June 1986, one of Habermas's most extreme ideological opponents, the historian Ernst Nolte, published an article in the *Frankfurter Allgemeine Zeitung* entitled "Eine Vergangenheit die nicht vergehen will," a past that refuses to go away. Both Habermas and Nolte, from entirely opposite points of view and for entirely different reasons, were pointing to the as yet massive presence of the Nazi epoch in contemporary German memory.

Indeed, when one considers the last two years, one gets the impression that, notwithstanding an explicit yearning for a "normalization" of the Nazi past, this epoch is more present than ever, that we are witnessing a kind of upsurge of something that, over long periods of time, had been partially repressed: the Bitburg affair may have triggered this return of the repressed; it was followed by the Fassbinder controversy and, more recently, by the historians' debate, which still simmers on. As Hans-Magnus Enzensberger remarked in relation to the historians' controversy, those who wanted Auschwitz to fade away, failed: never before, over the last twenty years, had Auschwitz been discussed so much in West Germany as during 1986.

Our frame of reference in this presentation will be the contemporary West German scene, and the analysis itself will concentrate on some major historical representations and shifts in representations of the Nazi era and, more specifically, of the annihilation of the Jews. But as this book does not deal with historiography in a professional sense, but rather with writing on the Holocaust (that is, with various kinds of narratives in a more general way), the basic narratives underlying the historical representations will be the main object of my query.

The simplest form of narrative is what becomes embedded in memory; as understood here, it should be considered as the most basic form of emplotment of the past. Most people are not aware of all the components of even one narrative. Their representations of the past, however, simply and lacunary as they may be, nonetheless follow the main lines of one narrative or another. These basic structures of memory are determined by the selection of representative aspects of the past, in accordance with the present needs of various groups. The symbolic networks carrying these narratives are most commonly commemorative ceremonies, monuments, artistic representations of past events, museums, and so forth. In France, for instance, since the end of the war, no fewer than four or five new films dealing with the Nazi epoch are produced every year: they bear the most diverse narratives. *Lacombe, Lucien* and *Shoah* tell very different stories. By the same token, complex historiographical presentations can also be reduced to basic narratives.

Over the years, the competing narratives shift, change, interact, and disappear from the scene. Silence concerning some massive event is possibly the most explicit narrative of all.

Some years ago, the main contending representations of the Nazi regime probably would have been an essentially linear, ideologically determined representation of Nazi policies, on the one hand, against a more haphazard, chaotic, but nonetheless structurally interpreted picture of the events of that period, on the other. Nowadays, these two representations can be put together under the same heading, and two further narratives can be added. The shift in representations that has recently occurred is significant enough to have been considered by many as the breakdown of some accepted consensus, a consensus more or less valid since the very end of the war.

Within the first category of narratives, one must distinguish within the basic overall consensus two different versions of the events. The first version, which could be called "the liberal interpretation of the Nazi period," to use the terminology coined by Geoffrey Barraclough in a well-known series of articles published in the *New York Review of Books* in 1972, was represented by such historians and political scientists as Hajo Holborn or Karl-Dietrich Bracher. It emphasizes the ideological, political, and criminal aspects of the Nazi phenomenon, that is, the destruction of the democratic system, the expansion of state control over society and of terror over those considered enemies of the regime or outcasts; it stresses the "conquest of *Lebensraum*," racial policies, and global struggle against the Jews, as well as other massive expressions of the criminality of the system.

This representation places ideology and modes of domination and terror at its very core and considers the developments leading to the Third Reich, as well as those which occurred within the system itself, in a partially linear way, although everybody would agree that, at each stage, various diverging paths would have been possible. Such a representation, like the others we will deal with further on, can be reduced to a series of basic narratives according to the central focus chosen. One possible focus could be that of historical continuity; another, probably the most compelling, is that of historical responsibility. Responsibility is understood here not as that of individuals, which, for the historian, is only of peripheral significance, but that of various collective agents linked to the criminal policies of the Nazi regime.

If one reduces the historiographical representations to narratives focused around the problem of responsibility, one necessarily has to take into account three collective actors: the perpetrators, the bystanders, and the victims. Each narrative will be based on a specific interaction between these three collective actors, or on a redefinition of the concrete groups encompassed within each of these categories.

In the "liberal" representation, the perpetrators are clearly the Nazi party and its periphery, including its bureaucratic instruments. The bystanders—and here we are dealing with the German scene only—include German society at large, with limited exceptions. These bystanders are characterized by partial knowledge of crimes committed and by more or less sustained indifference and passivity. The victims range from political opponents imprisoned in concentration camps, mentally-ill killed in the "euthanasia" program, Gypsies, Slavs and other victimized populations to the Jews. Here, we will concentrate on the Jews only, as their persecution was the most extreme, the most total, and they have therefore become, for many, the symbol of Nazi victims in general.

In this case, there is no opacity in the interaction between perpetrators, bystanders, and victims. By their passivity, the bystanders indirectly helped the perpetrators, as the lack of any major resistance and the existence of pervasive tacit acquiescence allowed the regime to pursue its policies to their most extreme limits. As for the victims, well-identified in this case, there is little they could have done to alter their fate, on a global level, no matter what possibilities for some kind of resistance are discussed.

In terms of self-perception within contemporary West German society, this narrative implies global historical responsibility. The overall background for the events may well be found in various trends in European history, but the immediate supporting system is firmly rooted in German soil. The perpetrators and the bystanders are part of German society. After the war, this representation seeped into German memory and into Western memory as well. It is the representation most of us have of what happened. In West Germany, the acceptance of this representation and of the responsibility it entails was clearly expressed by leaders from President Theodor Heuss during the early years of the Federal Republic to President Richard von Weizsäcker in his May, 1985 Bundestag speech. It has found manifold modes of expression, over the last forty years, in the news media, in literature and film, in rituals and monuments: from texts of Heinrich Böll to the maintenance of the Dachau and Bergen-Belsen camps, for instance.

The structuralist approach to the history of the Third Reich differs on many counts from the traditional, ideologically centered liberal vision: it puts a much greater stress on the continuity of social structures, rooted in nineteenth-century Imperial Germany, that offered the necessary breeding ground for Nazism in its rise and development, structures that, more often than not, still exist within the West German republic. This left-wing questioning of the liberal image has put much stress on the dynamics of institutions and on the relatively secondary importance of personalities within the Nazi system, including Adolf Hitler himself, whatever essential symbolic role the myth of the "Führer" may have fulfilled.

This mode of historiographical interpretation of the Nazi system offered an explanation of the "Final Solution" in terms quite different from those of the liberal approach: if ideology and stage-by-stage progression in the persecution of the Jews were essential aspects of the first representation, here we are faced with the dynamics of political rhetoric leading haphazardly to unforeseen results, or with the no-less-blind interaction of competing institutions initiating what Hans Mommsen called a process of "cumulative radicalization," by a lack of centralized decisions and a more or less chaotic development toward the most extreme results.

However, if one focuses on the problem of historical responsibility, the structural approach is not essentially different from the liberal one, although some nuances have to be pointed out briefly. The same three collective actors we encountered in the first presentation also interact within the structuralist view of the Nazi epoch. The difference lies in the fact that, in the structuralist view, there are many active and almost independent subgroups within the wide category of perpetrators; these subgroups interact with one another in such a way that it becomes extremely difficult to pinpoint where the responsibility lies, as each partial decision flows, in a haphazard way, from some partially perceived context. One may argue that such a view of the perpetrators considerably widens the field of responsibility and encompasses many more elements of German society within the tortuous process of destruction; on the other hand, it may be argued that the very fluid and nebulous aspect of the process itself made targeted resistance much more difficult. In any case, we are faced with a somewhat paradoxical image of mass murder, of a totally unprecedented kind, being enacted without any clear definition of the central group of decisionmakers.

Within this structuralist approach, the bystanders are, of necessity, much more widely implicated in the process than in the previous representation. We are offered a model of fascist society that puts heavier weight on the responsibility of traditional elites than the liberal view, which tends to concentrate on the central decisionmaking function of some institutions of the Nazi party, particularly its leadership.

These diverging representations of responsibility have not really seeped into the public debate because of their technicality. On the other hand, for professional historians—from the early 1970s to the mid-1980s or thereabouts—the opposition between "intentionalists" and "functionalists" has been one of the main historiographical controversies concerning the Nazi epoch.

In my opinion, as already stated, it can still be argued that both the liberal and the structuralist approach belong to a common consensus about basic responsibilities and basic victimization, notwithstanding the divergences just described. Whatever the dynamics of the process that led to ultimate destruction of the victims, whatever the groups and institutions involved, whatever the relative passivity or collaboration of the most varied strata of the German population, both representations would still focus on the unique responsibility of perpetrators as a German group within a system, the roots of which were to be found within German society; and both would identify the bystanders within that same society, with only nuanced divergences about degrees of conformism, passivity, tacit acceptance, and so forth. In a way, in both cases, at least up to the mid-1980s, some kind of implicit moral stand suffused the representation of this past, clearly considering the problem of responsibility from the viewpoint of the victims.

For reasons that cannot be developed here, and that may have something to do with the very passage of four decades since the end of the war, with changes in the political climate within West Germany, with the search for a new national identity, and with some haphazard catalytic incidents, too, such as the Bitburg controversy, this consensual vision of the past—consensual at least on the level of an explicit intellectual majority—seems to have been changing over the last two years in some rather fundamental ways.

The revision of the traditional and consensual narrative concerning the Nazi epoch should not, as a matter of fact, be considered as a phenomenon that started during the second half of the 1980s. The new versions of the past with which we will now deal have been present on the German scene since the very end of the war, but it is their current intellectual salience that allows one to consider the mid-1980s as a turning point. Among these new representations one may consider two different interpretations of past events, each of which implies a change in the fundamental structure previously described. Let me first present these two new narratives in the most general terms and focus only later on their implications for structural change within the former representations.

Let us call the first of the two new narrations the "symmetric vision of the past." The most obvious feature of the symmetric vision is an equation of crimes—and therefore of responsibilities—established between the atrocities perpetrated by the Nazis and those committed by the Allies, particularly by the Soviets: Auschwitz = Katyn = the expulsions of the German population from the East = Dresden = Hiroshima, etc. But the symmetric vision is more multifaceted than this.

At the end of World War I, a majority of Germans may have felt the need for, and had the possibility of referring to, the archetypal figure of the *Frontkämpfer*, dead or alive, as a source of patriotic pride and as a crystallization point for representations of the Great War. This emblem became more problematic at the end of World War II, however, for obvious reasons. Nonetheless, some select figures were integrated by the common imagination (Rommel, Odet, Guderian, and others), and an immense production of memoirs or popular literature (the vast number of copies of the weekly or monthly *Landserhefte*, and of the best-selling novels of Heinz G. Konsalik or Sven Hassell, for instance, immediately come to mind) fused with the personal reminiscences of millions of ex-soldiers of the Wehrmacht to keep an idealized memory of the fighting troops alive. This memory was possibly much more massive than the ritualized one of the anti-Hitler resistance officially considered to be the only acceptable link between the new society and its past.

This representation of the *Frontkämpfer* of World War II makes a clear distinction between the bravery and nonideological commitment of the Wehrmacht and the evil represented by such armed units as the Waffen-SS, although even the idealization of the latter soon became an accepted *topos* of postwar literary endeavors. All in all, however, the symmetric vision is based on a double symmetry, insofar as the central problem of responsibility is concerned: the symmetry of potential and actual criminal behavior established between Germany and its enemies, on the one hand; and the symmetry of courage and noninvolvement in criminal activity on the part of the immense majority of soldiers and civilians, on the other hand. This double symmetry creates a very peculiar image of the past when such an idealized Wehrmacht is evoked in its heroic resistance against the barbarity of Soviet troops invading German soil, during the last year of the war. Even if the wide acceptance of this narrative was not in any way new, its relative and rather sudden intellectual prominence of late may be considered significant.

The more extreme version of the current narratives, putting the main emphasis on the Soviet perpetrator, partly inverts what we call the basic consensual image. The Soviets—or, more precisely, the Bolshevik perpetrators—become the original perpetrators, the initiators of policies of total annihilation in history, at least in modern history. The Nazis, as perpetrators, copied the methods of the Bolsheviks, and their own crimes could be explained in part by their fear of becoming themselves victims of Bolshevik annihilation. Within this new narrative, not only are the crimes of the Nazis relativized, but the Nazis themselves become the potential victims of the archcriminals, the Soviets. The traditional perpetrators and their victims indeed exist within the new narrative, but the presentation of the Nazis as potential victims, too, tends to invert the basic roles.

It is difficult to know how widespread among the West German people this new representation of responsibility is or was. The descriptions of Soviet atrocities can fit either the "symmetric vision" or the latter one. In a Konsalik novel such as *Der letzte Gefangene* [The Last Prisoner], scenes of Soviet bestiality, such as the killing of German prisoners who have surrendered, may mean that, *ex post*, the reality of the Soviet threat is understood and that, for those who grasped the nature of the Bolshevik regime, there were good reasons for anxiety and preemptive action. The issue boils down to an alternative: who would liquidate whom first? Incidentally, the spate of recent publications telling of the imminence of a Soviet attack on Germany in the summer of 1941 reinforces this new narrative about the past.

In these two narratives, the reader somewhat familiar with the German scene will have recognized the very general outlines of some of the recent historical reinterpretations of the Nazi epoch that the Frankfurt philosopher Jürgen Habermas denounced in his *Die Zeit* article of July 11, 1986, as "apologetic," thereby starting the notorious "historians' controversy." The "symmetric vision" was historiographically expressed in no uncertain terms in Andreas Hillgruber's *Zweierlei Untergang* (1986); the more extreme "Bolshevik cause" version was expressed in Ernst Nolte's articles "Between Myth and Revisionism: National Socialism from the Perspective of the 80s" (1985) and "Eine Vergangenheit die nicht vergehen will" (1986).

In the first narrative, the symmetry implies two equivalent frameworks of responsibility: the responsibility of the Nazis in killing their victims is not denied but is, in a way, balanced against the responsibility of the Soviets for the horrors committed on German soil in 1944/45 and, more generally, against the evil intentions of the allies against Germany and its population, long before anything was known of the German crimes. This last point is very central in Hillgruber's argument and should be considered as no less important than the stress on Soviet criminality and the heroism of the Wehrmacht during the last year of the war. Instead of the three initial collective actors that we identified in the consensual narratives, we are now facing, at first glance, four actors, including two categories of perpetrators: the Nazis and, facing them, some mixed representation of Allied intent and Soviet behavior.

The bystanders, that is, the passive German population which facilitated the task of the perpetrators according to the initial interpretations, become, in Hillgruber's representation, the pitiful victims of the Allies and, in particular, of the Soviets. Therefore, the doubling of the perpetrator image leads, of necessity, to some kind of doubling of the collective victims' representation and to the transformation of the erstwhile tacit or explicit supporters of the Nazi system into victims of the Soviets and the Western Allies—not unlike, in their sufferings, the other victims, such as the Jews. In fact, we could say here that both the perpetrators and the victims are symmetrically doubled by an inverted image: there are two opposite kinds of perpetrators and two opposite categories of victims, whereby some of the erstwhile bystanders become the new category of victims. Such symmetry may help to deal with the problem of historical responsibility and reinstate an acceptable national vision of that period of German history.

A case in point is the image of the Wehrmacht. By most traditional accounts, the Wehrmacht was directly involved in the perpetration of the Nazi crimes, and it was certainly identified as part of the criminal system in massive studies published during the late 1970s and the early 1980s. In the new representation, the Wehrmacht becomes the heroic defender of the victims threatened by the Soviet onslaught. The crimes of the Wehrmacht are not denied by Hillgruber, although he prefers to speak of the "revenge orgy" of the Red Army. Whereas this revenge orgy is described with considerable pathos, however, its origin, the tens of millions of dead left by the Wehrmacht in the wake of its onslaughts on Germany's neighbors—particularly on the Soviet Union—does not seem to reenter the picture with any forcefulness.

The last narrative, exemplified in Ernst Nolte's articles, could be considered as approaching a reversal of the traditional representation of the Nazi epoch. The central actor within the global historical context that Nolte has described in his various publications is, by now, the Bolshevik. The Bolsheviks are the original perpetrators of atrocity and annihilation, and the Nazis—whose own atrocities are certainly not denied, but who "merely" copy the Bolsheviks—become, moreover, perpetrators who may well have acted out of anguish at the idea of being potential victims of the Red Terror. In short, the traditional perpetrator of the early narratives becomes a potential victim; the traditional by-stander becomes an actual victim; and, as for the traditional victim, although his or her fate is not denied, it is rendered in these recent presentations in what has more than once been shown to be a rather ambiguous light. In any case, the source of all evil is clearly placed outside the traditional representation of responsibility.

In a February 1985 article published in *Die Zeit*, in connection with the fortieth anniversary of the defeat of the Third Reich, the German historian Golo Mann asked who, in France, would have insisted on remembering Waterloo thirty or forty years later. Nobody would have thought of commemorating such an event. Why, asked Mann, dig up past accusations of wrong done on one side or the other? How long must one continue to mark the anniversaries of Nazi misdeeds?

The Waterloo image implies that, for posterity, whatever the crimes committed by the Nazi regime, one national defeat equals another, and that the historical fates of Napoleon and Hitler can ultimately be considered in the same terms. This comparison, although somewhat simplified, expresses in a nutshell what may well be the real sense of the growing urge for normalization of the past, as it appears today in West German society, notwithstanding the controversies just analyzed: after more than four decades, the Nazi epoch should finally be consid-ered as any other. This means, in other words, that the Nazi epoch should be removed from the field of ever-recurring memory to that of distant history. The real tension here is between memory and history;

or, more precisely, between memory and the various forms of "historicization" of National Socialism, to use a concept that has entered common discourse over the last two years. The shift in narratives that we have analyzed would be reduced by some to a necessary process of historicization.

At this final stage, however, these transformations of some German narratives about the past have to be considered against a much broader background. A basic question cannot be avoided—it could be formulated as follows: is there anything, in the very nature of the Nazi regime and, more specifically, in the nature of its crimes, that defies the reinsertion of that past into the framework of "normal" historical narrative, that impedes its transformation into an historical epoch like any other, into a story of events of as much or as little significance for posterity as, let us say, those which marked the Napoleonic era, whether in German memory or Western memory in general?

In other words, does this segment of history impress the imagination in such a way that the memory of it continues to be a source of constant fixation and reelaboration, notwithstanding the passage of time?

In "Fascinating Fascism," Susan Sontag noted, more than ten years ago, the widespread use of Nazi symbols in pornography and representations of sadism. In *Imagining Hitler,* Alvin Rosenfeld has further explored the murky field of an ever wider use of Nazi symbols and stories in the subcultures of the West. There is little doubt that at this peculiar level, involving the hidden or not-so-hidden fantasies of sadism and their commercial exploitation, Nazism and its symbols seem to offer a satisfaction, the roots of which may be interpretable in different ways, but the reality of which is incontrovertible.

On May 15, 1987, the *International Herald Tribune* reproduced the poster of a film on Josef Mengele with the legend "Nazi films abound" and the following details: "Distribution rights have been sold in the United States to New World Pictures, which has retitled the film and redrawn the artwork, eliminating the Commando Mengele turning-to-blood title in favour of a smaller, non-pink 'Angel of Death'. (The blood of millions is on his hands. The power of evil is on his side . . .)." The poster itself, as well as the text printed on either side of Mengele's civilian-attired figure in the foreground, with a ghostlike reproduction of his picture in SS uniform in the background, searchlights scanning a black sky, would be worth a thorough interpretation. There, in any case, lies some aspect of our question, and there one might search for part of the answer.

At a somewhat different level, the morbid fascination with Nazism may be due (as I tried to show in *Reflections of Nazism: An Essay on Kitsch and Death*) to the juxtaposition, within the representation of Nazism, of the warmth of the herd and its expression in the most varied forms of *Kitsch* sentimentality, with fantasies of Apocalyptic destruction. These two apparently contradictory longings, both of them deep-seated reactions to the challenges of modernity, of individualism and of freedom, found their expression in Nazi fantasies and in basic aspects of Nazi reality. They remain undercurrents of the modern imagination.

But, obviously, the basis of the permanence of present-day fantasies about Nazism is the feeling that Nazi crimes carry some specificity, some peculiar aspects not easily compared with other atrocities. In the concluding lines of her book *Eichmann in Jerusalem,* Hannah Arendt may have unintentionally given us the clue as to what distinguished Nazi crimes from others. The Nazis, argued Arendt, tried "to determine who should or who should not inhabit the world." This, in fact, is something no other regime, whatever its criminality, has attempted to do. In that sense, the Nazi regime attained what seems to be some sort of theoretical outer limit: one may envision an even larger number of victims, and a technologically more efficient way of killing, but once a regime decides that whole groups, whatever the criteria may be, should be annihilated there and then and not allowed to live on earth, the ultimate has been achieved. This limit, one may suggest, has been reached only once in modern history—by the Nazis. In other words, the Nazis destroyed, industrially, methodically, entire segments of the human race, not because of any act committed, be it actual or potential, but because of their definition of who was human and who was not. The Nazis thereby touched, in Habermas's terms, upon some fundamental feeling of human solidarity that may have definitively changed the nature of human relations. This, possibly, in one form or another, is what has haunted the human imagination ever since.

Commentary by Emmanuel Le Roy Ladurie

Mr. Friedländer raises some important issues for the historian. I first have to apologize for my lack of competence in his topic; the only viewpoint I can share here is that of comparative history. Dealing with periods I know a bit better as a specialist—for example, the period on the European continent that has been dubbed the Old Regime—I realize, could be quite strange or boring for people who essentially have an interest in literature and general topics and not historiography, and who also have an interest, of course, in Holocaust history. My comments, at least, will be brief.

My point of comparison will be the religious persecutions of the seventeenth century, especially the persecution against the French Protestants, or Huguenots, as symbolized by the revocation of the Edict of Nantes in 1685. Some of you, of course, may find the comparison ridiculous or insulting, since, after all, the Huguenots were not killed— or at least not too many were killed—by Louis XIV's authorities. But, to put it simply, some of them *were* killed, and the great majority were constrained either to convert or to endure dangerous self-exile, jail, or the galleys. Let me remind you, though, that before the Holocaust the revocation of the Edict of Nantes was considered one of the most atrocious acts of intolerance ever committed. Of course, we have made progress since then.

By the way, the persecution against the Protestants nearly degenerated into a persecution against the Jews in 1686, an event that, for various reasons, was averted in the end. So my subject may be a little more relevant than you would think.

An historical analysis of the revocation of the Edict of Nantes yields at least two or three of the schools of thought that Saul Friedländer mentioned. On the one hand, there would be the liberal—historicist, intentionalist—view. Like Hitler, Louis XIV, from the very top of society, was a responsible perpetrator of a terrible act of repression and exclusion. This does not at all mean, of course, that we may call Louis XIV another "Hitler." In other respects that would be ridiculous, but Louis XIV actually did operate as a determined ideologist, very different from the kings who were his predecessors and successors. As a matter of fact, from the beginning of the time when Protestants appeared in France (that is to say, from the 1520s) up to the good and final

Edict of Toleration in 1787, only two kinds determinedly persecuted Protestants during their entire reign—Henry II and Louis XIV. All the other kings (there are eight or ten, depending on whether you include the Regency periods) showed a certain degree of flexibility toward their Huguenot subjects. Louis XIV, during his entire personal reign from 1661 to 1715, consistently waged a war of repression against Protestants and thus deserves the title of chief ideologist of that campaign.

But then, there is also room in French history for views of the structuralist-functionalist approach much like those described by Friedländer. Actually, the bystanders, the nonpolitical majority, were often passive and even sympathetic to the whole repressive policy of the Sun King. The logic of the French absolutist regime and society, the preexisting social structures, were working in favor of the edict's revocation. As a matter of fact, it was in the interest of the state to give advantages to the Catholic church, and authoritarian suppression of the Protestant heresy gave certain obvious advantages to the Roman Catholic clergy. The Catholic priests and bishops, by the way, reciprocated: they advised their faithful to be loyal to the French king in exchange for the favor he did them by crushing the Calvinists. Thus, we can even retain the image of organized chaos that Friedländer mentioned, as we consider the local initiative of people such as Foucault (Foucault of the seventeenth century), who gave ideas to Louis XIV and his government, which then acted. This would be a nonlinear history of the revocation as triggered by various institutions, and there would be a pattern of widespread responsibility similar to the one that has been referred to by Friedländer; this, too, at the beginning at least, would be an act without actors.

Finally, the perspective of comparative history that Friedländer has evoked should not be absent from an analysis of the seventeenth century. Louis XIV persecuted the Protestants, but European kings in Spain and Austria also did. Protestant kings persecuted the Catholics in a very harsh way, especially the English kings and governments with respect to popish Ireland. The czar, emperor of Russia in the seventeenth century, severely punished the old believers of Archpriest Avvakumm; the Ukrainians killed Jews (at least some Ukrainians did—I should not put this in terms of collective responsibility). And the Japanese shogun, at the beginning of the same century, literally exterminated the already important Christian minority in southern Japan.

Apart from anti-Jewish pogroms in the Ukraine, this Japanese initiative is the only case of mass extermination in the otherwise tragic history of religious persecution in seventeenth-century Eurasia. Quite remarkably, some Japanese historians now, even left-wing and progressive ones, justify this destruction of early local Christianity by saying that it allowed Japan to escape Western and especially Spanish colonization and thus escape the fate of the Philippines. That might be so, but it is still objectionable, of course, from a moral viewpoint.

To return to our subject, we should not overlook the moral indignation that, in an absolutely legitimate way, must be raised against the Holocaust. We cannot look at this fact with quiet and cold objectivity. But neither can we escape the problem of comparative history. There have been several massive and planned exterminations in the twentieth century. In chronological order: against the Armenians; then the peasant collectivization and the Gulag in the Soviet Union, where the lowest and most reasonable estimates speak of 17 million dead; then, of course, the Holocaust with its 6 million dead; and, of late, Cambodia, where so many people have been destroyed in such a small country (French colonization, by the way, enjoyed a much better record than recently "independent" Cambodia).

In no sense does this comparison attenuate the horrendous, stupefying and, so to speak, metaphysical ferocity of the Holocaust. I want to be quite definite on this essential point. But a sound and fertile analysis, a very normally indignant analysis, I think, has nothing to lose by putting the great tragedy of the Holocaust in the context of an almost equally horrendous twentieth century, as it has been experienced from 1914 through the 1970s throughout Europe and Asia. After all, the expression of Hannah Arendt—the "banality of evil" (should we say the "trivializing" of evil, the normalcy in the abnormality?)—is also relevant for many other aspects of our whole century, even if it best applies in its worst form to the Holocaust.

PART · II

The Representation of Evil

6 · *Aharon Appelfeld*

After the Holocaust

*T*he subject to be discussed here is horror and art. Can they coexist? Perhaps combining the two is merely another expression of horror, revealing the depths of human degradation. In the concentration camps they forced the prisoners' orchestras to play classical music. For whom were those performances intended, and for what?

The famous saying of Theodor Adorno, that after Auschwitz it would be barbaric to write lyric poetry, is more than understandable. We must agree with it with all our being. A religious person will certainly argue in favor of silence, but what can we do? By his very nature and, if you will, because of his weakness, man has a kind of inner need for ritualization, not only of his joy, but also, and perhaps essentially, of his pain and grief. In the ghettos and the concentration camps, people used to sing a lot, sometimes for hours at a time, in order to banish fear and fortify courage. From the depths, I called Thee, God—sometimes those songs were as mighty as the suffering from which they arose.

The need for self-expression in a time of sorrow is ancient and long-standing, and is interwoven throughout the length and breadth of Jewish history. I am repeating that simple fact because one sometimes hears this argument and warning: "Keep literature out of that fire zone. Let the numbers speak, let the documents and the well-established facts speak." I have no wish to belittle that claim, but I do wish to point out that the numbers and the facts were the murderers' own well-proven means. Man as a number is one of the horrors of dehumanization. They never asked anyone who he was or what he was. They tattooed a number on his arm. Should we seek to tread that path and speak of man in the language of statistics?

In the meantime, however, life has made its own determinations. A great deal has already been written about the Holocaust, but if we inquire how much of what has been written is actually literature, we will find that it is quite a small part. When I refer to literature, I do not include all those fantasies about the Holocaust, those commercial productions, perverted stories, and sensational and scandalous writings which have inundated us since the end of the Second World War. Literature with a true voice and a face one can trust is very scarce. The number of such works could be counted by a child.

What we do have in abundance are memoirs, and we sometimes confuse them with literature. Why has no literature been written or, if you will, *yet* been written about the Holocaust? I shall try to answer that question in a personal way, and of course partially. But before I get to the personal part, I must venture a few words about the quality of the expression that has taken shape so far.

A rich body of testimony has been written about the Holocaust, the testimony of the survivors, and it embodies their whole psychology: haste, inarticulateness, and the lack of all introspection. It is as if what had happened had only happened outside them. The spiritual reckoning, if there is such a thing, was principally concerned with conclusions about society, not with the realm of the soul.

All that was revealed to the Jew during those years was vaster than his reason and his soul. He had been at the very point where the horror took place, and after leaving it he wished to see it as nothing but a nightmare, a rift in life that had to be healed as quickly as possible, a horror that could provide no moral lesson, only a curse.

While the survivor recounts and reveals, at the very same time he also conceals. For it is impossible not to tell, and it is also impossible to admit that what happened did not change him. He remained the same person, bound to the same civil concepts. That revelation and concealment continues to this very day. It seems to me mainly characteristic of the literature of testimony. Such writing must be read with caution, so that one sees not only what is in it, but also, and essentially, what is lacking in it. The survivor's testimony is first of all a search for relief; and as with any burden, the one who bears it seeks also to rid himself of it as hastily as possible. What transpired between him and the dread horrors during his years of suffering? What changed within him, and what will be his way of life from now on? You will not, it seems to me, find answers to these questions. People could not bear witness without encountering obstacles. Agonies of guilt, sometimes alternating with reproaches against the heavens, show up in almost all the testimony, but they are only marginal signs and not the essence of the writing, which is, as I said, in relief.

To avoid misunderstanding, I shall immediately add that the literature of testimony is undoubtedly the authentic literature of the Holocaust. It is an enormous reservoir of Jewish chronology, but it embodies too many inner constraints to become literature as that concept has taken shape over the generations. Those inner constraints are not only psychological.

However, why should I get ahead of myself? Let me return to the descriptive flow, which, more than anything, is personal experience, fragmentary of course, an attempt to trace the development of literary expression, and, if you will, literary nonexpression.

The war revealed to us, to our surprise, that even the most dreadful life of all was nonetheless life. In the ghettos and the camps, people loved, sang sentimental songs, and discussed political party programs. Evening courses in French were given, and people drank coffee, if they had any, in the afternoon. On the threshold of death a man still sewed on his buttons. There should be no need to mention that the children played, too. The closer death came to us, the greater was our refusal to admit its existence. Fear faded. Everyone held onto his little hopes—mostly trivial matters, such as taking a bath, for example. As for me, I remember a young man who absolutely refused to be deprived of his mathematics textbooks; he did problems all the time. He did not want to miss out on the second-year course. Those strange mathematics exercises, done between deportation and deportation, made him a tranquil person. In the camps and the ghettos, people played cards a lot, also dominoes and chess. Sometimes, in the good, forgetful moments, it did not seem like a death camp but, rather, like a summer camp for overgrown children deeply engrossed in their play.

For years we lived in the closest proximity to death, but very little thought, if it may be permitted to say so, was devoted to it. The selfish grasping at every crumb of bread and scrap of clothing, that grasping, which was sometimes ugly, was a kind of denial of death. What did people not do to escape it? The world was divided, let us not forget, between black and white in the most unambiguous fashion. That clear division between good and evil gave meaning and purpose to the struggle. And when I say "struggle" I do not refer to any kind of heroics, but to the encouragement one whispered to oneself: just a little more, it's worth it.

After the war when the wings of death were folded up, the meaning of life suddenly lost its power and purpose. Sadness, like an iron lid, descended upon the remnants and enclosed them. Reality, which no one could see or wished to see during the war, was now visible in all its starkness: nothing remained except you yourself. That nakedness of yours became a clear writ of accusation. I remember people whose sadness dragged them down with a whisper into a slumber from which they did not rouse again. The wish to sleep was dreadful and tangible. We drank coffee and alcohol in order to stay awake. During the war it seemed that, for years, until we reached a ripe old age, we would not cease telling of the horrors of the war. There were people who remained alive only because of the power of that hope: after the war, they would tell. That was, of course, one of the delusions that kept people alive. But, beyond that, people felt that they ought to tell about that Apocalyptic experience—to interpret it, to analyze it in the tiniest detail, and to examine it from every possible angle.

The struggle for physical survival was harsh and ugly, but that commandment, to remain alive at any price, was, in this case, far more than the commandment to live. It bore within it something of the spirit of a mission. Immediately after the war, that desire was overturned. People were filled with silence. Everything that happened was so gigantic, so inconceivable, that the witness even seemed like a fabricator to himself. The feeling that your experience cannot be told, that no one can understand it, is perhaps one of the worst that was felt by the survivors after the war. Add to that the feeling of guilt, and you find that with your own hands you have built a vast platform of misunderstanding for yourself. The feeling of vocation that throbbed within you in the camps and in the woods became, imperceptibly, an indictment of yourself.

The inability to express your experience and the feeling of guilt combined together and created silence. People have not yet been sufficiently cognizant of that silence. It is true that over the years it has lost some of its strength, it has slipped into the books of testimony. Sometimes it has been fraudulent, but its essence will always remain within that sphere which no expression can encompass.

Not everyone remained within that isolation. The desire to tell, which was latent all those years, broke out and took on strange and different forms of expression. Since new words had not been invented, people made use of the old ones, which had served them before. That was, of course, contemptible and painful.

I would like to take up some of those expressions now. Right after the war, the first entertainment troupes popped up: a mixture of old and young people, among them former actors, singers, youths who had grown up in bunkers, and all sorts of emaciated people who found relief in that distraction. Those troupes were formed spontaneously and went from one transit camp to another; they sang, recited poetry, and told jokes. Were it not for certain grotesque features, they would have been similar to the wandering troupes that used to circulate among the villages to amuse the peasants before the war.

What did those troupes express? It is hard, of course, to generalize. Essentially it was the latent, instinctive desire to live and to restore us to the round of life; on another level it was a kind of protest against suffering and sorrow; but, above all, it was forgetfulness. No one knew what to do with the life that had been saved. Sorrow and grief had passed the point of pain and had become something that could no longer be called sorrow and grief.

Since no one knew how to assuage his pain and grief, people sank into shady business deals and smuggling. The latent feeling of guilt created its own destructive means for lowering people to the lowest level of existence. Feverish activity drew people into the depths of oblivion, and at night the entertainment troupes would come and finish the job. Anything, just so as not to be alone with yourself.

At the time, I found these efforts at entertainment disgusting and repugnant. But we ourselves had not yet grasped the depth of the need for them, the innovation, if it may be permitted to say so, in that form. I remember people who protested vehemently against those cheap spectacles and saw them as desecrations. We did not yet understand that we had been deprived of tragedy as well. The regions we inhabited after the war were well beyond the tragic. Tragedy is distinguished by, among other things, conscious knowledge, by the hero's wish to confront his fate directly: tragedy is manifest in the individual, in his well-defined personal suffering. The dimensions of our suffering could not be fully expressed in an individual soul. When the individual attempted merely to become aware of his own consciousness, he collapsed. In the liberated camps, some actors tried to revive the classic Jewish repertory, particularly the tragic plays. Those efforts were, ultimately, more ridiculous than the cheap entertainment troupes. Today, I understand better those inchoate and spontaneous expressions of cheap entertainment. They filled the emptiness that threatened to engulf us. Today, I understand that they were the first harbingers of another form of expression: the comic and grotesque, which then, of course, was still in its infancy.

Alongside light entertainment other forms of expression appeared, of the religious sort, for example. After that enormous catastrophe, the soul seeks a foothold in superstition or, on the contrary, in metaphysics. On the warm coasts of Italy after the war, penitents would wander— rebukers, comforters, preachers, and all sorts of characters within whom metaphysical feelings kindled fiery words. In the great, drunken hurly-burly everything seemed like madness. It was the beginning of an inner discussion that evolved and became, over the course of time, the metaphysics of the Holocaust. Light entertainment and religious feelings intermingled after the war, creating a new kind of grotesque. Moral expression was missing. Moral expressions are always of a particular sort, and they arise from norms. The war destroyed, along with the rest, the accepted norms of good and evil. Choice and determination were stolen away completely. It was not who you were, not what you had done, but your being a Jew that was the determining factor in every case. For years we were subject to the blindness of fate. It is no wonder that we came to see the world as a kind of violent caprice. How can you come and say, "Do this" or "Do that," "This is good, that is bad"? Who knows what is good and what is evil? That void left room for a lot of arbitrariness, but also for a great deal of spiritual generosity and self-sacrifice.

Between our quest and our stammerings a great many distortions arose. People published journals that split the suffering down into its minute elements, politicians passed judgment, pseudo-romantic religious writers indulged themselves in reproaches directed against the Supreme Authorities. I do not mean to judge one form of expression or another, but it does seem to be permissible to say that they surrounded the bitter experience with misunderstandings and cheap, simplistic interpretations.

Artistic expression after the Holocaust seems repugnant, disgusting. The pain and suffering called either for silence or for wild outcries. Any embellishment or sweetening was jarring. Moreover, art, and not without reason, was linked in our minds with a sphere of European culture of which we had been the victims.

One evening an old actor from the Vilna troupe appeared in our transit camp. He read the works of the Yiddish poet Raizin. For a moment it seemed as if he was about to lead us back to the past, to what remained of ourselves, but it was precisely that delight which made everyone furious. There was an uproar, and the man left the stage in embarrassment, weeping.

The wish to forget was the strongest of all. It was then that the marvelous instruments of oblivion were created: sleep, bathing in the sea, and, above all, entertainment. Let there be no mention of the war. If it were not for those few who could not repress their experiences, the victims themselves would have denied the horror.

I am purposely mentioning the days right after the war. Then there arose, inchoate and inarticulate, the first efforts at expression. That which came later was only an expansion on those beginnings, or their impoverishment. The desire to keep silence and the desire to speak became deeper; and only artistic expression, which came years later, could attempt to bridge those two difficult imperatives. Artistic expression did not arise quickly. It called for a human form that would hint at the available possibilities.

The new "form," if one may call it that, was discovered by the children. They were survivors, and the war years in forests and monasteries had molded their faces and expression. Some of them sang well. I say well, even though their voices were generally cracked. Their songs were the remnants of melodies from their Jewish homes and scraps from the monastery organs. It all came together in them in a new kind of melody that only children, in their blindness, could create. You could call it innocent or just inelegant. They stood up on crates and sang. At the end of their performance, they would pass around their tattered hats and ask for payment. Violent managers quickly took them under their protection, and they would drag them from camp to camp. There were also girls. I remember one of them well. Her name was Amalia. She was about ten, and she would perform every night. Her repertory was a mixture of Yiddish songs and forest noises. Her thin, birdlike body always seemed as if it were about to fly away.

There were child acrobats who walked tightropes with marvelous skill. In the woods they had learned how to climb in the highest, thinnest branches. Among them was a set of twins, boys of about ten, who juggled wooden balls fantastically. There were also child mimics who would imitate animals and birds. Dozens of children like that wandered around the camps. While the adults tried to forget what had happened and to forget themselves, to get back into the fabric of life, the children refined their suffering as, perhaps, can be done only in a folk song.

I have discussed the children because it was from them, in the course of time, that artistic expression arose. I shall try to explain myself. Ultimately the children did not absorb the full horror, only that portion of it which children could take in. Children lack a sense of chronology, of comparison with the past. While the adults spoke about what had been, for the children the Holocaust was the present, their childhood and youth. They knew no other childhood. Or happiness. They grew up in dread. They knew no other life.

While the adults fled from themselves and from their memories, repressing them and building up a new life in place of their previous one, the children had no previous life or, if they had, it was now effaced. The Holocaust was the black milk, as the poet said, that they suckled morning, noon, and night.

That psychological aspect also had ideological significance. The Holocaust is sometimes conceived, even among its victims, as an episode, as madness, as an eclipse that does not belong to the normal flow of time, a volcanic eruption of which one must beware, but which indicates nothing about the rest of life.

The Holocaust as life, as life in its most dreadfully concentrated form from both the existential and social point of view—that approach was rejected by the victim. The numerous books of testimony that were written about the Holocaust are, if you will, a desperate effort to force the Holocaust into a remote recess of madness, to cut it off from life and, in other cases, to envelop it in a kind of mystical aura, intangible, which must be discussed as a kind of experience that cannot be expressed in words, but rather in prolonged silence. In the case of the children who grew up in the Holocaust, life during the Holocaust was something they could understand, for they had absorbed it in their blood. They knew man as a beast of prey, not metaphorically, but as a physical reality with his full stature and clothing, his way of standing and sitting, his way of caressing his own child and of beating a Jewish child.

We would sit for hours and observe. Hunger, thirst, and weakness made us observant creatures. Rather than the murderers, we observed their victims, in their weakness and in their heroism. Those tortured faces on the brink of the chasm will not be forgotten. To "be forgotten" is not the correct expression. They were stamped upon us the way childhood is stamped upon the matrix of one's flesh.

Most of us had no words, and it is therefore no wonder that our first artistic expressions were drawings. The children made a lot of drawings, even in the death camps. The poems and drawings created by the children in Theresienstadt bear witness to that power, which in its refinement is close to the folk song and naive art.

Artistic consciousness came later. There was a need not only for perspective, but also for some new orientation. Orientation after the Holocaust meant oblivion, flight from oneself and from one's Jewishness. Only a few of the Holocaust survivors reached Israel. Most of them preferred to be scattered throughout the world, to distant and remote places. The land of Israel was considered, and not incorrectly, to be Judaism, itself a danger that must be fled.

The children, of course, had no choice. No one wanted orphans. The ships of the Illegal Immigration accepted people indiscriminately— children, old people, and the sick.

It is strange to say so, but one must say so. There was a need for some kind of unmediated relation, simple and straightforward, to those horrible events in order to speak about them in artistic terms. Neither sublimation nor apologetics, and not glorification, but rather the way a person speaks about the events of his life, as terrible as they may be, but still and all, life. That way of speaking was the children's lot. That is how they expressed themselves when they were in the concentration camps, and afterward in the liberated camps; and something of that unmediated quality remained with them even after they grew up and sought themselves as human beings and as Jews.

Over the years the problem, and not only the artistic problem, has been to remove the Holocaust from its enormous, inhuman dimensions and bring it close to human beings. Without that effort it would remain a distant and unseen nightmare, somewhere off in the distance of time, where it would be easy to forget. It is the great Jewish experience, also a non-Jewish experience, and if it is not assimilated as it ought to be, one day we will be like grown-up children who have been deprived of a basic truth of life.

By its nature, when it comes to describing reality, art always demands a certain intensification, for many and various reasons. However, that is not the case with the Holocaust. Everything in it already seems so thoroughly unreal, as if it no longer belongs to the experience of our generation, but to mythology. Thence comes the need to bring it down to the human realm. That is not a mechanical problem, but an essential one. When I say "to bring it down," I do not mean to simplify, to attenuate, or to sweeten the horror, but to attempt to make the events speak through the individual and in his language, to rescue the suffering from huge numbers, from dreadful anonymity, and to restore the person's given and family name, to give the tortured person back his human form, which was snatched away from him.

There is a tendency to speak of the Holocaust in mystical terms, to link the events to the incomprehensible, the mysterious, the insane, and the meaningless. That tendency is both understandable and dangerous, from every point of view. Murder that was committed with evil intentions must not be interpreted in mystical terms. A vile hand was raised against mankind: we do not have mysticism here, but a blow directed against the central pillar of the Ten Commandments.

[Translated by Jeffrey M. Green]

7 · *Philip Hallie*

Writing about Ethical Ambivalence during the Holocaust

*F*or decades I have been a practitioner of the art of understanding ethics in terms of people's proper names and in terms of people's special circumstances. Mind you, I have always loved and I have always used the uncommon common nouns and the tenseless, actionless, and passionless verbs and adjectives of philosophy, but I have loved and used them in relationship with human experience, and not simply as pieces of a great verbal jigsaw puzzle called "The History of Philosophy."

What I am about to relate is the story of what has happened in my thinking in the course of three decades spent using the classical language of philosophical ethics to make some sense out of what Wittgenstein once called the "Umstände und Gelegenheiten," the circumstances and occasions of human helping and human harming. I think that ethics dwells in stories about the circumstances and occasions of human life, and so my story may show you something about ethics, as well as something about a person who is somewhat skeptical of language that is innocent of the sufferings and the joys of human experience.

For many years of doing narrative ethics I lived in a Manichaean world, a universe of discourse in which goodness and evil were as separate and as different from each other as torture is from efficacious love. Involved as I was in the richness of history, I still found myself involved in ethical melodrama.

The first proper name I studied in any depth was that of Frederick

Douglass, one of the morally heroic figures of American history, whose autobiography tells of his personal and public struggles with slavery in America. His book, entitled *Life and Times of Frederick Douglass*, along with the many other accounts I read of black slavery, took me more deeply into the meaning of such terms as "evil" and "good" than any book of philosophical and theological ethics ever took me. His life and times taught me that the word "cruelty" is often a better term to use than "evil," because cruelty has to do with *a reported experience* that does not require the principles of philosophy or theology to explain it. Cruelty, with all of its gray areas and ambiguities, happens in ordinary situations and in extreme situations like that of slavery, and it has its authoritative reporters, who need not know philosophy or theology to report it.

Those authoritative reporters, I discovered, are its victims. The perpetrators and defenders of black slavery in America, for instance, do not have the empirical authority to report it. Victimizers, such as the compact white majority in America in the life and times of Douglass, could humiliate and torture without caring and, therefore, without knowing that they were maiming lives down to their very centers. But Douglass knew when cruelty was happening to him and to his fellow blacks, even though habit and necessity often dulled that knowledge. In the relationship of cruelty, do not ask the *sword* if cruelty is happening; ask the person upon whose life that sword is falling. To understand cruelty is to understand in detail the immense importance of *empirical authority* in ethics. For instance, a slaveholder can give a bun or a penny to a slave and be fully convinced that he is being kind, that he is making more bearable the chains of slavery. But as Douglass points out again and again, the condescending, self-satisfied smile on the face of the master can be the ultimate cruelty to the slave who knows that his self-respect and his very life have been stolen from him, that he has been given a penny or a bun in exchange by this smirking white.

Another thing I learned from Douglass and other black authorities on the institutionalized cruelty of slavery was that a *disparity of power* between the white majority and the black slave was at the center of the dynamism of that "peculiar institution," as slavery was called. The political, economic, and verbal power-ascendancy of the whites over the blacks in America was the very nerve of the cruel relationship between the two groups, and to cut that nerve the blacks had to have not only unity with each other, but help from whites. For only by solidarity could they hope to change the grotesquely imbalanced power relationship they had with white slaveholders and their allies.

What all this meant for me was that there was a pitched battle between good and evil, between dignity and cruelty. On the one hand, there was the slaveholder with his cruel kindnesses and, on the other, the innocent, tortured slave.

Because narrative ethics involves narrators—stories need story-tellers—I found myself personally as well as philosophically involved in a Manichaean nightmare. And the nightmare deepened and darkened for me when I decided to study institutionalized cruelty during the twelve-year empire of Adolf Hitler. What I had learned about the disparity of power and the disparity of perspective led me directly into studying the Nazis' so-called medical experiments upon primarily Jewish and Gypsy children. What greater disparity of power could there be than the disparity between the power of an adult, "Aryan" doctor in a killing camp and the power of a Jewish or Gypsy child lying on a bloody table under that doctor's knife? And what greater disparity of point of view could there be than that between the murderous ideology of such a doctor and the horror of a child of three or four or five or six years old having its limbs or organs cut off without anesthesia?

But the medical tortures of children were too much for me. As I worked on the records of these tortures, I found myself imitating the victims and the monsters I was studying. I found myself wanting to strangle and smash the so-called doctors, thereby imitating them, and I felt myself lying there on the blood tables inside the skins of those children, who, incidentally, often resembled my own son and daughter in appearance. And when I was not being one more Jewish victim of Hitler, or one more victimizer in this cruelly murderous world, I was being detached, objective, cold—like a Josef Mengele who could maim and destroy human beings while whistling melodies from *Madame Butterfly*. In short, I found myself to be not merely a student of evil, but an embodiment of evil.

It was at this time that I found myself—for the first time in my life—envying my fellow students of ethics who were spending all their time jigsawing abstractions into philosophical patterns. But I was never tempted to join them. I was *embarqué,* committed to being a moralist of seeing, a student of ethics who felt *obliged* to see, in all the sense of that word, the factual and affective details of human moral experience.

What I learned from my work on the Nazi doctors was that the Shoah was of special moral significance to me, especially the Shoah with regard to children, Jewish and otherwise. I found that the fact that I am a Jewish father was directly relevant to my capacity to see and to feel the victim's perspective in the cruel relationship the Nazis created between Jews and non-Jews. The source of the pain I felt in studying the medical experiments was also the source of my power to see and feel my way into the heart of darkness, the center of evil, the mind and body of the victim.

But cruelty during the Shoah was too cruel to me, and so I turned to stories about those people who did their best to save children. Maybe, I thought, instead of mimicking cruelty I would mimic goodness, and find joy in my work, not just horror.

And so it was that I began a study of a tiny French mountain village that saved thousands of Jewish children from the killing camps of Central Europe. The Protestant village of Le Chambon, perched on a high plateau amongst the mountainous sources of the Loire River, spent the first four years of the 1940s, when the Germans were occupying France, sheltering children most of whose parents were being tortured and killed in the concentration camps. In great poverty and in constant danger of being massacred by the German occupiers of France, or by their puppets the Vichy police and *milice,* they not only sheltered children, but in many cases took them across the terrible mountains of southeastern France to Geneva, Switzerland.

The proper name I found at the center of almost all the stories about the rescue machine of Le Chambon was Pastor André Trocmé, the Huguenot minister of this gray little Huguenot village that never betrayed and never turned away a single child. In the course of living in Le Chambon and learning how Trocmé and his villagers fought cruelty and murder, I discovered that my previous work on cruelty had a serious flaw. I had seen cruelty as the result of an imbalance of power between victimizer and victim; but, in the stories of the *Chambonnais* during the Occupation, I learned that power, broadly construed, need not produce cruelty. I found that the religious and moral force that Pastor Trocmé generated in the granite, boxy church of Le Chambon created a little world of unsentimental, sacrificial loving. If we think of power in general in analogy with the idea of power in physics—that is, if we think of it as force overcoming resistance more or less swiftly—then the village of Le Chambon had great power. The villagers managed during those four years to keep at bay not only the German occupiers and their French collaborators, but also their own fears and their own poverty and hunger.

Whatever else ethics is, it is involved with the enhancement and the preservation of life. This involvement takes two forms: negative guidelines, or laws or rules, and positive ones. In a world where killing is as much a force as caring, people, somehow, have carved out ethical space, room for caring. The negative guidelines are the Thou Shalt Nots of secular and religious life: do not murder; do not betray; do not hate unto death. The positive guidelines adjure us, somehow, to prevent murder, betrayal, and hatred; to be our brothers' and sisters' keepers. Our ethical power is our capacity to resist temptations to murder, betray, and hate, and to resist temptations to fail to be our brothers' and sisters' keepers. The person of greatest moral power resists all of these temptations, even when the temptations to rage, cowardice, and indifference are greatest.

In these terms, the nonviolent village of Le Chambon during the German Occupation had great moral power. Led by Pastor Trocmé in his ugly granite church, the villagers did not hate, betray, or kill anyone during those four terrible years; and not only did they observe the airy negative "rules" of ethics—they also observed the positive rules that Jesus exhibited in the story of the Good Samaritan in the Gospel according to Luke. And they did these things in the course of four of the bloodiest years in the history of our species. They resisted the temptations of cowardice, hatred, greed, and, above all, indifference that were afoot in their world. The motto above the main door of their granite temple was "Love one another," and they obeyed it not only with moral power, but with aesthetic power as well: they observed the old ethical ideals with the virtuosity of a great performer performing an old musical score with fresh, passionate insight, and with glorious skill. The score they performed was not as detailed or explicit as classical musical scores are, but they played that ancient score better than any people I had ever encountered.

But after I wrote *Lest Innocent Blood Be Shed*, about detailed goodness, I realized that I had spent much of my professional life indulging in ethical melodrama. Whether I was studying the slaves and the slaveholders or studying Jewish and Gypsy children and the Nazis, I was seeing the world in a Manichaean mode, a mode that I came to feel was irrelevant to much of my own personal life. I was neither a villain nor a saint, pure and simple, and neither were my friends and my family members. We were mixtures of caring and indifference, helping and hurting.

I even found myself resenting these villagers I had learned to admire and to love personally. They had not tried to stop Hitler's armies, and I had. I had been an artilleryman in combat during the Second World War, and I had killed Germans with my 155-millimeter howitzer, even though my profoundest ethical and personal conviction is that every human being is a universe, the only concrete universe we know, and also that to destroy a universe is the fundamental evil. But, I found myself thinking, it was people like me, decent killers, who had stopped Hitler and had made the world safe for the pure ones, who violated neither the positive nor the negative ideals of ethics. A hundred Le Chambons would not have stopped Hitler—only people like me stopped him and kept him from killing millions more, and enslaving the "non-Aryans" on the planet. Ethical purity was irrelevant to my life, especially since I have not the slightest regret over what I did as a combat soldier.

In fact, I found myself thinking, their ethical purity was irrelevant to the world I actually lived in. As an American, I was part of a country that had been born in bloodshed, like, perhaps, every other country in the history of the world, and that had all but extinguished the native American tribes in its midst, *and* had enslaved blacks for hundreds of years, torturing and murdering many of them in the process. Whatever goodness there is in our history is not unmixed with cruelty and murder.

And even as a part of nature I felt ethically compromised. I was part of a vast system wherein each creature has three functions: to eat freshly killed other-creatures, to protect itself from being killed by other creatures, and to propagate itself so that others of its kind might continue to kill and keep from being killed. The caring of creatures for their own kind, like the presumed moral beauties of my country, the Land of the

Free, was tainted, when you dared to look on the underside of their stories.

What all of these questions came down to was this: how could one apply a term such as "good" to a person—or a nation, or a world—that both cared and killed? How could I find decency not in a melodramatic world, but in a world of ethical ambivalence?

Then I remembered what the villagers of Le Chambon had told me about *le Major,* "the Major." Throughout my research on the village, I kept asking them how Le Chambon managed to survive without a massacre for four long and bloody years, with the bitterest enemies of the Germans—Jews—living there in large numbers. The Germans knew what was happening there: in fact, they called Le Chambon "that nest of Jews in Huguenot country." They also knew about the little steam-train that came into Le Chambon almost every afternoon with more Jewish children on it. The Germans were masters in the art and science of murder, and there were more than four hundred of the most vicious auxiliaries the Germans had, the Volga-Tatar Legion, stationed only two dozen miles to the west of Le Chambon. Whenever I asked the villagers how the largest rescue machine in Europe could have been spared for all those years when other villagers were being massacred and burned to the ground, I got the same answer: "Ah! C'était le Major" ("Well, it was the Major").

All I could learn from them was that "the Major" was head of the German occupation troops in the High Loire during the two bloodiest years of the Occupation, 1943 and 1944. He had his headquarters in Le Puy, about twenty miles west of Le Chambon, and he did not let his Volga-Tatar Legion strike the village; nor did he let the Gestapo come near it during the most murderous year of the Occupation, 1944.

After I finished writing *Lest Innocent Blood Be Shed,* in my need to understand the ethics of *tainted* decency, this major in the German army became very important to me. Here was a trusted officer in Hitler's army, in full charge of a part of France where the armed Resistance fighters were plentiful and adroit, and yet he protected a village full of his nation's worst enemies, full of the disease germs of mankind, Jews. Here was a man praised by the villagers of Le Chambon as their protector, and yet here was a man who was a trusted part of the most murderous killing-machine in human history. He seemed to be the embodiment of tainted decency; and if I could come to understand why the villagers praised him, I felt, I could learn much about understanding decency in myself and in the morally tainted world around me.

The name of that major was Julius Schmahling, and he was not a professional soldier. Before the Second World War he was a schoolteacher in and around Munich, the Bavarian city that was the cradle of Hitler's career and of the hate-filled philosophy of Nazism. After the war, he went back to Munich, taught again for a few years, then retired; he died in 1973 at age eighty-nine.

During the war, at the end of 1942 when the Germans occupied the south of France, Schmahling became what he once described as "king" of the mountainous department in southeastern France called the High Loire. As I have mentioned, his headquarters were in the medieval city of Le Puy, a short drive from Le Chambon; and, because he was in a part of France where many Resistance fighters were hiding out in the mountains, he had a very large number of auxiliary troops at his command. And yet, despite the great power he held in the region, and despite the fact that he had the most ferocious auxiliary troops in Hitler's Third Reich under his command, he would return after the war three times to the High Loire as an honored and beloved guest. As far as I know, and this is a matter I have studied, no other German officer serving in France was the recipient of such respect and such affection after the end of the war.

What did he do? As my distinction between negative and positive ethics implies, what one does *not* do can be a vital part of decency. He never allowed his auxiliary troops to leave the limits of Le Puy before the German retreat in August 1944. He never let them strike either Le Chambon or any of the armed Resistance groups stationed throughout the mountains of the High Loire. And he never permitted the Gestapo to strike Le Chambon or any other area of resistance within his jurisdiction. He had the power and, as some servants of Hitler would have put it, the duty to destroy the known enemies of his country, and yet he did not destroy them.

In his own headquarters city of Le Puy, Jews from the region and from other parts of France lived openly, without threats or action from the Germans. For instance, the elder members of one of the wealthiest and most conspicuous Jewish families, the family that controlled Franck et Fils in Paris, lived openly in the Bristol Hotel in downtown Le Puy until the end of the war, and many other Jews worked openly in various other places in the city.

What he *did* do to preserve human life and human dignity has much to do with what he and his fellow Germans did not do. One of his ways of following the positive ideals of ethics that adjure us to prevent murder and betrayal was to develop a way of alerting the Jews in Le Puy and in nearby Le Chambon when there was going to be a Gestapo "visit." Either he or someone on his office staff would call the mayor of Le Puy, Eugene Pebellier, or the chief of Le Chambon, Pastor André Trocmé, before such a "visit"; then, the operation that the people of Le Chambon called the "Disappearance of the Jews" would take place, and the Gestapo would find a *Judenrein*, or "Jew-free," city or town.

Perhaps the sort of action that established his reputation in the High Loire was his personal intervention with the Gestapo in order to— literally—drag people out of their prisons. Again and again he would turn up at 2 Royat Avenue in Clermont-Ferrand, where the Gestapo headquarters and prison were, and storm his way through the offices and into the prisons themselves, in a loud German rage. And, in a little while, he would usually emerge from the Gestapo building with a disheveled and bleary-eyed Frenchman on his arm, who could not believe what had just happened to him.

When I heard such stories about what this German did to save lives in the High Loire, I found myself asking how he did it. The Gestapo had far more power in the Nazi hierarchy than a German army officer who had no combat record, and Major Schmahling had on his own staff in Le Puy some zealous Nazis who hated the Jews and who all but worship-ped the watchdogs of Nazi Germany, the Gestapo. How did he do what the French and what Jewish refugees abundantly attest that he did do?

In answering this question, we enter a region where the ethical ambiguity of this man looms large. One of the main reasons he could do some of the things I have been describing is that it was his duty as the leader of the German presence in the High Loire to keep the peace there. His main job as head of the *Verbindungsstab* was to keep the French from rising up against the Germans and resisting. The Germans were relieving France of personnel and materials, including food; the occupying troops were there to see that nobody would disturb those who were raping this rich country. If no German was killed, then only a few German troops were necessary to keep the peace, and the bulk of

Germany's troops could go about their main business, which was winning the war so that Hitler's dream of a Thousand-Year Empire could become reality. The good that Schmahling was doing in the High Loire was tightly intertwined with the evil Nazi Germany was perpetrating—and was planning to keep perpetrating for a thousand years. He was an efficient rear shield that would keep the French from stabbing the Germans in the back while they went about their business of murdering and subjugating millions of human beings.

But there is another answer to my question. Schmahling's defiance of the Gestapo in Clermont-Ferrand, his success in keeping the Gestapo from destroying the largest rescue machine in France—these are not explained by the back-shield theory. Not only were the Gestapo in nearby Clermont-Ferrand, but the star of the Gestapo in France, Klaus Barbie, was stationed in Lyon, and Barbie had the authority to strike anywhere in southern France. How could a noncombatant army reserve officer manage to fend off and even defy the darlings of Nazi Germany, the Gestapo?

The only answer I can find to this question deepens and darkens Schmahling's complicity with evil. One of his friends in the Nazi empire was Waffen-SS Lieutenant General Josef (Sepp) Dietrich. Dietrich was one of the original henchmen of Adolf Hitler in the streets and beer halls of Munich; he had been one of the assassins Hitler used in the "Night of the Long Knives" of 1934, when Hitler decided to murder the SA leadership. Dietrich was rightly called the "Learned Butcher."

Schmahling and Dietrich first met in the north of France shortly after the fall of France in June 1940. Dietrich apparently learned to like this fellow Bavarian who was bold enough to criticize Dietrich's SS troops for harassing the French, and who had the same outgoing, sensual temperament as Dietrich himself. They occasionally drank together, and according to testimonies from both French and German sources, they conversed on the telephone after Schmahling came down to take over the High Loire.

The SS and the Gestapo were at the pinnacle of the Nazi power structure, and they shared not only theories and procedures, but personnel as well. A word from Dietrich on the telephone could, and I am convinced did, keep the Gestapo away from the High Loire, especially in the bloody year of 1944, when Le Chambon was by far the biggest rescue machine in France and when the German massacres of French villages reached their peak. Barbie, for example, destroyed the tiny rescue operation in Izieu during that last year of German power in France, and I believe that only a Nazi with the power of General Dietrich could have kept him from striking Le Chambon.

In the relationship between these two Bavarians, the ethical ambiguity of Schmahling is writ very large indeed. By being friendly with and getting favors from one of Hitler's most trusted assassins, Schmahling was supping with the devil. Dietrich would never betray or resist Nazism, and so Schmahling, if he was to get Dietrich's help, had to make a case to the general that was absolutely consistent with the aims of Nazism. He had to demonstrate that if the Germans struck against the peaceful activities under way in the High Loire, they would be stirring up a hornet's nest of resistance in the whole of southern France, just when the Germans needed all their troops on the Russian and African fronts. And Dietrich would have accepted such an argument from Schmahling, whom Dietrich respected and whose job was primarily to keep his region peaceful—a job at which he was succeeding admirably. Schmahling's relationship with Dietrich—which is the only explanation I can find as to how Schmahling managed to protect the High Loire from the Gestapo—is the very embodiment of his complicity with mass murder. By keeping the peace in the High Loire, he was serving the Nazi cause in a way that could please one of Hitler's most zealous followers, Lieutenant General of the Waffen-SS Josef Dietrich.

The third question I found myself asking about Schmahling's role in keeping the peace in the High Loire, especially in 1944, had to do with why he did it. The obvious answer was that it was his duty to keep the peace. But why did he perform that duty by protecting not only the French, but the bitterest enemies of the Germans, the Jews? His political life before the war was that of a passionate anti-Nazi, and Jews he knew before the war attest warmly to his strong distaste for anti-Semitism. Did he do what he did out of sheer expediency, just to keep the peace, and in a calculating spirit? This was one of the main questions I found myself asking about him: was he helping to protect the Jews so that the Thousand-Year Empire would come, thinking that the Jews could be taken care of later? His bitterness toward both

Nazism and anti-Semitism went a long way toward answering that question in the negative.

Did he protect Jews and others out of some deep religious conviction, as was the case with Pastor André Trocmé? Like many Bavarians, Schmahling was a Roman Catholic; but the answer to this question is also in the negative. He was almost totally nonreligious, totally secular. From his young adulthood on, he refused to go to church, except when it was empty and he could admire the architecture in peace. When a friend would meet him in the street and ask him why he was not seeing Schmahling in church, Schmahling would answer, "It's lighter out here. We can see each other better outside of a church."

Then I started looking for his ethical principles. After all, he was a teacher of history and literature, and he had to be articulate about what he believed. But when any of his students or colleagues would ask him what he meant by calling somebody or some deed "good" or "bad," he would—instead of presenting some ethical rule or theory—invariably utter one empty little phrase: "What's right is obvious, obvious." Certainly he was no theorist, no moralist.

Then, I asked myself, did he protect the defenseless out of sheer expediency, in the calm, orderly performance of his job as a peace-keeper in France? But everything I learned about him from both French and German sources, as well as from his own letters to his wife, Emma, said no to that question, too. He was a man who lived in, as he once called it in a letter to his wife, "hot-blooded indignation." He had an immense capacity for anger, and for sudden, overwhelming compassion and affection. All of my sources, including my French Resistance friends in the High Loire, told me that Schmahling did whatever he did by impulse. He loved the Now, and he was totally innocent of calculated expediency. With his rages and hugs and enthusiasms, he was the exact opposite of the "orders are orders" personality. In Munich he would yell in the ears of friends who were driving him somewhere, "Run that light! Run that stop sign! Are you a sheep!?" He was not a calculating man who *had things to do;* he was a boiling man who *had to do things* out of the wellspring of an immense physical and mental vigor.

To use a word from the history of art, he was baroque, unruly, exuberant, not classical or restrained or deliberative. He was a man possessed of a baroque superabundance of passion, and that passion is the best answer I know as to why he did what he did to protect people's lives in the High Loire.

But his passion and his compassion were not simply forces of nature in him. There is a story behind them. In his old age he wrote about the one crucial experience in his life, as he remembered that life. One day, shortly after the turn of the century, he walked into his classroom in northern Bavaria, a young teacher full of his plans to give a lesson on lions. But before he could get past his first few words, a boy who had been sitting dumbly upon his wooden bench for the whole term started waving his hand frantically. The young teacher set his jaw and talked on, but the boy suddenly leaped up off his bench and yelled out, "Herr Professor! Herr Professor! Yesterday I saw a rabbit! Yesterday a rabbit!" Schmahling thundered down on the boy: "Sit down you little jackass!" And the boy fell down onto the bench, silent, and silent he remained for the rest of the year, despite everything Schmahling did to encourage him to speak again.

In his old age, a few months before he died, in 1973, Schmahling saw this incident as the turning point of his life as a person and as a teacher. He saw that his anger could crush not only the joy of living out of his students, but his own compassionate urges out of himself. And he vowed that he would never do such a thing to a human being again, and that he would do all he could to keep others from doing it.

And he kept his vow. It was as simple as that, and as infinitely complex as keeping such a vow during the German Occupation of France. If he had had a complicated ideology or ethical theory, he might well have been recognized as a *Gegner*, or enemy of the Third Reich, and he might well have been smashed, and Le Chambon might well have been smashed, too. As it was, he was no ideological threat to the Nazis around him, only a rather lovable, passionate man. That, I think, is why Dietrich could find him unthreateningly likable.

My way of understanding good and evil, I have noted, involves proper names and particular circumstances, and a felt obligation to look closely at these. One of those proper names is my own. Narratives need narrators, and storytellers have much to do with the nature and style of their stories. For me, ethics is partly a matter of autobiography, partly a matter of history and philosophy. Personal candor is part of narrative ethics for me, just as it was an important part of my master Montaigne's skeptical concern for essaying human thought and experience.

The fact is that there are two kinds of ethical ambivalence involved in my understanding of this German officer under Hitler, Major Julius Schmahling. One kind is external ambivalence, the ethical paradox, if you will, of a compassionate person serving the most brutal cause our ingenious and dangerous species has ever generated. The other kind is internal, inside me, Philip Hallie. My intimate, inward ambivalence toward this man is embodied in my relationship with my mother. When, years ago, she discovered that I was planning to study and even to find some good in a German who held a responsible position in Hitler's Third Reich, she began to beg me to give up the project. For her, all the Germans in that empire were murderers of the *Faegele*, the "little birds," the Jewish children, so much like my children Louie and Michelena. And her pleas were not alien to me: in fact, they voiced my own deepest fears and anger. My studies of the Nazi medical experiments and my killing of Germans as a combat soldier in the Second World War had helped make a Manichaean view of life an essential part of my way of approaching life. And even today, at this moment, the very idea of Germans in the Third Reich is an idea that carries anger and horror with it. In my mother's pleas not to go on studying Schmahling, I felt and I feel the ethical ambiguity I saw and see in that man.

When my mother died, in the course of my research on Schmahling, I felt that since she could no longer speak for herself, I had an obligation to speak and to feel from her point of view. It was not only the obligation of a loving son, nor only of a Jew whose people had suffered horribly under the Third Reich, and whose people are always in danger of suffering again, it was also the felt obligation of a student of ethics who saw a Manichaean world of difference between cruel murder and loving help.

The two kinds of ambiguity about Schmahling strengthened, and still strengthen, each other: Schmahling's complicity in evil arouses the fearful and angry Jew in me, as well as the ethicist in me. And my feelings and beliefs as a Jew and as student of ethics and history make me see his complicity in evil as sharply as I see the help he gave to Jews and many others in the High Loire.

How, then, have I learned to live with these ambivalences? How have I learned to live with the ambivalences not only in this man Schmahling, but in myself, my friends, my nation, and in nature itself?

I have learned that when I think of the proper name and the actions and passions of this man Julius Schmahling, he becomes foreground to me, and the country he served becomes background, smaller than he in my eyes. When I think not mainly of him but mainly of his country, which tortured and murdered millions, and which used him to keep the "peace" while it did so, the Third Reich becomes foreground, as it was when I killed as many Germans as I could as a combat soldier.

Now that I am no longer a combat soldier who has to treat every German alike, lest I endanger my own life by hesitating to shoot, this man Julius Schmahling can be foreground to me. Now I can afford to judge Germans ethically—one at a time—to look closely at the *ethos*, at the characteristic spirit of individual Germans. By a kind of art not totally unlike the art of portraiture, with its use of foregrounds and backgrounds, I have found myself making room in my caring for both my mother and Julius Schmahling.

Unlike the art of portraiture, there is no deliberate skill in the foregrounding and the backgrounding I am describing. That which is foreground *interests* me powerfully. When I think of his name and his story, I think of him with the passions and beliefs of a Jew and of a father, and I see writ large the fact that he did not hate or hurt Jewish children in the High Loire. On the contrary, he did much to save their lives there, and if he had been one of *them*, one of the murderous Nazis of his country, Le Chambon and its Jewish refugee children would surely have perished. When I think of him, all of this is foreground, large, and so is he, because he touches my feelings as a Jewish father, and touches them hard.

But it is not only my deep self-preservational passions that make him foreground. Not only my being a Jewish father and the son of my particular Jewish mother: ethical beliefs that I coolly and carefully hold also make him interesting, large, important for me. I believe that a human life is the center of its experienced universe and that, therefore, from the point of view of that human life, destroying that life is the same as destroying a universe. This is the foundation of all my ethical reasoning and observation, and it is for me the concrete meaning of the Hebrew saying that to save a life is to save a world. On these grounds he touches me as strongly as do those who have saved the lives and the dignity not only of Jews, but of blacks, of native Americans, of Armenians, or of any other defenseless universe.

Ethical beliefs, deeply personal as they are, and subject to endless dispute, are as real as the largely unscrupulous natural and international world that surrounds them. According to these beliefs as I see them, Julius Schmahling was better than many people at performing the ancient score of ethics, at observing the ancient guidelines or rules or ideals of ethics, and because of this he is large in my mind when I concentrate on him. Others have played that ancient score of ethics more immaculately than he: Pastor André Trocmé of Le Chambon, for one. But Schmahling did well at a time when it was both hard and dangerous to be decent; and so do some of my not-so-immaculate friends in less difficult and dangerous times; and so do I, I believe, and so, perhaps, do you. Sometimes we make decency large in our imperfect lives.

In the end, I do not see Schmahling mainly in terms of art. I see him and his ethical ambivalence in terms of the impersonal forces of nature. I see him as one who resembles the eye of a hurricane. In the eye of a hurricane, the sky is blue, and birds can fly there without suffering harm, even *Faegele*, "little birds." The eye of the hurricane is in the middle of pitiless power, and that power is always near, always surrounding it.

There are those who carve out a large space for compassion in their lives. In them, the eye of the hurricane is very wide. Such people are our moral aristocracy. And there are those who mainly hurt and murder their fellow human beings. Such a person was Heinrich Himmler, head of the SS and of the Gestapo, a man who was directly responsible for the humiliation and torture of many millions of people. There was an eye of the hurricane within Himmler, as there is in every living creature that has found a home in the universe: when Himmler returned from his work late at night, he would enter his house through the back door, quietly; he was being careful not to disturb his pet canary. This was the extent of his caring. It was so slight that it made his murderousness all the more murderous.

And there was Julius Schmahling, whose effective caring was narrower than a Trocmé's or a Mother Teresa's, but far wider than a

Himmler's. The most hospitable people amongst us do not compromise much with the indifference and hatred in the world; but those of us who do compromise much can nonetheless push away the choking circle of unscrupulous force that is around and within us. We may not be able to push it very far away, but when we have carved out such ethical space as we can or as we dare, we, and those we help, can know a joy that the hate-filled or the cold, indifferent murderer or bystander can never know.

8 · Kenneth Seeskin

Coming to Terms with Failure:
A Philosophical Dilemma

Although there is considerable disagreement about what caused the Holocaust or whether there is any historical precedent for it, there is a great deal of agreement on one point—that it is fundamentally unintelligible. According to Arthur Cohen:

> There is something in the nature of thought—its patient deliberateness and care for logical order—that is alien to the enormity of the death camps.[1]

And Emil Fackenheim:

> To explain an action or event is to show how they were possible. In the case of the Holocaust, however, the mind can accept the possibility of both how and why it was done, in the final analysis, solely because it was done, so that the more the psychologist, historian, or "psychohistorian" succeeds in explaining the event or action, the more nakedly he comes to confront its ultimate inexplicability.[2]

And finally Irving Howe:

> Our subject resists the usual capacities of mind. We may read the Holocaust as the central event of this century; we may register the pain of its unhealed wounds; but finally we must acknowledge that it leaves us intellectually disarmed, staring helplessly at the reality or, if you prefer, the mystery of mass extermination. There is little likelihood of finding a rational structure of explanation for the Holocaust: it forms a sequence of events without historical

or moral precedent. To think about ways in which the literary imagination might "use" the Holocaust is to entangle ourselves with a multitude of problems for which no aesthetic can prepare us. Neither encompassing theory nor religious faith enables us to reach a firm conviction that now, at last, we understand what happened during the "Final Solution."[3]

All of this talk about explanation and comprehension leads to an obvious question: how does one write about something that neither the reader nor the author has any hope of understanding?

One solution is not to write about the subject at all. If it is really unintelligible, why not pass over it in silence? To the writer concerned about the Holocaust, this answer is unacceptable. Silence can be taken for acquiescence or, in some circles, lack of interest. Neither is a legitimate response to the death of the six million. To an author concerned about these deaths, there seems little choice but to speak the unspeakable, think the unthinkable, and attempt to communicate what no sane person can fathom. In this respect, the author concerned about the death of the six million is in a Sisyphean dilemma: if it is intellectually dishonest to ignore the Holocaust, it is equally dishonest to pretend to wisdom. We want to know how people with all the outward signs of rationality could have driven the trains, turned on the gas, or manufactured the lamp shades. An obvious way of proceeding is to ask what constitutes rationality in the first place. Is it possible to offer a rational justification for genocide? And if a justification can be given, is it rational for someone to act on it—to participate in the day-to-day activity of exterminating human life? Large-scale questions of this sort put us in the domain of philosophy. It is to philosophy that we turn to find out about the limits of rationality and what happens when a rational agent chooses evil.

Traditional philosophers have always regarded evil as a mystery. That is why many of them, particularly those in the Platonic tradition, have characterized it as a lack or privation. For the traditional philosopher, goodness and intelligibility are related. To understand something is to understand its purpose or function. A traditional philosopher myself, I intend to argue that evil is outside the bounds of rationality. But unlike many traditional philosophers, I do not intend to stop there. If, as Irving Howe maintains, we can never really understand what happened during the Final Solution, we must still write about it. But if we do, we must look for a paradigm other than that of comprehension. My suggestion is that the person writing on the Holocaust think of himself or herself as making the move from theory to practice. In this way, writing is more a case of doing than a case of seeing.

One way of answering the question of what happens when a rational agent chooses evil is to say that no rational agent ever chooses evil wittingly. In well-known sections of the *Protagoras, Gorgias,* and *Meno,* Plato's Socrates advances the idea that all evil is the result of ignorance or intellectual error. On this view, it is impossible for a person to choose evil *as* evil. If a person murders or degrades another human being, the person does so not out of depravity, but in the mistaken belief that the action is good. In *The Republic* (505e), Socrates describes goodness as "that which every soul pursues as the end of all its activities, dimly perceiving its existence, perplexed and unable to grasp its nature with the same clearness and assurance as in dealing with other things, thereby missing whatever value those other things may have." It is a consequence of Socrates' view that both the hero and the criminal act with the intention of securing their own welfare. The difference is that one sees (correctly) that this welfare is dependent on moral behavior, while the other does not. This is another way of saying that the difference between them is a matter of correct or incorrect perception.

The immediate consequence of Socrates' theory is a strong connection between thought and action. Since all action is undertaken in pursuit of the good, no one acts contrary to what he or she takes that good to be. It follows that to understand an action is to explain what value the agent saw in it. There is a long history of people who have attacked this theory on the grounds that it does not account for moral weakness. Is it not possible for a person to overindulge in sex, food, or drink in full knowledge that the action is wrong and will lead to harm? In the *Protagoras,* Socrates says no; but generations of critics regard his denial as contrary to experience. From the standpoint of a person writing on the Holocaust, the issue is not how we understand isolated cases of moral weakness, but how we understand repeated cases of—indeed, a national commitment to—moral atrocity. Are such actions to be explained as misperception of the good or as deliberately choosing its opposite?

There is no simple way to answer the question. It is always open to Socrates to say that no matter how repulsive an action seems to us, the fact that someone undertook it shows that it was not repulsive to the agent. *We* recoil at the thought of genocide, but the agent has a different perception. So the issue is not whether we approve of what the agent did, but whether we can understand what goal the agent was trying to realize. To understand the Nazis, we must clarify the perverted values they lived for. On this view, the problem with the Nazis is not that they consciously affirmed evil, but that they had a highly distorted view of their own self-interest. The Jew was perceived as the ultimate threat to that interest. Therefore, the Jew had to be exterminated. The premises and conclusion of this argument are repulsive. But, to the degree that people accepted them, they constitute the framework with which to explain Nazi genocide. The task of a person writing about the Holocaust is to show how Nazi ideology constitutes a self-consistent, albeit morally repugnant, worldview.

There are, however, several problems with the Socratic theory. If the crux of the Nazi worldview is bad science, a dispassionate but unsustainable reading of the evidence, we could explain their actions in terms of faulty perception. They saw the extermination of Jews as no different from the extermination of lice. But how dispassionate was the "science" that affirmed Jewish racial inferiority? Surely this is a case where science was made to serve cultural needs having nothing to do with argument or evidence. Put otherwise, the decision to hate the Jews is what led to the faulty perception of them as a threat to society, what motivated the process of looking for scientific corroboration. If so, faulty perception is the effect, not the cause. It is the outcome of a willful effort to destroy the Jewish people, an effort that involves a denial of the very rationality in whose name evidence was sought.

There is, in addition, the question of whether self-interest is sufficient to explain the full extent of the Nazi horror. A distorted view of self-interest might explain the desire to kill Jews, but as Berel Lang has shown, it would not explain the elaborate efforts to humiliate them: torture, meaningless work assignments, babies killed before their mothers' eyes, and, in general, an attempt to make Jewish prisoners hate themselves.[4] An analysis of the historical evidence shows conclusively that the Final Solution involved more than the elimination of a perceived threat. No one devises "ingenious" ways to dispose of lice. No one takes the killing so seriously that critical resources are diverted from other projects to permit the killing to continue.

Rather than a necessary evil motivated by a distorted view of self-interest, the killing of Jews often became an end in itself. When soldiers intent on world conquest complained about working in concentration camps, they were told that their own happiness had to be sacrificed to a higher purpose. When people complained about turning in Jewish friends, they were told it was their duty to do so. In a famous speech, Heinrich Himmler urged his subordinates not to weaken when arresting Jews or viewing piles of corpses—to endure and remain strong.[5] The language of duty and purpose is a deliberate inversion of Kantian moral categories. It is well known, for example, that in his trial in Jerusalem, Adolf Eichmann invoked the categorical imperative.[6] It is questionable whether every person responsible for the killing of Jews would defend his behavior in quite this way. But to the degree that the Nazi hierarchy glorified such killing, and endured costly sacrifices to prolong it, self-interest is beside the point.

My claim is not that the Holocaust somehow "refutes" the Socratic understanding of behavior. Rather, it is that the Socratic understanding is not very illuminating in respect to the demonic. The only way Socrates can account for the demonic is to say that it represents the ultimate level of ignorance. It is always possible to argue that there are moral truths the demon has overlooked. But simple ignorance does not lead to nationally supervised genocide. The tyrant described in book VII of *The Republic* is given to lawlessness and uncontrolled thirst for pleasure. People who get in his way are killed or tortured without hesitation. Still, Socrates' picture of him is not a study in moral inversion. For the tyrant, killing is a means to an end. Socrates compares him to a wolf.[7] The comparison is apt because the tyrant has no "higher values" to justify his cruelty. He would never think of undergoing personal sacrifice to humiliate victims that pose no threat to him. He may have an impoverished understanding of his own welfare, but Socrates never doubts that, like us, he is pursuing it. It is this assumption that allows Socrates to answer potential tyrants such as Callicles and Thrasymachus. But neither character contemplates mass killing or killing for its own sake. As far as the dialogues are concerned, Socrates never comes face to face with an Eichmann or a Himmler. If there were a level of ignorance beyond the tyrant, it would be a moron incapable of any sustained activity. That is a far cry from the architects of the Final Solution.

The great alternative to Socrates is the account provided by Augustine. If Socrates' model of evil is the tyrant, who seeks his own welfare but does not know where to find it, Augustine's is the fallen angel, which is to say, the demon. Unlike the tyrant, the fallen angel is not lacking in intelligence. He is a creature endowed with a free will whose welfare depends on God. But in a primordial act of sin, the angel turns away from God and pursues a course destined to end in wretchedness. The cause of this sin is the will: it decides of its own to defy God and to court evil. If we ask *why* the will decides to court evil, Augustine insists there is no answer: "If one seeks for the efficient cause of their [the fallen angels'] evil will, none is to be found. For what can make the will bad when it is the will itself which makes an action bad? Thus an evil will is the efficient cause of a bad action, but there is no efficient cause of an evil will."[8]

Augustine's reasoning is straightforward. If there were an efficient cause of the will, either the cause would have a will or not. If the cause had a will of its own, and this will, too, is evil, we only put the problem off. For we would then want to know why the second will is evil and so on *ad infinitum*. If, on the other hand, the cause does not have a will of its own, it would be a being inferior to the fallen angel and, therefore, could not turn the angel's will away from God. The result is that there is no efficient cause of the will.

The problem is that if there is no efficient cause, there is no explanation, either. If we press the issue of why a flawless creature not subject to human frailties could will evil, Augustine readily admits that he does not know: "there is no point in anyone trying to learn from me what I do not know—unless, perhaps, he wants to know how not to know what, as he ought to know, no one can know."[9] At bottom, evil is unintelligible. If the will were not free, it could not be responsible for sin. But if it is free, it is a self-originating act that has no prior cause. We can see this unintelligibility in another way. According to Augustine, evil does not exist in itself. It is like a parasite in that the source of its existence is something else, something good. It follows that, insofar as evil attempts to *destroy* goodness, it destroys the only thing capable of sustaining it. In a word, it destroys itself. Whether we look at evil from the standpoint of the individual will or the metaphysical privation it represents, we do not have an explanation. We have the grounds for saying *that* the demonic exists, but as to why it does, we are forever in the dark.

The nature of this predicament was seen clearly by Kant. At the beginning of *Religion within the Limits of Reason Alone,* Kant inquires into the propensity to evil in human nature. He is adamant that the ground of this evil cannot be our sensuous nature or the inclinations that arise from it. Evil implies responsibility, and people are not responsible for the sensuous nature with which they are endowed. If the cause of evil were in the flesh, one could no more blame a person for doing something wrong than one could blame a person for having brown eyes. To put this in a different way, animals cannot be evil, only rational agents can. But Kant is equally adamant that the ground of evil cannot be found in a corruption of our moral reason. He regards it as impossible for reason to destroy the authority of its own law. The ground must lie in the will, and since the will is determined by incentives that the agent incorporates into a maxim, evil arises when an agent adopts the incentive to deviate from the moral law. The point is that unless evil is chosen freely, it is not really evil. But why would someone choose to subvert the law that follows from his or her awareness of being a rational agent? In short, why does the agent will evil in the first place? To this question, Kant, too, responds with a confession of ignorance: "the rational origin of this perversion of our will whereby it makes lower incentives supreme among its maxims, that is, of the propensity to evil, remains inscrutable to us. . . . [T]here is then for us no conceivable ground from which the moral evil in us could originally have come."[10] We cannot inquire into the subjective ground for why the will adopts the disposition to do good or evil. We are, then, in the position of Othello. At a crucial point in the play, he asks Iago why the entire scheme to trap him was hatched and is told: "Demand me nothing: what you know, you know" (*Othello* V, 7).

Notice, however, that Kant does not stop with an admission of skepticism. For while we cannot inquire into the subjective ground for the determination of the will, Kant thinks it is inevitable that we should.[11] We might rephrase this by saying that if, like Othello, we have been victimized by outrageous evil, how can we not inquire into its cause? How can we look evil in the face and be satisfied with a discourse on the limits of human knowledge? So we are back to Sisyphus. We cannot succeed in getting the rock to the top of the hill, but neither can we give up the attempt. Camus argued that we have to imagine Sisyphus as happy. This may be true of the character in the original Greek myth, but it is not true of the person writing about the Holocaust. When *we* push the rock up the hill, the inevitable failure has catastrophic potential. There is always the fear that if we do not make the world understand, the killing will recur.

If the previous argument is correct, we are no closer to answering the question of *why* evil occurs than we were in the time of Plato. Let me qualify this by saying that we are no closer to explaining how lucid, stable, and well-integrated personalities can choose to subvert the moral law. The reason is not that the various attempts to understand evil have been halfhearted. It is rather that this sort of evil cannot be incorporated into rational structures. To return to the character of Iago, one of the distinguishing features of the demonic is that it resists our efforts to understand it. The final words he speaks to Othello are an ultimate act of defiance. We can explain evil as ignorance, but the cost of doing so is that we assume the evildoer is pursuing the same ends we are. To the person who scoffs at those ends, we have nothing to say. Or we can explain evil as a self-originating act. But then we concede Iago's point: the decision to subvert the moral law is essentially surd. Between the conditions that permitted extermination and extermination itself, there is, as Claude Lanzmann remarked, a hiatus or abyss. It is that abyss which prevents us from saying we understand what happened in the Holocaust.

The understanding I speak of is philosophical. To say that the enactment of the Final Solution is incomprehensible is not to deny that historians can keep accurate records or that jurists can find cause for assessing blame. We have much to learn about the events that led from traditional hatred of Jews to the construction of gas chambers. What I am denying is that we will have a general theory to answer the questions we most want to ask. How could people with outward signs of rationality drive the trains or drop the crystals into the gas chambers? How could millions of other people look on as they did so? We want to probe the psyche of the perpetrators and claim we understand the logic of genocide. I submit, however, that all of the film clips, interviews, personal accounts, and philosophical reflections have not made that logic any more comprehensible. The universe they describe is rule-governed and internally consistent.[12] But it is a universe without redeeming value, a universe whose existence does not make it any more accessible.

It will be objected that the comparison between Iago and the Nazis is instructive only to a point. If there is no explanation of why an agent chooses to subvert morality and revel in human degradation, then the Holocaust is not the only event for which the philosopher must plead ignorance. Put otherwise, if there is no explanation for Iago's activity, there is no explanation for the activities of any psychopathic criminal. But then there is nothing distinctive about the Holocaust—at least not from a philosophical perspective. Of course, we cannot explain how people with outward signs of rationality could plan and execute the Final Solution. Still, if Kant is right, we cannot explain many of the brutal crimes reported in the daily newspaper, either. From Kant's perspective, the problem is not changed by increase in size. In one case, we have a brutal murder committed by a seemingly rational person; in the other, a nation has chosen to put a *group* of murderers in power and assist them with their work. Kant would argue, however, that philosophy is as incapable of explaining one as it is of explaining the other. So the people who maintain that the Holocaust is at bottom unintelligible do not establish that it is unique. There may be a thousand other events in history for which the claim of unintelligibility can be made. Although they may not be as comprehensive as the Final Solution, they, too, defy understanding. It is like the discovery of surd numbers. There was a great upheaval when the first one was found; but eventually mathematicians came to see that there were many others.

Needless to say, there is long and heated debate on the uniqueness of the Holocaust. It should be understood that I am not here taking sides in that debate. The immediate conditions that led to the death of the 6 million may have no historical precedent. Nazi ideology may be without equal in depravity. There may be no other case in which demonic forces took hold of an entire nation. My argument is simply this: if it is unique, it is not its unintelligibility that makes it so. Iago's actions are unintelligible, as well. And even though there is a world of difference between the plot to humiliate Othello and the attempt to destroy European Jewry, Iago is not any easier to understand when we point out those differences.

It may be said, therefore, that the person writing on the Holocaust confronts the unintelligible on a grand scale. Here it is realized not in the person of a disgruntled lieutenant, but in the national will. But the problem of writing about the Holocaust remains. If we can never understand it, we are back to the same dilemma: either (1) silence or (2) another attempt to complete an impossible task.

We may regret that the majority of philosophers have chosen silence, but their decision is not irrational. The history of philosophy is laden with examples of people extending human reason beyond its limits. The notion that there *are* limits that can be formulated in a precise way is one of the insights we inherit from the Enlightenment. To some philosophers, intellectual limits are like forbidden fruit. Once a person recognizes them, there is an immediate urge to ask about the territory that lies beyond. But, strong as that urge might be, a critical philosopher has to resist it. Having questioned Socrates' account of evil, we can agree with him on this much: there is an obligation to admit what we do not know. In fact, the recognition that there is something we do not know is itself a philosophical achievement.

On the other hand, if there is an obligation to admit what we do not know, there is an equally strong obligation not to remain silent in the face of mass murder. Some issues loom so large in the minds of modern intellectuals that a discipline such as philosophy cannot ignore them without running the risk of marginalization. That is, it cannot ignore them and still claim to provide a global perspective on culture. If the Holocaust has become an important issue for historians, theologians, filmmakers, novelists, and literary critics, then silence on the part of philosophers would indicate that the discipline has relinquished its position as cultural overseer. In many instances, this is exactly what has happened. According to Richard Rorty, people still believe it would be a good idea to have a view of how different parts of culture "hang together."[13] But, he continues, few people in this century have turned to philosophy to provide one. The Holocaust is no exception.

It seems that the philosopher's dilemma resolves itself into a choice between intellectual dishonesty, on the one hand, and marginalization, on the other. I suggest that the only exit from this dilemma is to adopt the Kantian strategy of shifting the focus from theory to practice. The goal of the philosopher writing about the Holocaust is not to probe the psyche of a concentration camp guard and say what makes it tick. It is to offer a program by which we can oppose the concentration camp guard and everything he stands for. This move is already apparent in the work of Emil Fackenheim. At a crucial place in *To Mend the World*, he writes: "The truth is that to grasp the Holocaust whole-of-horror is not to comprehend or transcend it, but rather *to say no to it, or resist it.*"[14]

The greatness of Fackenheim is, as his critic Jacob Neusner once remarked, that he discusses the Holocaust in such a way that theodicy is not the issue.[15] Unanswerable questions about God are ignored in favor of more pointed questions about humans. But here, too, Fackenheim knows when reason has met its limits. The real question is not why it happened, but what we do after we have seen what happened. This is not to say that Fackenheim is entirely successful. There are well-known problems associated with the 614th Commandment, Fackenheim's position on the State of Israel, and the claim that resistance to evil is an ontological category. The problem is that Fackenheim's shift from theory to practice is not as clean as we might like, so that often he avoids one dilemma only to find himself faced with another.[16] But that is a subject for another occasion. The basic insight—that we must try not to comprehend, but to resist—is sound.

On the question of writing, this insight implies a second one: writing itself can be an act of resistance. The Holocaust is not like the issues one finds in an introductory textbook on philosophy. It does not call for sharper-edged concepts or more elegantly formulated axioms. The person who discusses the meaning and implications of evil on this scale has one overriding concern: to bring the world to its senses. The hope is that having shown people the destructive potential of the human mind, the philosopher can set a course for a world in which such potential will never again be realized. If so, the philosophical implications of the Holocaust are normative. The task is to defend the values that the Nazis denied their victims—to explain what respect for human life requires of us. It should be said that this project, too, involves the possibility of failure. Pol Pot and the Gulag are evidence enough that it is unfinished.

The point is, however, that in this case, failure is not inevitable. Unlike the task of pushing the rock up the hill, that of bringing the world to its senses has a chance of success. To the degree that it does, the predicament of the philosopher writing about the Holocaust is not tragic, but prophetic—the correct analogue is not Sisyphus but Jeremiah. The difference is that if Jeremiah used a vision of the future to make his point, the philosopher writing about the Holocaust uses a vision of the past. Still, their functions are the same. Both have looked into a bottomless pit and returned with a call to action. The responsibility of the philosopher is to be specific about what such action requires. Unless we recognize this, the writing we produce will be an exercise in futility. If I am right, the author confronting an incomprehensible subject can do more than point out its incomprehensibility. Having looked into the bottomless pit, it is the job of such an author to lead us out of it.

Notes

1 · Arthur A. Cohen, *The Tremendum* (New York: Crossroad, 1981), p. 1.

2 · Emil Fackenheim, *To Mend the World* (New York: Schocken Books, 1982), p. 233.

3 · Irving Howe, "Writing and the Holocaust," *The New Republic*, October 24, 1986, p. 27; reprinted here, pp. 175–99.

4 · Berel Lang, "The Concept of Genocide," *The Philosophical Forum* 16 (1985/86): 11–14.

5 · Himmler's speech of October 4, 1943, can be found in L. Dawidowicz, ed., *A Holocaust Reader* (New York: Behrmann, 1976), p. 120ff.

6 · See Hannah Arendt, *Eichmann in Jerusalem* (New York: Viking Press, 1963), p. 136. For more on the Nazi use of Kant, see Fackenheim, *To Mend the World*, p. 296ff., and Lang, "The Concept of Genocide," pp. 12–13.

7 · *The Republic* 565e–566a.

8 · Augustine, *The City of God*, trans. G. G. Walsh et al. (New York: Doubleday, 1958) 12.6; cf. *On Free Choice of the Will* 3.17.

9 · Augustine, *The City of God* 12.7.

10 · Immanuel Kant, *Religion within the Limits of Reason Alone*, trans. T. M. Greene and H. H. Hudson (New York: Harper & Row, 1960), p. 38.

11 · Ibid., p. 20.

12 · On the Nazi "logic of destruction," see Fackenheim, *To Mend the World*, pp. 130–131, 206–215.

13 · Richard Rorty, *Consequences of Pragmatism* (Minneapolis: University of Minnesota Press, 1982), pp. 168–169.

14 · Fackenheim, *To Mend the World*, p. 239.

15 · Jacob Neusner, "The Implications of the Holocaust," in Neusner, ed., *Understanding Jewish Theology* (New York: KTAV, 1973), p. 187.

16 · See the dilemma into which Fackenheim's argument (*To Mend the World*) forces him at p. 309ff.

9 · *William Heyen*

Unwilled "Chaos": In Poem We Trust

*E*very time I have thought of how to begin this essay, I have thought of something that comes before, something that needs to be said first. I will try to begin with a poem I often use at poetry readings to suggest how it was I came to the writing of poetry. This is called "The Crane at Gibbs Pond." I wrote it about twenty years ago:

> The boy stood by the darkening pond
> watching the other shore.
> Against pines,
> a ghostly crane floated
> from side to side,
> crooning. Maybe
> its mate had drowned. Maybe
> its song lamented
> the failing sun. Maybe
> its plaint was joy,
> heart-stricken praise
> for its place of perfect loneliness. Maybe,
> hearing its own echoing,
> taking its own phantom gliding the sky mirror of the pond
> for its lost mother in her other world,
> it tried to reach her
> in the only way it could. Maybe,
> as night diminished
> all but the pond's black radiance,
> the boy standing there

knew he would some day sing
of the crane, the crane's song,
and the soulful water.

That poem came out of my idyllic Long Island childhood. As a boy, I did sense something in the water of the ponds I waded and fished. I felt they were "soulful," in some way full of souls. And now I think that my own movement from innocence to experience has to do with the realization that people of my own blood flushed the ashes of millions of people into the pond at Auschwitz.

Another little poem occurs to me. It is called "The Eye," and because it seems to suggest so many of the things I think I have been up to in my poetry, I will probably someday use it as the prefatory poem to a book of selected poems:

As I begin, not knowing what, to write,
the sun, from the clip on my pen,
turns on this page, such a streaked,

burst gold eye,

all I have, all I have ever wanted,
you to see this, to see *with* this,
in case it is dark where you live.

"The Eye" carries my sense of the process by which poems come to me, and carries my desire that the poem be a means of perception and a help. The purpose of poetry, I believe, is to help us live our lives. But how could a book of poems—this was my worry when I first began, after about ten years of writing them, to think of gathering my Holocaust poems together—how could a book of poems about the Holocaust help anyone in any way?

I will begin, now, where I first thought to begin. I will trust a poem to be what I need it to be now, a vessel to hold within its form, at least for a little while, my whirling thoughts and feelings about writing about the Holocaust.

This poem is called "Poem Touching the Gestapo." It has two epigraphs. One is from Edward Crankshaw, an English historian of the SS. His phrase "willed chaos" is important to my poem, and to what I would like to edge in on, if I can. The second epigraph is from Olga

Lengyel, a survivor. You will hear the echo of "willed chaos" again. At Auschwitz, for example, tall women would be issued very short dresses, short women would be issued very long dresses—all for the sake of gratuitous confusion and humiliation.

Behind the apparently iron front of Teutonic organization, there was a sort of willed chaos.

—*Edward Crankshaw*

The system of administration [at Auschwitz] was completely without logic. It was stupefying to see how little the orders which followed one another had in common. This was only partly due to negligence.

—*Olga Lengyel*

You now, you in the next century, and the next,
hear what you'll almost remember,
see into photos where he still stands, Himmler,
whose round and puffy face concealed visions,

cortege of the condemned winding toward Birkenau,

and how to preserve Jews' heads in hermetically sealed tins,

der Ritter, knight, *treuer Heinrich,*

visions of death's head returning in Reich's light,
the Aryan skull ascending the misformed skull of the beast,
the Jew, Gypsy, lunatic, Slav, syphilitic, homosexual,

ravens and wolves, the Blood Flag, composer Wagner
whose heart went out to frogs, who, like Martin Luther,
wanted to drive Jews "like mad dogs out of the land,"

Heydrich dead but given Lidice,
Mengele injecting dye into Jewish eyes—
Ist das die deutsche Kultur?—
this vomit at last this last
cleansing and an end to it,
if it is possible, if I will it now,

Lebensborn stud farms, *Rassenschande, Protocols
of the Elders of Zion, SS* dancing in nuns' clothes,

Otto Ohlendorf, who left his Berlin desk to command
Einsatzgruppe D and roam the East killing
one million undesirables in less than two years' time,

lamenting the mental strain on his men,
the stench of inadequate graves,
corpses that fouled themselves in the gas vans,

the graves rupturing, backs, backs of heads, limbs
above ground as they are here, if I will it now,

the day-in, day-out shootings of Jews, some attractive,
brave, even intelligent, but to be dealt with
in strict military order, not like at Treblinka where
gas chambers were too small, and converted gas vans' engines
sometimes wouldn't start, the thousands already
packed into the showers for history,

their hands up so more would fit, and smaller children
thrown in at the space left at the top,
and we knew they were all dead, said Hoess of Auschwitz,
when the screaming stopped,

Endlösung, Edelweiss, Lebensraum, Mussulmen, Cyklon B,

"and his large blue eyes like stars," as Goebbels wrote,
and the Fuehrer's films of conspirators on meathooks,

we cannot keep it all, an end to it,
visions of loyal Heinrich, what engineer Grabe saw at Dubno,
he and two postmen allowed to watch, the vans arriving,
a father holding his boy and pointing to that sky,
explaining something, when the *SS* shouted and counted off
twenty more or less and pushed them behind the earth mound,

Stahlhelm, Horst Wessel, Goering in a toga at *Karinhalle,*
redbeard Barbarossa rising,

that father and son, and the sister remembered by Grabe
as pointing to herself, slim girl with black hair,
and saying, "twenty-three years old,"
as Grabe behind the mound saw a tremendous grave,

the holy orders of the *SS,* Lorelei, the Reichstag fire,
Befehl ist Befehl, Anne Frank in Belsen, jackboots, Krupp,

bodies wedged together tightly on top of one another,
some still moving, lifting arms to show life,

the pit two-thirds full, maybe a thousand dead,
the German who did the shooting sitting at the edge,
his gun on his knees, and he's smoking a cigarette,
as more naked victims descend steps cut in the pit's clay,
clamber over the heads of those already dead there,
and lay themselves down. Grabe heard some speak
in low voice, . . . listen . . .
before the shooting, the twitching, the spurting blood,

competition for the highest extermination counts,
flesh sometimes splashed on field reports,
seldom time even to save skulls with perfect teeth
for perfect paperweights,

his will be done, and kill them, something deeper dying,
but kill them, cognac and nightmares but kill them,
Eichmann's "units," the visions, the trenches
angled with ditches to drain off the human fat,

the twins and dwarfs, the dissidents *aus Nacht und Nebel,*

Professor Dr. Hans Kramer of the University of Munster
who stood on a platform to channel new arrivals—
gas chamber, forced labor, gas chamber—and later,
in special action, saw live women and children thrown into pits
and soaked with gasoline and set on fire—
Kramer, a doctor, who kept a diary filled with
"excellent lunch: tomato soup, half a hen with
potatoes and red cabbage, sweets and marvellous vanilla ice,"
while trains kept coming, families with
photograph albums falling out of the cars, the books
of the camps and prisons, the albums imprinting the air,
as here, we close our eyes, and the rain falling from photos
onto the earth, dried in the sun and raining again,
no way to them now but this way, willed chaos,

visions deeper in time than even the graves of the murdered
daughter who tells us her age,
in the round face of the man with glasses and weak chin,
Himmler, *Geheime Staats Polizei*, twisting his snake ring,

as now the millions approach, these trucks arriving with more,
these trains arriving with more, from *Prinz Albrecht Strasse,*
from the mental strain on Ohlendorf's men,
from the ravine at Babi Yar, from the future,
from the pond at Auschwitz and the clouds of ash,
from numberless mass graves where Xian prayer and Kaddish
now slow into undersong, O Deutschland, my soul, this soil
resettled forever here, remembered, poem touching the Gestapo,
the families, the children, the visions,
the visions . . .

I do not know, clearly, what it is that I have done in this poem or in my book, *Erika,* which came together over about twenty years. Many of my Holocaust poems, it seems to me—these are probably either the best ones or the worst ones (though I am probably wrong to separate them)—begin simply, logically, as though toward some traditional poetic coherence, but then the speaking voice begins to lose grasp, begins to rave or hallucinate or become hysterical or speak in tongues. For better or worse, I have come to trust such poems in a deeper way than I trust my more definite and controlled ones, the ones that I understand.

It may be that traditionally most poems have managed, at least momentarily, to compose self and world. Bless such poems that manage to do this, but my heart goes out to those that remain behind the barbed wire of their saying—are they themselves metaphoric concentration camps?—poems that I cannot quite free by means of rational paraphrase. But they shimmer with meanings, with witness, if I could just hear.

Perhaps my root assumption is that the Holocaust is "opaque," as Susan Sontag says it is. We may be able to quantify it, to find out its shape and weight in time and space, but its sources and meanings and losses glimmer in black light into which we try to see, into which we *must* keep trying to see, instance by instance. Some poems enable me to keep trying to feel my way into that which remains beyond my imagining. I think of what is perhaps the best-known of all Holocaust poems, Paul Celan's "Todesfuge," in this regard.

I remember that I had sat down to work on something else when "Poem Touching the Gestapo" came quickly, almost of a piece. It seemed to choose me and, writing it, I did not consciously adopt discursive strategies or aim for chaos and ambiguity. But I do believe, and this seems to have come through, that our best poems and stories are written with a kind of intellectual passion, with what Emerson called the "flower of the intellect." When they are, they can be read over and over. They hold to their mysteries even as they keep giving of themselves. They create in us the feeling that if we read them once more, once more, we will surely know them. But we won't. But something in them makes us want to keep trying.

It may be that an assumption of mine even deeper than that of the Holocaust's opacity is that it is morally best for me not to be sure of myself. If I think I know how it was that a so-called civilized German engineer could design and build crematoriums to precise human specifications, how a so-called civilized German soldier could execute innocent people all day long, then I might find myself becoming lax about my own potential for evil. I am tall, I was a blond youth, an athlete—if I had been born in Germany in 1920 instead of Brooklyn in 1940, might I not have aspired to membership in the SS? My father-in-law, a Nazi who died after Stalingrad in a prisoner-of-war camp in the Urals, had worked for Goebbels in the Propaganda Ministry in Berlin. When I was with my wife and family in Germany in 1971–1972, a relative gave us a cache of the dead man's belongings that had been packed away since the war, including many smoldering obscenely anti-Semitic books sent to the Propaganda Ministry. I have stared at them, from their color frontispieces of Hitler to their long bibliographies of similar publications—how could I have escaped such poisoning of mind and soul? My point is that if I do not know, finally, how it was that a man such as myself could act demonically, I can fearfully guard against this in me. Maybe. Perhaps I am swimming in waters too deep for me here. But I noticed that many were against Gerald Green's television miniseries on the Holocaust because, for one thing, they felt that viewers coming away from such a melodrama could say forever after, "Oh, yes, we know all about the Holocaust now. We know what it was and what caused it. We do not need to know more or think about it any longer. We are bored." Such an attitude is very dangerous, of course. On the other hand, the series, seen by millions, acquainted many for the first time with the basic reality of what it was that happened to the Jewish people during the Third Reich.

I sent a poet-friend "Poem Touching the Gestapo" in manuscript. He told me not to publish it. He asked me, "Who would want to touch the

Gestapo?" I have been afraid of my poem, but I have trusted it, in part, because I have not quite understood it. It is not simple enough for me to put in simple terms just what position its voice has achieved in its single-sentence cry/wail/lament/moan/madsong/curse. I am not even sure about the implications of its title. *Concerning* them? *Moving* them? *Laying hands* on them? Making them *"touched,"* that is, pushing them vengefully toward insanity? Every time I wrote a Holocaust poem such as that, I had to resist, for better or worse—and this is something only a reader can decide—working on it to the point where I knew, consciously, just what it was saying. At the end, my speaker says that his soul is "resettled forever here." Where? In the poem, I suppose, in the rhyme of "ash" and "Kaddish," in the black bed of this history, in the rush and breakdown of the rendering. After the Holocaust, we are all refugees from the human dream. My speaker's attempt at resettlement seems to me to be—and I have not thought about my poem in these terms before I began writing this paragraph—pathetic, heartbreaking. Whoever he is, he has taken Gestapo visions inside himself and gone wild with them.

I try to make rational sense of my poem, but it knows more than I do. It goes on speaking itself, turning and turning darkly on itself even while I try to spade its soil up to air and sunlight.

In contrast, here is a poem more willing to reveal itself. I feel I know what is inside this one, "The Numinous":

> *Our language has no term that can isolate distinctly and gather into one word the total numinous impression a thing may make on the mind.*
>
> —*Rudolf Otto*

We are walking a sidewalk
in a German city.
We are watching gray smoke
gutter along the roofs
just as it must have
from other terrible chimneys.
We are walking our way
almost into a trance.
We are walking our way
almost into a dream
only those with blue

numbers along their wrists
can truly imagine.

Now, just in front of us, something
bursts into the air.
For a few moments
our bodies echo fear.
Pigeons, we say,
only an explosion
of beautiful blue-gray pigeons.
Only pigeons that gather
over the buildings
and begin to circle.

We are walking again, counting
all the red poinsettias
between the windowpanes
and lace curtains.
It was only
a flock of pigeons:
we can still see them
circling over the block buildings,
a hundred hearts
beating in the air.
Beautiful blue-gray pigeons.
We will always remember.

The word "numinous" concerns spirit of place, and my poem, though suggestive, is never quite irrational as it walks its way almost into a trance. But here is a poem called "Darkness." It begins with the speaker's lament that he will forget the camps:

Thirty, fifty, eighty years later,
it's getting darker.
The books read, the testimonies all taken,
the films seen through the eye's black lens,
darker. The words
remember: Treblinka green,
Nordhausen red,
Auschwitz blue, Mauthausen
orange, Belsen white—
colors considered
before those places named themselves. Thirty,
fifty, eighty years later. Now

the camps—I lose them—
where are they? Darker.
If it is true
that I've always loved him,
darker. If it is true
that I would kill again,
darker. If it is true
that nothing matters,
darker. If it is true
that I am jealous of them,
the Nazis' hooked crosses, the Jews' stripes . . .
He speaks inside me. Darker.
I lie on a table
in the Fuehrer's bunker,
outside his chamber,
in the hall. I am waiting.
They do not see me,
dogs nor people. This
dream begins again, the film
circles and burns. Eighty, fifty,
thirty years. Darker. He
touched my forehead. He
speaks now, says, somehow,
lower, tells me to speak to the lower power,
for once, to say,
come back, enter, I was once alive.
Darker. The air
swims with words, hair
twines the words, numbers
along a wrist, along
a red brick shower. Darker.
To forgive them,
killer and victim: darker.
Doctor, help me kill
the Goebbels children. Darker.
Across the street, now,
a cattlecar, stalled.
The skin lampshades darken under varnish.
Fragments. Can I call
him back? Millions still
call him back in deepest prayer,
but the light diffused
as spray, past
Andromeda, in spiral
shadows. Darker, always

darker. *SS*, death's head,
oval hollow deadface hole for boot—
fragments. The heroes
all dead in the first five minutes.
Darker. To enter
this darkness, to dig
this chancellery garden to my own
remains, to watch
as the black face and scrotum
lacking one egg stare up
at the sun, to speak
with that charred jaw,
carrying this with me. Darker.
Under the answer, under
the darkness, this love I have,
this lust to press these words.
He tells me *lower,*
and the black breastbone aches with it,
the last black liquid
cupped in the eyesockets smells of it,
odor of cyanide's bitter almond,
the viscera smeared to the backbone
shines with it, for me
to say it all, my
hands around his neck,
mouth to mouth, my lips
to kiss his eyes to sleep. We
will taste this history together,
my friend: take a deep breath.
Take it. Smell
almond in the air.
The leader lives.

One evening some years ago, I saw the film *The Man in the Glass Booth*. There were such strange psychological leaps. I walked home in a moonless darkness, swirling, and I wrote that poem. Writing it, I was not like a man in a train on a track, but like a man being dragged by a horse galloping wildly across a landscape that it knows better than he. The rider wants to give the horse its head, but wants to feel somewhat in control of the situation at the same time. When he manages, some-how, to bring the horse to a standstill, when he manages to dismount, he is too shaken to know for sure where he has been.

My metaphor, maybe, is too fanciful. My poem's voice has tried to say it all, has made some terrible admissions. I, as a writer finished with his poem, decided not to censor it. It plunges into psychic and sexual depths I do not completely fathom. That is its power. I must not (must I?) break its power with my conscious mind.

Am I using the Nazis' own method, willed chaos, to write about their victims? I do not think so. My "chaos" in certain obsessive poems such as "Poem Touching the Gestapo" and "Darkness" is *un*willed, I think. And I hope—here is my transition to the second point I wish to make— I fervently hope, unfashionable as it may be in our time for a poet to cherish such hope, that in the end my poetry is a moral poetry, is restorative, redemptive.

Although the sources and strategies of poetry must necessarily be oblique, on a slant, somewhat mysterious, indirect, I have always believed, simply, what Walt Whitman said—that literature is a "means of morally influencing the world." If I did not think it was more than a time-killing, whimsical entertainment, I would pick up my props and playthings and go home. In her essay in *Art and Ardor*, "Innovation and Redemption: What Literature Means," Cynthia Ozick explains very patiently, gritting her teeth, what a writer she overheard meant when he said, "For me, the Holocaust and a corncob are the same." For that writer, a phrase such as "a morally responsible literature" is an oxy- moron, since writing is pure imagination, dream, and language respon- sible only to itself. *But,* Ozick says clearly, "I want to stand against this view." "For me," she says, "with certain rapturous exceptions, liter- ature *is* the moral life." In a beautiful and charged simile she says that "the exceptions occur in lyric poetry, which bursts shadowless like flowers at noon."

But in most literature, she continues, "one expects a certain corona of moral purpose: not outright in the grain . . . itself, but in the form of a faintly incandescent envelope around it." And I wonder if she has not described what I have sensed as sometimes occurring in me as I wrote some of these poems (this is not a value judgment, but a prayer that, as I wrote and as vile things suggested themselves to me in my "lust to press" sometimes sensationalistic images, something deeper gusted into the poems, validating them as human painsongs): "The corona flickers, brightens, flares, clouds, grows faint. . . . The Evil Impulse fills its cheeks with a black wind, hoping to blow out the redemptive corona; but at the last moment steeples of light spurt up from the corona, and the world with its meaning is laid open to our astonished sight."

All things are not the same. A poem about the Holocaust needs to be responsible not only to its own language unfolding in the present, but to its particular subject. It must live in the dual world of the deepest racial being of its speaker, and in history. It must mean, and be meaningful.

I will conclude with two other poems from *Erika*. The first comes from a dream I had after reading about programs for killing children the Nazis believed were mentally retarded or physically handicapped and therefore unfit to live. I need to say one thing about this poem. Often in *Erika*, I, my speaking voice, does not know whether he is victim or murderer, whether he is wearing jackboots or whether he is dying in a gas shower. But here, for *once*, he does know who he is, what he did, and what he would do again. "The Children" may be my most affirmative poem:

> *I do not think we can save them.*
> I remember, within my dream, repeating
> *I do not think we can save them.*
> But our cars follow one another
> over the cobblestones. Our dim
> headlamps, yellow in fog, brush past,
> at the center of a market square,
> its cathedral's great arched doors.
> I know, now, this is a city
> in Germany, two years
> after the Crystal Night. I think ahead
> to the hospital, the children.
> *I do not think we can save them.*
>
> Inside this dream,
> in a crystal dashboard vase,
> one long-stemmed rose unfolds
> strata of soft red light.
> Its petals fall, tears, small
> flames. I cup my palm to hold them,
> and my palm fills to its brim,
> will overflow.
>
> Is this the secret, then? . . .
> Now I must spill the petal light, and drive.

We are here, in front of the hospital,
our engines murmuring. Inside,
I carry a child under each arm,
down stairs, out to my car.
One's right eyeball hangs on its cheek
on threads of nerve and tendon,
but he still smiles, and I love him.
The other has lost her chin—
I can see straight down her throat
to where her heart beats
black-red, black-red.
I do not think we can save them.

I am the last driver in this procession.
Many children huddle in my car.
We have left the city. Our lights
tunnel the fog beneath arches of linden,
toward Bremerhaven, toward
the western shore.
I do not think we can save them.
This time, at the thought, lights
whirl in my mirror, intense
fear, and the screams of sirens.
I begin to cry, for myself, for the children.
A voice in my dream says
this was the midnight you were born. . . .

Later, something brutal happened, of course,
but as to this life I had to, I woke,
and cannot, or will not, remember.
But the children, of course, were murdered,
their graves lost, their names lost,
even those two faces lost to me. Still,
this morning, inside the engine of my body,
for once, as I wept and breathed deep,
relief, waves of relief, as though the dreamed

rose would spill its petals forever.
I prayed thanks. For one night, at least,
I tried to save the children,
to keep them safe in my own body,
and knew I would again. Amen.

Finally, a two paragraph prose poem called "The Tree":

Not everyone can see the tree, its summer cloud of green leaves or its bare radiance under winter sunlight. Not everyone can see the tree, but it is still there, standing just outside the area that was once a name and a village: Lidice. Not everyone can see the tree, but most people, all those who can follow the forked stick, the divining rod of their heart to the tree's place, can hear it. The tree needs no wind to sound as though wind blows through its leaves. This listener hears voices of children, and of their mothers and fathers. There are moments of great joy, music, dancing, but all the sounds of the life of Lidice: drunks raving their systems, a woman moaning the old song of the toothache, strain of harness on plowhorse, whistle of flail in the golden fields. But under all these sounds is the hum of lamentation, the voices' future.

The tree is still there, but when its body fell, it was cut up and dragged away for the shredder. The tree's limbs and trunk were pulped at the paper-mill. And now there is a book made of this paper. When you find the book, when you turn its leaves, you will hear the villagers' voices. When you hold the leaves of this book to light, you will see the watermarks of their faces.

I would like to think that all of us, our whole lives, are reading and writing that book made from the leaves of that tree. When we hold the leaves of our book to light, we can almost see watermarks of all the lost faces.

10 · *Sidra DeKoven Ezrahi*

Considering the Apocalypse: Is the Writing on the Wall Only Graffiti?

*O*ur century has been divided almost equally between cataclysmic historical events and massive programs of reconstruction. If, in the shadow of atomic bombs, concentration camps and penal colonies, heroic efforts are required to regenerate any of the ruptured continuities in cultural and social visions, the phenomenon of Jewish rehabilitation is arguably one of the most complex. From those fragments of Jewish civilization which have survived massive displacement and decimation in the twentieth century, a discourse on history and theodicy is being recovered that attempts to address contemporary Jewish sensibilities.

Critical readings of Jewish responses to catastrophe tend to construe the literary manifestations of collective survival that span two millennia as a sustained and highly contrived anti-apocalyptic narrative. David Roskies, in his comprehensive survey of the resonances of destruction in Jewish literature, argues that "of all Jewish traditions, the response to catastrophe remains the most viable, coherent, and covenantal."[1] Roskies is taking his stand on the rather slippery terrain of an oxymoron—"viability" in response to catastrophe; yet he is not alone in arguing that defiance informed by faith, rather than surrender out of despair, characterizes the Jewish encounter with adversity. Along parallel lines, Alan Mintz grounds his study of Hebrew literary responses to catastrophe not in the landscape of destruction but in the strategies of what he calls "creative survival".[2] And, some years ago, Robert Alter elaborated on Martin Buber's thesis that the Jewish imagination tends to be prophetic rather than apocalyptic, marked by "courageous engagement in even the most threatening history," rather than by "a total withdrawal . . . from a history that has become unbearable."[3]

Historically, the anti-apocalyptic strain in Jewish letters is more or less coterminous with the evolution of rabbinic—hence "mainstream" or "normative"—Judaism. Much of the legal-religious enterprise was a response to and a defense against the apocalyptic sectarians who flourished in the wake of the destruction of the Second Temple and whose texts tested the boundaries of the scriptural canon and its theological norms.[4]

The Rabbis' own struggles—and martyrdoms—are incorporated into the legendary saga of the struggle to set limits to an imagination of the End: "R. Ishmael was flayed, suffering with great fortitude; he wept only when his executioners reached the place of the *tefillin*. The angels of heaven called in anguish, 'Is this the Torah, and this its reward? Behold, the foe blasphemes Thy great and revered name, and scorns Thy Torah!' Whereupon a voice cried from heaven: 'If I hear another sound uttered, I will turn the world to water! I will devastate both Heaven and earth. This is my decree; accept it, all of you who love the Torah that preceded creation by two thousand years.'"[5] Antinomianism followed by social anarchy is regarded as the inevitable consequence of the loss of perception of the universe *in its present state* as structured and beneficent. Profound suffering leading to ecstatic visions of deliverance were common to Jewish as well as early Christian martyrs[6] and aroused considerable anxiety among the rabbinic architects of the new social and religious order ("Let the spirit of those who ponder upon the end expire"). The talmudic enterprise is largely a construction of *fences* against the encroaching threat of chaos—and they proved no less binding for being rhetorical.

In what amounted to a radical reorientation, the central arena of cultic activity was displaced from the sacrificial altar onto the written word. The Temple, which had been reconstructed once before from the ground up, could not be rebuilt again and acquired the status of a governing myth: an edifice of words was erected as a defense against the reality of ruin and desolation and as a movable property that made the Diaspora possible as a shifting Jewish province. The reciting of Talmudic, Midrashic, and liturgical texts came to replace priestly rites as primary acts of devotion. The scattered exiles who had returned once before to the center would not be ingathered again in the foreseeable future:[7] as the Jews came to live more and more within the elastic bounds of their own internal discourse, the significant historical and geographic coordinates of collective life were located in the suspended time and place of sacred texts, and a lamentation tradition based on archetypal rather than historical memory evolved. The cyclical nature of Jewish memory has been explored by Yosef Ḥayim Yerushalmi in a series of essays (*Zakhor*, 1982) demonstrating that even the most diastrous of contemporary events—massacres, expulsions, pogroms—were coded as but pale recapitulations of such primary biblical moments as the *Akedah*, or the Exodus from Egypt.[8] The destruction that gave rise to a state of geographical and spiritual exile is balanced by the promise of ultimate redemption ("on the day the Temple was destroyed, the Messiah was born"); yet, stretched between these two poles, history as present time loops back upon itself, endlessly deferring the End.

It is this reading of the connections between catastrophe, the dynamics of collective memory, and resistance to eschatological calculations that informs the writing of a number of scholars working in related fields, including both Roskies and Mintz, who trace the lamentation tradition along a continuum of Yiddish and Hebrew letters, respectively. Whereas Mintz's study of Hebrew responses to catastrophe proceeds by a close reading of certain canonic texts, Roskies diversifies and contextualizes his readings to convey the dialectics and the scope of an ongoing encounter with adversity. Mintz's focus on a few select texts derives from a model that sees cultural changes as emerging through paradigmatic shifts, and from a perception of the constitutive role of interpretative, textual activity.[9] Roskies, on the other hand, bolsters his argument by reference to a totalistic and diachronically consistent cultural idea. Whether roaming through biblical spaces or modern Jewish territory, he finds his evidence everywhere—in poetry and prose, in folk song, in ritual behavior, in visual art—construing a tradition not only in terms of its major texts, but in the extent of its diffusion in the culture at large. What emerges from these studies, taken together, is a mosaic of a vibrant culture that managed to incorporate periodic disaster into its vision of suffering and redemption and into the calendar of its life cycle. Roskies introduces the voice of the engaged writer into the scholarly conversation, defining the pursuit as both intensely personal and culturally urgent. A critical assessment of his hermeneutic strategies can, I think, bring into focus the far-ranging implications of this approach.

Running just ahead of the Crusaders or the Cossacks, rather than following in their wake, Roskies surveys not just the ruins and threnodies, but the sustaining structures that have withstood every destruction. As a longitudinal survey of the repeated dynamic of catastrophe and regeneration, *Against the Apocalypse* differs from many other books in the field in moving forward, rather than backward, striking a delicate balance between the dangers of *thanatopsis*, or a sustained contemplation of death, on the one hand, and of a kind of Darwinian celebration of survivalism on the other. Roskies begins not with the bones and the broken glass, but with the "keys," metonymic figures that presuppose the doors they have outlived and that yield access to a myriad of untried doorways in the "ruined cities of the mind" (p. 1).

The selection of texts and of exegetical procedures is thus carefully and deliberately geared to substantiating the thesis that Jewish culture is a bulwark "against the apocalypse." This is, admittedly, an ideologically weighted excursus through Jewish civilization; yet it is by no means a sentimental affirmation of the anti-apocalyptic, yea-saying rituals of a homogeneous community of the faithful. Responses to catastrophe are seen as alternating between "literal recall" and "sacred parody" of ancient archetypes. Both resist the temptation to submit to cosmic despair in the first place by denuding contemporary events of their specific historical properties and "disassembl[ing] the worst disasters into their recognizable parts" (p. 202). Literal recall then proceeds to engage the past innocently in its effort to decipher and accommodate to present circumstances: "On seeing what the Russians did to [the town of] Hysiatyn in the twentieth century, I could easily imagine what the Romans must have done to Jerusalem some two thousand years ago" (p. 15), writes a Jewish medic serving in the tsarist army in 1916. Analogues provide consolation; the locus of a vast primal destruction in the remote but accessible past contextualizes, disciplines, and codifies the tribulations of the present. This analogical reasoning relates to that basic metaphoric function of poetry as consolation which is so forcefully enacted in the Book of Lamentations: "What can I compare or liken to you, O fair Jerusalem? What can I match with you *so that I may comfort you?*")[10]

"Sacred parody," on the other hand, as Roskies and others have defined it, is an ironizing appropriation of the consecrated past or of constitutive texts that still manages to preserve their normative valence. The process by which the text threatens to subvert its own foundations may be as old as the Bible itself.[11] One of its earliest post-biblical expressions, which still sounds sacrilegious even to modern ears, is found in the *Mekhilta* of R. Ishmael where the doxological "who is like unto Thee among the mighty [*elim*]" is rendered as "Who is like unto thee among the *mute* [*ilmim*]?"[12] By incorporating the anger, and even the blasphemy, into the normative response to catastrophe, the language of sacred parody remains contained yet infinitely expandable; scriptural and liturgical texts can be appropriated while registering the enormity of the violation of central precepts.

It comes as no surprise that the parodic, subversive mode begins to dominate modern sensibilities and that contemporary literary history is punctuated by ironic transmigrations of inherited symbols. The critical stance of the post-Enlightenment writer vis-à-vis traditionalist society finds expression even in his encounter with adversity, and Roskies highlights some of the most relentless instances of self-castigation in the Yiddish and Hebrew prose and poetry of the late nineteenth and early twentieth centuries. In this literature, the *shtetl* becomes a microcosm of the corrosive forces undermining East European Jewish civilization from within on the very eve of its destruction by external powers. S. Y. Abramovitsh's Mendele Moykher Sforim, "torn between tirade and tears," arrives at a "precarious and outrageous blend of the sacred and the profane" (p. 68). Sholem Aleichem erects a self-mocking wall of defense and brings us to the very brink of the abyss, "laughing off the trauma of history" (p. 163) by recapitulating or inventing a "language that might still protect the Jews from harm" (p. 182). But whereas satire and humor are the likely tools of the parodist, a deadly bitterness permeates the Hebrew "Songs of Rage" of H. N. Bialik. Roskies suggests that Bialik's poems "On the Slaughter" and "In the City of Slaughter," written in the wake of the Kishinev pogrom of 1903, "desacralize history in God's own name" (p. 89):

> See, see, the slaughtered calves, so smitten and so laid:
> Is there a price for their death? How shall that price be paid?
> Forgive, ye shamed of the earth, yours is a pauper-Lord!
> Poor was He during your life, and poorer still of late.

> When to my door you come to ask for your reward,
> I'll open wide; see, I am fallen from my high estate
> > [*yaradeti minekhasai*]
> I grieve for you, my children. My heart is sad for you.
> Your dead were vainly dead; and neither I nor you
> Know why you died or wherefore, for whom, nor by what laws;
> Your deaths are without reason; your lives are without cause.

A. M. Klein's archaic and sonorous English translation hardly conveys the linguistic violence inflicted on the lamentation tradition through the wrenched metaphors of consolation and the anthropomorphism of God as a loser in real estate. A close modern reading of "In the City of Slaughter" such as Roskies, Mintz and other critics provide reveals a series of ruptures that should have proved utterly subversive to the genre: God has been stripped of His omnipotence, the martyrs and survivors of their dignity and innocence, and the poet of his vocation. Yet the biography of this poem teaches us that the vehicle of resilient response to catastrophe proves stronger than the tenor, that even when the parodic process reaches beyond sacrilege, this literature can still answer public needs and acquire canonic status. (Consider, for instance, that in the Warsaw ghetto, the historian Chaim Kaplan invoked Bialik as the poet who might have written the sorrows of his dying people; and that, decades later, "In the City of Slaughter," which had been construed as a platform in the struggle for self-defense when it first appeared in 1903, was piously incorporated into the memorial Holocaust liturgy of a number of American synagogues.)

Between the world wars, however, the pressure of events and centifugal forces of secularism, modernism and competing ideologies seemed to overcome even the elasticity of these conventions, and the literature of catastrophe reflected a near-breakdown in the traditional concepts of theodicy and community. Only a total catastrophe could "rescue" the lamentational mode from the utter profanation of its normative base. Roskies argues that while in the early part of the century writers such as Abramovitsh and Warshawski in Yiddish and Bialik and Agnon in Hebrew could focus on the internal seeds of corruption and dissolution, and poets like Halpern or Leivick could carry the subversive mode to the very limits of its form, this was an option no longer available to the writers incarcerated in the ghettos and utterly unavailable to those who survived the camps. For a very brief and tragic period, he claims, beginning in 1939, the internal dissensions between the assimilated and the committed, between the religious and the secular, between the elite and the masses, between the Yiddishists and the Hebraists, were bridged by the shared deprivation that preceded annihilation—and a strange and terrible process of *ingathering* recreated a community of fate and recuperated the writer's forfeited public role: "The modernists became, despite their long battles against it, part of the literature of consolation. With the ghetto's intellectuals moving closer to the people, the writers could . . . restore conceptually and socially the idea of a Jewish nation that was the penultimate consolation for the ultimate destruction" (p. 198). This view of a last-minute repair of deep divisions within the community speaks, at least in part, to our own aesthetic and ideological need for a reconciliation scene before the denouement. Roskies' chapter on "Scribes of the Ghetto" recreates the literary and cultural activities of the war years from a large number of documents which have been preserved, and attributes to a persistent—and desperate—faith in the Jewish word the fact that ghetto leaders could promote new forms of creative expression and even award prizes to outstanding poets and artists.[13]

The dynamic of consolidation and of closing of ranks that began in the ghetto continued after the war as a cleansing process which, as it is narrated, seems to resemble nothing so much as a *tahara* or ritual purification of the corpse. The self-censorship of Yiddish writers Avraham Sutzkever and Isaiah Spiegel who expunged, in the postwar years, references to Jewish collaboration or ignominy *from their own ghetto poetry or fiction* as well as from the documents they rescued from the ashes, is understood as a reversal of the maskilic activity of self-castigation and as reflecting the writer's reappropriation of the discarded mantle of consolation and mourning. Sutzkever, who in the immediate aftermath of the war engaged in frantic acts of testimony and retrieval that were a race against time, gradually despaired of the prospects of rescue and rededicated himself to the act of re-creation—and to verbal symbols as the only markers of a vanished world:

> It is not just because my words quiver
> like broken hands grasping for aid,
> or that they sharpen themselves
> like teeth on the prowl in darkness,

that you, written word, substitute for my world,
flare up the coals of my anger. . . .

> Vilna Ghetto
> July 28, 1943[14]

Yet all these elements, which appear to cohere, are but fragments of a language that has lost its syntax. Roskies' narrative effectively ends in the ghetto. While he relates to the postwar poetry and art of such writers and painters as Uri Zvi Greenberg, Avraham Sutzkever, Yosl Bergner and Samuel Bak—all of whom are identified as "eastern European Jewish writers and artists," although after the war they lived and created in Israel—he isolates their texts and canvases and does not continue to explore the social and cultural matrix of their art. Whereas he is guided by the presumption of "internal bilingualism" as the natural condition of East European Jewish literacy, it is *Yiddish* language and culture, and not the Hebrew enterprise that was to diverge from it in ideology and in practice in the late nineteenth and twentieth centuries, that is Roskies' real subject. When he talks of Sinai and of Vilna as primary Jewish spaces or—once both have entered the realm of myth—as primary moments in the march of Jewish consciousness, he refrains from according the same status to Tel Aviv. He makes passing references to rituals and documents of mourning in modern-day Israel, and acknowledges the "archetype of miraculous survival" (p. 254) in the poetry of Sutzkever or Greenberg; yet in his narrative these remain concepts never naturalized in their cultural surroundings. The implicit assumption is that the *Yiddishe folk* died in the ghetto and that the last flickerings of their life can be recorded there alone. A few solo voices remain, but the chorus has been silenced (a "break deeper by far than existential despair [is] the end of the dialogue between eastern European Jewish writers and their Jewish audience" [p. 302]). Those Jewish writers and artists who survived the Holocaust and cast their lot with the emerging Jewish nation in Palestine are presumed, then, to have constituted a community not only decimated by the war, but so transfigured that all the continuities are lost except for a handful of free-floating symbols which still provide the ongoing vocabulary for their art.

I would submit that the linguistic heirs to a tradition originating in Hebrew scriptures present a resounding challenge to the presumption of a total loss of community. The procession of Hebrew writers and their readers could, in fact, serve as a central proving ground for the fundamental thesis that, under stress, Jews have learned to marshal all their cultural resources "against the apocalypse."

Alan Mintz, by contrast, does devote an entire section to Hebrew resonances of the Holocaust, providing close textual readings of major poetry and fiction. Yet it is here that even his argument for "creative survival" loses conviction and coherence. This is only partly attributable to the inevitable fact that in moving from liturgy to *belles lettres*, post-Enlightenment Hebrew literature entered an entirely different semantic field, forfeiting some of the norms of consistency and fundamental conformity that had shaped its tropes and conventions over the centuries. But an even more fundamental issue is at stake here. In the course of his overview of Hebrew literary responses to the Holocaust, Mintz maintains that despite the magnitude of the destruction and the slowly evolving cultural responses to it, one can hardly identify a significant *paradigmatic* leap in philosophical presumption or literary practice—and the reason can be sought in the deep structures of Zionist thought: since Zionism was predicated on the "withering away" of the Diaspora, the cataclysmic realization of prophecies of doom could hardly have precipitated a fundamental crisis in prevailing Israeli perceptions of Jewish destiny. I have traced elsewhere[15] the slow but ideologically consistent process by which, in the decades after the war, the Holocaust was assimilated into the logic of Jewish regeneration so that it would not shake the foundations of the new state. We can find early poetic expressions of this kind of Zionist historicism, in which catastrophe becomes an enabling, not a paralyzing, force, in the original reception of Bialik's "Songs of Rage."

What we discover, in fact, is both a surprising continuity and a radical shift in Jewish consciousness whose implications are more far-reaching for their own thesis than either Mintz or Roskies acknowledges. Confronted with both a vast destruction of biblical proportions and an opportunity for (secular, political) redemption, the architects of national consciousness were engaged in constructing a response that is as consequential in the twentieth century as the rabbinic response was in the first and second. "I want to state . . . that I am opposed to Jewish history," states Yudke in H. Hazaz's story "The Sermon"—by which he means, clearly, the burden of Jewish *memory*.[16] This story, written in 1942, can be viewed as a proximate and radical response to catastrophe.

What is being put forward here is a daring proposal for *non-Apocalyptic closure*—and the antinomies are so great that it takes an ongoing collaborative effort to hold them together. The problem was how to appropriate the past for its redemptive vision without allowing archetypal memory to usurp the future; how to facilitate a selective forgetting of the past so that the new story could be written without surrender to deterministic models. The Zionist reading of Jewish history and its revolutionary platform partake, partially and selectively, of the messianic mode in envisioning a domain where the traditional defenses marshalled in the name of "creative survival" are transformed into collective acts of salvation.

While arguing that the Zionist enterprise in the immediate aftermath of the Holocaust was a life-affirming challenge to the forces of despair and capitulation, I think it is worth exploring the extent to which the utopian visions upon which the "Third Commonwealth" was founded were animated by yearnings of a messianic nature that had to actively resist the temptations of apocalyptic surrender. It is curious that neither Roskies nor Mintz mentions Gershom Scholem's study of the strains of apocalyptic-messianic thought which he identifies as a persistent undercurrent in Jewish culture over the centuries. Scholem elucidates the connection between catastrophe, redemption, and utopia in Jewish eschatology: the "catastrophic nature of redemption [is] a decisive characteristic of every such apocalypticism, which is then complemented by the utopian view of the content of realized redemption."[17] To leave the shadow-life of exilic Jewish time is to enter both "historical" *and* eschatological zones; although secular Zionism has been perceived, as Jacob Katz puts it, as "Jewish messianic belief . . . purged of its miraculous elements, and retain[ing] its political, social and some of its spiritual aspects,"[18] the discarded religious vocabulary continued to inform the perception of the return to Zion as a radical departure from unredeemed time. Once we view the anti-apocalyptic posture as coterminous with the apparatus of Exile and with the idea of homecoming as an endlessly deferred possibility, even a secular, political act of "return" will inevitably be measured against eschatological visions, both ancient and modern.

Scholem insists that one cannot overlook the "overtones of messianism [that] have accompanied the modern Jewish readiness for irrevocable action in the concrete realm, when it set out on the utopian return to Zion."[19] He is identifying here a dialectic that, I think, has only intensified with the passage of time and the appeal of militant millenarianism among growing numbers of religious Zionists:

> Born out of the horror and destruction that was Jewish history in our genera-
> tion, . . . [the Jewish readiness for action in the concrete realm] is bound to
> history itself and not to meta-history; it has not given itself up totally to
> Messianism. Whether or not Jewish history will be able to endure this entry
> into the concrete realm without perishing in the crisis of the Messianic claim
> which has virtually been conjured up—that is the question which out of his
> great and dangerous past the Jew of this age poses to his present and to his
> future.[20]

The signs of Armageddon that Scholem, before his death in 1982, was able to discern in Israeli social thought and political rhetoric become even more pervasive as we move inexorably toward our own *fin de siècle*,[21] and they both reinforce and undermine fundamental myths of return and redemption.[22]

It emerges, then, that the critical and the creative stand "against the apocalypse" is no less an act of faith today—in Israel at least—than it was for our rabbinic ancestors. Plays like Samuel HaSafri's *Tashmad* (1984)[23] or Motti Lerner's *Ḥevlai mashiaḥ* [Pangs of the Messiah] are political theater, enacting visions of a war of Gog and Magog on the West Bank of the River Jordan (that rough beast slouching toward Bethlehem to be born?). At this level, Israel's ongoing struggle is not only with its enemies but also within itself, between those forces that would capitulate to a metahistorical, metapolitical model—forces which would celebrate death meted out and sustained in the name of a heavenly blueprint of Eretz Yisrael—and those which would insist on living humanely in the inglorious, compromised reality of a deferred redemption; between those who would invoke messianic time to collec-tivize death as a necessary component of the redemptive process ("pangs of the Messiah") and those who personalize death as irretrievable loss.

The struggle against capitulation to absolutist visions in Israeli drama, fiction, and poetry can be measured in their distance from the poetics of Uri Zvi Greenberg, whose *Streets of the River* was the earliest sustained poetic response to the Holocaust. Roskies and Mintz both acknowledge the apocalyptic strains in Greenberg's poetry and the appearance of messianic figures in his interbellum poems. The connection between his poetics and his revisionist politics is also perceived—but not the subversive effect of his presence in the canon. Mintz goes so far as to make a bold comparison between Greenberg's poetry and early rabbinic Midrashim, viewing the two as resourceful efforts at a "recovery of meaning" and bringing his own discussion full circle:

> For both enterprises, the possibility of success relies on the fact that the catastrophe has left something crucial undestroyed: in the case of the Rabbis it was the inviolability of Scripture and its potential for exegesis and intertextuality; in the case of Greenberg it is the inviolability of the mythopoeic imagination and the maneuvers made possible by it. Admittedly, there is no small difference between collective exegesis and individual mythopoesis, yet both presume the persistence, after destruction, of discourse and textuality as a ground in which the seeds of recovery can be sown [*Ḥurban*, p. 200].

The analogy may be more apt in drawing attention to what is *dissimilar* than what is similar in these two creative projects—and the difference lies, I believe, not only between collective exegesis and individual mythopoesis. Greenberg, who is probably, as Mintz suggests, the only modern Hebrew poet to construct a coherent, sustained system of meaning and theosophy out of the most recent catastrophe in Jewish history, seems to represent, in his apocalyptic vision and mythopoeic practice, both an anachronism and a challenge to the anti-apocalyptic edifice so carefully constructed by the Rabbis and sustained for nearly two thousand years. Apocalypticism, as Amos Funkenstein points out, was suspect in the Rabbis' eyes partly because "it smacked of mythology, of mythopoetic mentality."[24] Yet these temptations sometimes prove no less compelling for the modern maker of fictive worlds poised at the edge of a ruined universe; apocalyptic modernists like D. H. Lawrence or W. B. Yeats share what Frank Kermode defines as the "conviction that [they] exist at the end of an epoch, in a time of transition, on a ridge of history from which the contours of the whole are visible. That vision [encompasses] . . . the design of history . . . the outcome of the great narrative plot."[25]

Among those western writers who lived to see the realization of their absolutist fantasies in the spectacle of the Third Reich, many redrafted their vision of the "great narrative plot" to reduce it to human dimensions. Regarding his "supreme fiction," Wallace Stevens wrote after the war: *"It must be Human."*[26] It is as if the monumental cosmic narratives of apocalypse and redemption were constantly being checked and defied at the borders of the domain in which the local and contemporary narratives of individual lives reign.

In the Jewish civilization that was decimated by the apocalyptic fantasies of others, both apocalyptic and anti-apocalyptic visions have survived in the encoding of catastrophe. While Greenberg's poetry is the most coherent and strident articulation of what persists as a sensibility, a nerve, a force active in Jewish consciousness, messianic figures such as Shabbetai Zevi—and even Jesus—have fired the imagination of a number of other Yiddish and Hebrew writers in the twentieth century, from Scholem Asch through Bashevis Singer to Hayyim Hazaz. A powerful vision of apocalypse appears as the concluding chapter of Leib Rochman's novel, *Mit blinde trit iber der erd* [With Blind Footsteps over the Earth]; this pageant of transmigration and resurrection of the souls of Hitler's victims, enacted in the Judean Desert, resembles some of the most majestic scenes in Greenberg's poetry.[27]

Sometimes it is a very subtle line that divides the innocent from the ironic appropriations (or, if you will, "innocent recall" from "sacred parody") of apocalyptic themes and images.[28] The antimythological, antimythopoetic and anti-apocalyptic stand of most of Greenberg's compatriots in the poetry and prose of contemporary Israel is, at the very least, dialectical evidence of the enduring power of visions of destruction and surrender and of the aesthetic appeal of visible "contours of the whole," and underscores the tremendous creative energies required to resist them. All of modern Hebrew literature evolves in the shadow of Israel's annihilation in Europe and Israel's ongoing wars in the Holy Land. Against the imposing and colossal figure of Uri Zvi Greenberg, against the power of prevailing myths of regeneration, manifest destiny, and redemption, irony continually seeks to replace pathos, and the profanities of the quotidian challenge sacred space and existential disorders preempt messianic order.

While the eschatological vision of Greenberg or Rochman is saturated with the images of Jewish martyrdom and regeneration, and the transcription of this vision into a theodicy of a Jewish kingdom resurrected from the ashes has had very specific political ramifications, it is the anti-apocalyptic stand in modern Hebrew letters which is continuous with the antimythological orientation of the rabbinic literature. What emerges here is a long tradition of Jewish resistance to the subsuming of the voice of the reflective, wondering individual into the loud noises of divine acts;[29] it reaffirms, in its intertextual ironies, the covenantal logic of the dualism of human and divine voices and the unresolvable tensions between man's endless, open-ended quest and the never-realized divine promise of a final judgment.

When parodic versions of apocalypse in contemporary Israeli poetry incorporate midrashic subtexts, they address, across two thousand years of collective memory, a discourse on the probability and parameters of redemption that has not lost its hold on the Jewish imagination. The midrash which presents the Messiah binding his wounds among the beggars of Rome—all the while assuring R. Yehoshua that he will come "today" (that is, as it is glossed, when the created world will "hearken to His voice")[30] acknowledges the human longing for apocalyptic surrender but places it in an endlessly deferred future and a compassionate human landscape. Yehuda Amichai's ironic voice provides a strong reading of the classical source which deflates messianic pathos by resacralizing the banal and repositioning the individual at the center of the cosmic drama:

> Once I sat on the steps by a gate at David's Tower, I placed my two heavy baskets at my side. A group of tourists was standing around their guide and I became their target marker. "You see that man with the baskets? Just right of his head there's an arch from the Roman period. Just right of his head." "But he's moving, he's moving!" I said to myself: redemption will come only if their guide tells them, "You see that arch from the Roman period? It's not important: but next to it, left and down a bit, there sits a man who's bought fruit and vegetables for his family."[31]

Notes

1 · David Roskies, *Against the Apocalypse: Responses to Catastrophe in Modern Jewish Culture* (Cambridge: Harvard University Press, 1984), p. 10. All further references to this work will be noted in the text.

2 · Alan Mintz, *Ḥurban: Responses to Catastrophe in Hebrew Literature* (New York: Columbia University Press, 1984), p. x.

3 · Robert Alter, "The Apocalyptic Temper," in Alter, *After the Tradition: Essays on Modern Jewish Writing* (New York: Dutton, 1971), p. 50.

4 · See, on this subject, Roskies, *Against the Apocalypse;* Mintz, *Ḥurban;* Gershom

Scholem, *The Messianic Idea in Judaism and Other Essays on Jewish Spirituality* (Schocken Books, 1971); Amos Funkenstein, "A Schedule for the End of the World: The Origins and Persistence of the Apocalyptic Mentality," in *Visions of Apocalypse: End or Rebirth?*, eds. Saul Friedländer, Gerald Holton, Leo Marx, and Eugene Skolnikoff (New York: Holmes & Meier, 1985)

5 · What is translated here as "two thousand years" appears in the Hebrew original as "two days"—"Eleh Ezkerah," medieval *piyyut* whose author has not been definitively determined, based on four different versions of a *midrash* dating from the *geonic* period describing the martyrdom suffered by ten teachers who defied the Hadrianic decrees against teaching Torah; incorporated into the Yom Kippur liturgy (trans. Philip Bernbaum, *High Holiday Prayer Book* [New York: Hebrew Publishing Co., 1951], p. 842). Alter argues that "nothing expresses more clearly Judaism's concern with the 'factual character of human existence, as existence that factually meets transcendence' than the Jewish preoccupation with law [Torah, *halakhah*]. . . . There is, moreover, a clear connection between Christianity's rejection of law and its expectations of an imminent apocalypse" (*After the Tradition*, pp. 54, 55).

6 · The ambiguous status of the martyr in Jewish tradition can be traced back to a polemic between Rabbi Akiva—who preached on behalf of "ahavat havisurim" (the love of suffering) and who also embraced Bar Kokhba as the Messiah—and Rabbi Ishmael and others who would not accept the redemptive power of suffering and who denied any superior measure of piety to Bar Kokhba. See A. J. Heschel, *Torah Min Shamayim* [Torah from Heaven], vol. 1, Soncino, 1962, pp. 100ff.; and Louis Finkelstein, "The Ten Martyrs," *Essays and Studies in Memory of Linda R. Miller,* ed. I. Davidson, *Jewish Theological Seminary Annual,* 1938, pp. 29ff.

7 · See Arnold Eisen's exegesis of mishnaic tractate *Avoda Zarah* in terms of the rabbinic construction of the parameters of *Galut* (exile) in the wake of the destruction of the Second Temple (*Galut: Modern Jewish Reflection on Home-lessness and Homecoming* (Bloomington: Indiana University Press, 1986), pp. 35ff.

8 · Yosef Ḥayim Yerushalmi, *Zakhor: Jewish History and Jewish Memory* (Seattle, University of Washington Press, 1982).

9 · "The depiction of catastrophe . . . does not relate directly to the question of pain and suffering caused by historical events. The catastrophic element in events is defined as the power to shatter the existing paradigms of meaning, especially as regards the bonds between God and the people of Israel. Crucial to creative survival was the reconstruction of these paradigms through interpre-tation, and in this enterprise the literary imagination was paramount" (Mintz, *Ḥurban*, p. x).

10 · See Mintz's discussion of poetic reflexivity and commensurability in *Lamenta-tions* (Ibid., pp. 28ff.).

11 · Roskies' understanding of sacred parody is, however, stronger than the biblical passage he cites as its original source—an emended and highly questionable reading of the verse in Lamentations "ani hagever ra'ah 'oni" (p. 19). Generally translated as "I am the man who has seen [or experienced] affliction", Roskies'

emended reading translates as "I am the man whom the Lord has shep-
herded," thereby asserting the subversive resonance of the pastoral image in
Psalm 23. The same procedure of scriptural revision or parody could have been
demonstrated through other passages, without recourse to such philological
calisthenics. For a detailed discussion of Midrash-like procedures in the Bible,
see Michael Fishbane, *Biblical Interpretation in Ancient Israel* (Oxford: Claren-
don Press, 1985). My own understanding of Midrash was also enhanced by
conversations with him in the course of writing this essay.

12 · On this passage see Ezrahi, *By Words Alone: The Holocaust in Literature* (Chicago:
University of Chicago Press, 1980), p. 234.

13 · For a painstaking and illuminating study of ghetto literature, see Yeḥiel Shein-
tuch, *Yiddish and Hebrew Literature under the Nazi Rule in Eastern Europe: Yitzḥak
Katznelson's Last Bilingual Writings and the Ghetto Writings of A. Sutzkever and I.
Spiegel* [Hebrew], Hebrew University dissertation, 1978.

14 · "Burnt Pearls," in *Burnt Pearls: Ghetto Poems*, trans. Seymour Mayne (Ontario:
Mosaic Press, 1982), p. 38. The postwar phenomenon of "return" among
modernist Yiddish poets has been widely discussed in the critical literature.

15 · "Revisioning the Past: The Changing Legacy of the Holocaust in Hebrew
Literature," in *Salmagundi*, Fall 1985–Winter 1986, No. 68–69.

16 · "The Sermon," trans. Ben Halpern, in Robert Alter, ed., *Modern Hebrew
Literature* (New York: Behrman House, 1975), p. 273.

17 · *The Messianic Idea in Judaism*, p. 10.

18 · "Jewish National Movement: A Sociological Analysis," in *Emancipation and
Assimilation* (Farnborough, Hants, 1972), p. 130.

19 · *The Messianic Idea in Judaism*, p. 35. See also, on these and related issues, Eisen,
Galut.

20 · Ibid., p. 36.

21 · The phenomenon of millenarian movements at the end of each century—and
most acutely at the end of each millennium—has been defined by Henri
Focillan as "centurial mysticism" (quoted in Frank Kermode, "Apocalypse and
the Modern," in *Visions of the Apocalypse*, p. 93).

22 · When such redemptive and apocalyptic scenarios—which proved dangerous
enough to the collective psyche when played out in the second century around
the figure of Bar Kokhba or in the seventeenth century around the figure of
Shabbetai Zevi—enter the orientations of religious zealots in the contemporary
context of the Arab-Israeli conflict, they become powerful political strategies by
which the zealots depersonalize the employment of Jewish power and integrate
it into a deterministic scheme which releases them from personal or moral
responsibility for the actions taken.

23 · The Hebrew calendar year 5744, corresponding to the Gregorian 1984, is
designated by alphabetic notation as "tashmad," which spells out the word
"destruction".

24 · Funkenstein, "A Schedule for the End of the World," p. 50.

25 · Frank Kermode, "Apocalypse and the Modern," p. 94. On the connection
bet̨ween "Absolute Poetry and Absolute Politics," see also Michael Ham-

burger, *The Truth of Poetry: Tensions in Modern Poetry From Bandelaire to the 1960s* (London: Methuen, 1982), pp. 81–109.

26 · Letter to Robert Pack, 28 December, 1954. Quoted in Hamburger, p. 107.

27 · *Mit blinde trit iber der erd* (Tel Aviv: Hamnoyre, 1968). This apparition in the epic fiction of a major Yiddish survivor-writer, which complements Greenberg's poetry and should pose a serious challenge to Roskies' thesis, is missing from his encyclopedic account of Yiddish writers enlisted "against the apocalypse".

28 · See Hazaz's aforementioned story, "The Sermon" and his 1950 play, "In the End of Days"; see also Alter's discussion of it in *After the Tradition*, pp. 70ff.

29 · For a daring contemporary treatment of this theme, see Shulamith Hareven's novella, *Sonei hanisim* [Miracle Hater] (Jerusalem: Dvir, 1983).

30 · Sanhedrin, 98a.

31 · Yehuda Amichai, *Poems of Jerusalem* (Tel Aviv: Schocken, 1987), p. 177—trans. by Glenda Abramson and Tudor Parfitt.

11 · George Steiner

The Long Life of Metaphor:
An Approach to the "Shoah"

*I*n Christian theology, the question of whether there is a mode of human language in which to speak adequately of God is a classical and perennial motif. It constitutes the linguistic-philosophical sphere of hermeneutic theology. Prayer *to* God does not present a problem; discourse *about* God, a very nearly insoluble one. It is, precisely, the God concept which seems to transcend the capacities of language either to define or to analogize truthfully the object of conceptualization and expression. The Wittgensteinian precept that the limits of our language are those of our world simply restates the dilemma. Language cannot go beyond the constraints of the human intellect and imagination. By definition, God lies outside such constraints.

In Judaism, this problem of linguistic epistemology, or hermeneutic theology, has not been prominent. Indeed, the very notion of "theology," in the post-Pauline, post-Johannine, and post-Augustinian sense, has no real counterpart in Jewish religious feeling. The most authentic and lasting strength in Jewish sensibility is not a reflection or metaphysical discourse on the nature and attributes of God, but rather a "living in His presence." From Abraham onward, there has been a covenant of dialogue between the believing Jew and God. In this dialogue, the problem of language does not really obtrude. As, perhaps, in no other faith, the God of Abraham and Moses, and those to whom He has chosen to speak, individually and as a community, share the same language. We can almost define the language-world of Judaism in relation to God as one of idiomatic affinity.

One of the consequences of the Shoah, or Holocaust, is to have transported (violently, irreparably) into Judaism, both religious and secular, the hermeneutic dilemma. The problem as to whether there is a human form of language adequate to the conceptualization and understanding of Auschwitz, as to whether the limits of language do not fall short of the limits of the Shoah experience, is now ineradicably installed in Jewish existence.

This is true, first, on the theological level as such: in what conceivable language can a Jew speak *to* God after Auschwitz, and in what conceivable language can he speak *about* God? The challenge is deeper, more corrosive than that in Christian hermeneutics. In post-Shoah Judaism, the question of the language of prayer—how can it be anything but cynical, accusatory, or despairing?—is radically posed. I will come back to it via a text by Paul Celan that, alone I believe, is as profound and encompassing as the problem itself. As to speech *about* God: what forms can it take, what plausibility can it enlist, after the death camps?

But the possible absence of any mode of human expression relevant to the Shoah experience has consequences that extend beyond the ritual and the religious domain. Even the most secular Jew is the explicit creature of his past, of Jewish history. Even the Jewish atheist or most deliberate assimilationist orients his identity in reference to the historical destiny of the Jewish people and the enigma of their survival. What categories of intelligibility, what grammar of reason, indeed what vocabulary in the most concrete sense, can incorporate, can articulate, can give interpretation to, the abyss of 1938–1945? But if there can be no such intelligible and significant incorporation, what will befall that lived sense of an unbroken past, that ontological historicity, which has, until now, been the immediate context of Jewish self-recognition, both personally and communally? For a Jew to be silent about any determining part of his own history is self-mutilation.

There are no ready answers to this absolutely crucial dilemma. It is by no means clear that there can be, or that there ought to be, any form, style, or code of articulate, intelligible expression somehow adequate to the facts of the Shoah. Let us consider this point closely, bearing in mind both the existential (the *can*) and the morally prescriptive (the *ought*) elements of the situation.

It may be that the Auschwitz-universe, for it was that, precisely marks that realm of potential—now realized—human bestiality or, rather, abandonment of the human and regression to bestiality, which both precedes language, as it does in the animal, and comes after language as it does in death. On a collective, historical scale, Auschwitz would signify the *death of man* as a rational, "forward-dreaming" speech-organism (the *zoon phonanta* of Greek philosophy). The languages we are now speaking on this polluted and suicidal planet are "post-human." They are serving creatures less than man. They are loud with emptiness, a volume made the more evident and barbaric by electronic media. Where the language is still humane, in the root sense of that word, it is being spoken by survivors, remembrancers and ghosts. Its haunted music is that of the embers that continue to crackle in the cooling ash of a dead fire. Eloquence after Auschwitz would be a kind of obscenity (this is the meaning of Theodor Adorno's so often misunderstood call for "no poetry after Auschwitz").

But I ask further: since it is not eloquence that is at issue, what kind of rationality, what kind of ordered logic of the human social and psychological circumstance, what processes of rational analysis and causal explanation are available to language after the cancer of reason, the travesty of all meaningfulness, enacted in the Shoah? It is doubts of this order that have generated my own (provisional) feeling that silence is the only, though in its way suicidal, option; that to try to speak or write intelligibly, interpretatively, about Auschwitz is to misconceive totally the nature of that event and to misconstrue totally the necessary constraints of humanity within language.

What is more: it may be that after the Shoah, those metaphors, those projections and sublimations, which made it possible for human words and human syntax to speak about God are no longer available to us. (It could, quite precisely, be this nonavailability that now sickens, that now condemns to erosion or quarrelsome gossip the discourse worlds, the speech acts, of Christianity and Christian theologies.) It may be that after the gassing, starvation, live burial, slow torture, burning of millions of men, women, and children in the heartlands of so-called civilization, we no longer have cause or need to speak to or about a God whose overwhelming attribute became that of absence, of nothingness. Words fail *us*, as we have failed *them*. And it is this dialectic of reciprocal failing—*O Wort, du Wort das mir Fehlt!* is Moses' despairing cry at the unfinished close of Schönberg's *Moses und Aron*—which would come nearest to justifying the concept of the "death of God" or (as I prefer to think of it) the "exit of God" from language, which is to say, from the bounds of human experience.

Possibly the only language in which anything intelligible, anything responsible, about the Shoah can be attempted is German. It is in German, at the very source of its modern genius and linguistic conventions, that is, in Luther's pamphlets of the early 1540s, that the elimination, the *Ausrottung* of the Jew from Europe, that the burning alive of the Jew, is clearly enunciated. It is in the seminal call to German nationhood, in Fichte's *Addresses to the German Nation,* that Jew-hatred is given the sanction of a major philosophy. It is in German that Heine, as early as 1820, voices the plain warning that where certain books are being burned, human beings will be. It is Nietzsche who, with almost somnambular clarity, identifies murderous anti-Semitism as being the defining dynamism of the German spirit. It is Kafka's parable, notably "The Metamorphosis" and "In the Penal Colony," that exactly prevision the vocabulary, in technocracy, the politics and psychology of the subhuman, as these are fulfilled in the concentration-camp state. It is Karl Kraus who concretely dates "the last days of humanity," who gives the apocalypse of the inhuman its calendar. The literally unspeakable words that are used to plan, to prescribe, to record, to justify the Shoah; the words that entail and set down the burning alive of children in front of their parents' eyes; the slow drowning of old men and women in excrement; the eradication of millions in a verbose bureaucracy of murder—these are German words. They are words to which the hallucinatory fantastications, the death-*Kitsch* of Nazi oratory, gave a force, a consequence that few other words have possessed in human history.

It may be, therefore, that if there is to be a rehumanization of language after the Shoah, a restoration to language of its lost capacities to speak to and about God, to speak to and about man in any answerable *(verantwortlich)* sense, such reparation and restoration can come only from within the death-idiom itself. It is in German that we find the only poet—dare I say the only writer—on a level (and I use that eroded phrase with extreme, literal intent) with Auschwitz.

It would follow that the attitudes toward the Shoah in the earlier years of the State of Israel and of the new Israeli literature represent a counterpart to the destined singularity of German. For quite a long time, Israeli sensibility sought to look away from the European and East European catastrophe. Israeli poets and novelists wrote of other themes. This has changed, I know. But, even today, the relations between modern Hebrew and the realities of Auschwitz are problematic (as is, within Israel, the vestigial, spectral presence of Yiddish). How could the rebirth of Israel, how could the modulation of Hebrew into a future tense—one, precisely, lacking in the intemporal presentness of biblical Hebrew—incorporate the Shoah without risking self-destruction, without relinquishing the life-giving grammar of hope? Even as there is an urgent sense in which Auschwitz is the problem not of the Jew but of the Christian, in which it is now central to the terminal belief, so there is an urgent sense in which the language dilemma brought on by the Shoah is, above all, the problem of German and the nonproblem of Hebrew. I do not really believe this to be the case, but I register the logic and force of the proposition.

The questions I have posed, and the way in which I have posed them, postulate the uniqueness of the Shoah. They imply that the massacre of European and East European Jewry under National Socialism is an event unlike any other in the long history of massacres and mass extermination. The Shoah is seen to be what modern physics calls a "singularity," a phenomenon and event outside the rules or patterns of the general system of reality. Is this so? I find the question deeply unsettling, even repellent. But it must be considered.

Quantitatively—and this is, by itself, something of an obscene criterion—there have been worse killings. Responsible historians put at 10 or 12 million the number of human beings done to death by the Stalinist regime during the crisis of the kulaks and the subsequent purges and deportations. We have, over these past two decades, witnessed massacres in Indonesia and in Africa that run into the hundred thousands, perhaps millions. The insane blood lust that erupted in Cambodia under Pol Pot massacred an estimated 2 or 2.5 million men, women, and children in a much shorter time than that of the Shoah. With the very brief, inherently fragile exception of that armistice with history that benefited the middle and upper classes in Western Europe during the century from 1815 to 1914, massacre, torture, deportation, persecution of minorities, and exploitation of race hatreds have been the customary fabric of history. Men are murderous and murdering primates. See the Book of Joshua.

Is there a qualitative uniqueness in the Shoah? The argument that there is a bestial innovation in the Nazi decision to kill all Jews purely and simply on ethnic-racial grounds does not hold. Ask the Armenians, the Gypsies, the members—men, women, children—of those diverse African tribes methodically hounded to death in Uganda or Burundi. In ancient history, whole peoples, cultures, and languages were eradicated by deliberate political acts of homicide, vengeance, or enslavement. A number of Jewish thinkers and historians have argued that the Shoah differs from any other massacre in its application of a specifically designed bureaucracy and technology. I do not find this argument persuasive. In their own military-political terms, the mass exterminations carried out by the Vandals, by the Huns, by Islamic conquerors of Byzantium represent appalling feats of purposed and organized bestiality. Arrows and fire kill no less surely than gas ovens. *If* there are qualitative differences between the Shoah and the innumerable examples of mass murder that punctuate history both before and since, they must lie very deep: in that symbolic and metaphysical-theological realm I want to point toward.

But whatever the "objective" case, and here "objectivity" is near to being inconceivable, the presumed uniqueness of the Shoah has become vital to Judaism now. In numerous, complex ways it underlies and underwrites certain essential aspects of the re-creation of nationhood in Israel, a re-creation whose uniqueness, whose transcendence of normal probability even in secular perceptions, subtly counterbalances that of the world of Auschwitz, of Bergen-Belsen. Climaxing—but also overshadowing—all previous persecutions in the history of Jewish exclusion and suffering, the Shoah has given to that history a particularity of darkness, a seeming logic in which the sole categorical imperative is that of survival.[1]

The Shoah, the remembrance of Auschwitz, the haunting apprehension that, somewhere, somehow, the massacres could begin anew, is today the cement of Jewish identity. It is the one and only bond that unites the Orthodox Jew and the atheist, the practicing Jew and the total secularist, the people of Israel and the Diaspora, the Zionist and the anti-Zionist, the extreme conservative Jew (so prominent in the United States today) and the Jewish Trotskyite or Communist. Above all else, to be a Jew in the second half of this century is to be a survivor, and one who knows that his survival can again be put in question.

This bond is at once inevitable and psychologically ambiguous. It serves to mask the profound differences within current Judaism. Israel has too often invoked the Shoah as an apologia, as a justification for the more extreme gestures of its policies, both inside its borders and beyond them. The horror of the Shoah and of its recall—in books, in pictures, in the media—has provided the nonpracticing, the largely assimilated Jew in the West, notably in the United States, with a subtly self-flattering, self-dramatizing aura of tragic "belonging." A disturbingly commercialized pathos of horror has arisen around certain survivors and their all-too-eloquent and sometimes even theatrical witness. In other instances, the remembrance of the Shoah and the agonizing question of the absence or inadequacy of Jewish resistance have induced self-contempt and a compensating fascination with violence. We are, in certain respects, a traumatized, a crazed people. How could we not be? Especially where it is that trauma which keeps us from final dispersal.

Unavoidably, the idiom of singularity, the assumption that the Shoah must be thought about and studied (if at all) as extraterritorial to normal human history, has become intermixed with the usual modes of historical, sociological, and economic discourse. The instruments and disciplines of rational inquiry that apply, say, even to the apocalyptic massacres, starvation, manhunts, and lies of the decades of the Gulag, or that are currently being brought to bear on the horror of recent Cambodian history, are felt to be both relevant and, in the final analysis, irrelevant to an understanding of the Shoah. To *normalize* that understanding would, very precisely, signify an abandonment of the appalling, yet also ennobling and justifying, mystery of Jewish identity. My own reflections on and questions about Auschwitz, in fiction and nonfiction, my attempts to say something about the nature of human language after the Shoah (I now try to avoid that ritual, elevated, and therefore radically inappropriate Greek word "Holocaust") directly reflect this intermingling of different, perhaps irreconcilable levels of analysis and of method.

One major fact does seem clear. So far, the empirical, the positivist *(wissenschaftlich)* techniques and methodologies have failed to explain not only the sources of the Shoah in high European civilization; they have also failed to explain certain crucial elements in Nazi policy and in the aftermath of that policy.

I would not deny for a moment the value of economic-sociological investigations of European Jew-hatred from the beginnings of modern mercantilism and market-competition to the present. I fully recognize the endeavors of political theorists and political historians to analyze, to quantify the class conflicts, the demographic shifts, and the voting patterns that underlay the Dreyfus Affair and the rise of Nazism. Psychologists of the "totalitarian personality," of race relations under economic stress, have made stimulating suggestions. By simple virtue of their publication of the documentary records of the death camps, of the massacres at large, of Jewish resistance, the historians of the Shoah have performed an absolutely essential act of truthful remembrance, of resurrection. Theirs has been the *kaddish* against lies—and against that greatest lie, which is forgetting. Pragmatic, systematic studies of the Shoah are vital.

To my mind they have not, however, illuminated the deeper-lying roots of the inhuman. They have, quite markedly, failed to explain—except on the rather trivial level of Hitler's private pathology—the Nazi decision to press on with the "Final Solution" when even a brief suspension of the death transports, roundups, and extermination industry would have freed desperately needed resources for the defense and survival of the Reich. Nor do "rationalistic" and immanently grounded explanations explain the continuation of virulent Jew hatred in countries, in societies where there are virtually *no Jews left* (as in Poland, in Austria, in the Ukraine). The seeds of Auschwitz—the Nazi sense of victory over the Jews as outweighing the ruin of Germany; Jew-hatred where only phantoms are left. These are the questions that demand an attempt at an answer. And it is that attempt which leads me to test a different order or framework of thought and speech.

"Regardless of what anyone may personally think or believe about him, Jesus of Nazareth has been the dominant figure in the history of Western culture for almost twenty centuries." (Jaroslav Pelikan). At their peril, the Jews in the long ghetto of their waiting ignored this fact.

So did those Jews who, after the latter part of the eighteenth century, played so forceful a role in the history of the European Enlightenment and of the secularization (probably superficial) of our modern consciousness. Nor did many Jews read and ponder that early and perhaps most inspired of all documents in the history of Jewish self-hatred: Paul's Epistle to the Romans 9–12. It is in that fantastically charged, opaque, at moments schizophrenic text, and in the immense volume of development and interpretation to which it has given rise, that we find the dark font of the interminable tragedy of Jewish-Christian coexistence or, rather, of Christianity's destined, logical attempt to terminate that coexistence.

Embryonic or fully spelled out, several scenarios spring from the Pauline source. Christ was the long-awaited Messiah, the Davidic liberator and savior so accurately prefigured in the Psalms and in Isaiah's vision of the suffering servant and representative of God. It is this Messiah, foretold in their own Torah, prayers, and prophecy, whom the Jewish people handed over to abominable torment and death. In so doing, Judaism eradicated from within itself not only the act of divine election, the "chosenness" by and for God's unique purpose; it tore up from within its own flesh and spirit *the very right to hope.* Israel passed into the limbo of theological sterility and despair (and certain cardinal traditions in Christian doctrine define such despair precisely as the unforgivable sin).

A second scenario is no less ominous. By refusing to recognize Jesus of Nazareth as the foretold Messiah, the Jews have postponed the day of man's salvation, the apocalyptic enfranchisement of suffering humanity and the eternal justice and peace that are to attend the Second Coming. Israel's refusal of Christ has, literally, condemned mankind to the treadmill of history. The Jews therefore hold the *Ecclesia* in particular, and humanity in general, hostage. There can be no liberation, no salvation from the agonies, bloodshed, and injustice of history until Judaism recognizes the authentic messianic truth of Jesus' ministry and incarnation.

This second scenario can lead to one of two logical consequences. The first is that of the elimination of Israel from the otherwise captive community of man. The possible program for such elimination, either by violent destruction or forced conversion, is, as we know, all too clearly set out in the writings and preaching of certain Church Fathers.

It runs through early and medieval Christianity as a perennial black thread. The other alternative, fashionable since Auschwitz, is that of Christian patience and self-questioning. The Messianic purposes of Christ the Son of God were not accomplished either in His earthly sojourn or in His resurrection. They are a continuous, incomplete process that will find fulfillment only when Judaism enters *freely* into the *Ecclesia*, only when synagogue and church are united in a common tabernacle. Till that day, Christianity itself is a fragmentary, often self-contradictory and culpable institution. The Jew is sacred, he must be preserved from harm, just because the potentiality of the truly ecumenical contains within itself the only access to genuine realization of God's promise in and through Christ. This, for example, seems to be the reading of history in the later work of Karl Barth. It is emphatically present in such contemporary ecumenical theologians of hope as Jürgen Moltmann.

These several scenarios—call them metaphoric constructs, symbolic dramatizations, doctrinal mythologies, or what you will—are enormous in their implications. Or, to enforce the connotations of that word: they are charged with enormity. Even the present-day proposals of patience and conciliation are overladen with social and psychological tension. Barth's famous formula—"Israel leidet an Gott" ("Israel is sick 'with' God" or "Israel's sickness is God")—is ambiguous, and carries with it a burden of terror. Israel's "God sickness" infects not only itself, in a way that can be construed as a metaphysical-transcendent privilege (God, through Abraham and Moses, chose the Jewish people to be the particular carriers of His "virus"). It can also be held to infect other men, to render the human condition in some central respect *incurable*.

So far as our evidence goes, and in an historical development that remains largely enigmatic, the Jewish people invented monotheism. In radical hostility to all surrounding creeds and cultures, Judaism originated, and identified its own destiny with, the concept of an infinite, intangible, invisible, ethically imperative God. And of a God inseparable not only from every moment of the individual human being's day, but from the meaning and purpose of political and social history. In the Sermon on the Mount, in his parables, Jesus the Jew reiterated, sharpened to apocalyptic extremity, the moral demands, the uncompromising imperative of altruism and self-sacrifice, present in the Mosaic Law and in the visionary rigor of the Prophets. This summons to abnegation—to the abolition of the ego and of private property and privilege—this annunciation of the inevitable, sacrificially-prepared coming of the kingdom of justice on earth, constitutes the core of that utterly Judaic secular messianism which we call Marxism. When Marx asks that man "exchange love for love, and justice for justice," he is speaking the exact language of Isaiah, of Amos, of the anarchist from Nazareth and Galilee.

Three times, Judaism has confronted Western man with the merciless claims and exactions of the ideal. Three times—in its invention of monotheism, in the message of the radical Jesus, in Marxism and messianic socialism—Israel has asked of ordinary men and women more than human nature wishes to give; more, it may be, than it is organically and psychically able to give. Nothing is more cruel than the blackmail of perfection. We come to hate, to fear most those who demand of us a self-transcendence, a surpassing of our natural and common limits of being. Our hate and fear are the more intense precisely because we know the absolute rightness, the ultimate desirability of the demand. In failing to respond adequately, we fail ourselves. And it is of deeply-lying self-hatreds that hatreds spring.

It is not, I believe, as deicide, as "God killer," that the Jew has been loathed and feared in the Christian civilization of the West (although that hideous attribution does play its part). It is as *inventor* of God; it is as spokesman for and remembrancer of an almighty, all-seeing, all-demanding Deity. It is because Judaism has kept man awake, as do the Prophets in the sleeping city (Sigmund Freud would even take away from us the innocence of our dreams.) It is because Judaism has said to man, thrice over: "Be better than you are lest God curse you for your weakness and backsliding"; "Love your neighbor as yourself even if every instinct in you bids otherwise"; "Lose your life so that you may gain it in the kingdom of justice"; "Empty creation of those manifold, intelligible, supernatural presences with which polytheism and the Greek imagination had peopled the earth, and worship instead a desert god, inaccessible to understanding, a god of whom you may not even make a mental image. . . ." Reportedly, Hitler said in his tabletalk: "The Jews invented conscience." Which is simply another way of saying: "The Jew invented God." For this crime, what forgiveness?

Minds trained to reason, to an empirical view of evidence, find it difficult to grasp the possessive force of doctrine, even where—or especially where—such doctrine seems irrational and foreign to rational and evidential proof. The force, the obsessive depth, of a doctrine become greater as that doctrine passes into the individual and collective unconscious in the guise of symbol and metaphor. Such symbolic and metaphoric obsessions with the psyche become virulent when the doctrine they represent has lost or begun to lose its own plausibility and intellectual coherence.

This is only an apparent paradox. It is when they are exhausted or degenerating that organs and muscle tissues secrete contagious and maleficent substances into the human body. So it was that the original Pauline and Patristic theology of Jew hatred, together with the more general and even deeper-lying resentment of monotheism and sacrificial morality, took on their terrible, festering virulence precisely as Christianity and a belief in God as such began receding from the spiritual habits and intellectual-political adherence of Western civilization. There is a perfect logic in the anti-Semitism of a Voltaire. There is a clear pattern in the fact that the Auschwitz world erupts out of the subconscious, collective obsessions of an increasingly agnostic, even anti- or post-Christian society. Long-buried, and freed of doctrinal inhibitions and abstractions, the symbols and metaphors that cluster around the Judaic invention and "killing" of God (the two are, psychologically, twinned) turned murderous.

This hypothesis cannot be "proved"; the evidence for it is not of an empirical or quantifiable kind. What it does, I believe, is to provide a framework of reference, a measure of depth in some sense corresponding to the phenomenology of the Shoah. Only a theological-metaphysical scale of values, only an acute awareness of the life force of theological-metaphysical metaphor and symbolism (even vestigial) in Western collective consciousness and subconsciousness, can hope to throw some light—I do not lay claim to more—on the etiology, the causal dynamics of Jew hatred and of the Auschwitz experience as these arose from inside the core of European history and culture.

No other approach gives intelligible access to the National Socialist axiom that the eradication of the Jew and of Judaism from Europe was a goal worth achieving even at the cost of the (temporary) destruction of the German nation-state. No other hypothesis will help us understand the widespread, almost total, indifference with which this homicidal policy was met throughout Europe, Eastern Europe, and the Soviet Union. In regard to the "Jewish problem," Nazism spoke out loud and enacted what Christian and post-Christian Europe had long harbored as an obsessive, half-avowed dream and fantasy. And it is, I suggest, only a theological-metaphysical category of analysis that provides any possibility of understanding the survival—the flourishing—of Jew hatred where there are no Jews left. Ghosts are of particular menace when they emerge from within oneself.

It is, therefore, no accident that the theological-metaphysical levels of language, of metaphor, of symbolism should be the foundation and constant resource of the one writer who, to my knowledge, has not only taken us to the unspeakable center of the Shoah experience, but—and this is far more difficult and important—has located the sense of that experience within the definition of man, history, and human speech. Only a Jew compelling himself to write in German could have brought this about, as, before him, only a Jew writing in German could be Kafka the prophet. That Paul Celan is also among the greatest poets in the German tongue, indeed in modern European literature (being, perhaps, an even more *necessary* poet than Rilke); that Celan alone can stand beside Hölderlin in both his poetry and his prose—this is almost an extraneous wonder. The necessary and sufficient condition for Celan's poems is the situation of all human saying after the Shoah, a situation that Celan lived and articulated in the absent face of God. In this one supreme witness—"Wer," he asks, "zeugt für den Zeugen?" ("Who bears witness for the witness?")—the fate of the Jew, the night-charged genius of the German language, of the idiom of Auschwitz and Belsen, and a profound intimacy with the Hebraic and the Yiddish legacy coalesced; and they coalesced around the central criteria of the theological and the metaphysical orders of questioning.

There is hardly a poem or parable or address by Paul Celan that would not serve to illustrate this point. If I cite the famous "Psalm," it is because of its unsurpassed immensity of implication and nakedness of expression:

Niemand knetet uns wieder aus Erde und Lehm,
niemand bespricht unsern Staub.
Niemand.

Gelobt seist du, Niemand.
Dir zulieb wollen
wir blühn.
Dir
entgegen.

Ein Nichts
waren wir, sind wir, werden
wir bleiben, blühend:
die Nichts—, die
Niemandsrose.

Mit
dem Griffel seelenhell,
dem Staubfaden himmelswüst,
der Krone rot
vom Purpurwort, das wir sangen
über, o über
dem Dorn.

In rough, inadequate paraphrase:

No-one kneads us again out of earth and loam,
No-one bespeaks our dust.
No-one.

Praise unto thee, No-one.
For love of you will
we bloom.
Towards/against
You.

A nothing
were we, are we, will
we remain, blooming:
No-one's-rose.

With
the stylus soul-bright

the dust-thread sky-waste,
the crown reddened
by the purple word, which we sang
above, o above
the thorn.

It is not my aim to add yet another to the manifold commentaries and exercises in paraphrase that Celan's famous text has elicited. The very word *Niemandsrose* has passed into the German language and into the inward history of Jewish consciousness. All I wish to do is to underline what is evident: the radically theological and metaphysical (in the etymological sense of the transcendent) character of Celan's idiom and field of referral—here a stricter term than "reference."

The identification of the Creator with "No-one" and "nothingness" reaches into the ambiguous heart of both ascetic piety and kabbalistic speculation. It bears simultaneous witness to the inconceivable, unimaginable, unspeakable, antimetaphoric tenor of the God of Israel, and to the enigma of His withdrawal from that making of man, that shedding of Adam—*aus Erde und Lehm*—which, according to certain kabbalistic theories, represented a tragic self-division within God Himself. The liturgical-formulaic praise of the Lord—*Gelobt seist du, Niemand*—is at once of exemplary piety and resignation and of ultimate rebellion. The Jew in the *Aschenglorie* (another key Celan word) of the death camps, "blooms" both *toward* God—in *that* place, at *that* hour—and "against" God. *Entgegen* signifies "towardness" and "opposition."

The "nothingness" of the Jew at Auschwitz is, in a sense, the nothingness of man before God created him; it is the nothingness that constitutes every individual extinction; it is the nothingness, the zero point, of history for the Jewish people at the hands of its killers. Yet, it is a nothingness "in bloom," a terrible flowering toward and against the "no-oneness" of God's absence.

It is this accusation out of ash, this blossoming indictment that, alone, tells against the finality of annihilation. It is not only, *contra* Ezekiel, that there shall be no resurrection for the slain Jews; it is, more hideously, that there will be no bespeaking their dust. That tremendous phrase carries a twofold charge. *Bespricht unsern Staub*[2] refers to God's breathing of life into the clay of Adam, to God's "saying of being," in the precise sense in which Hellenistic Judaism will develop the concepts of *pneuma* and *Logos*. But *besprechen* also means "to talk about," "to talk to" (as one "addresses oneself to" a topic). No one—not, above all, God Himself—will speak to the condition of Auschwitz, will speak about it in adequate witness or commemoration. The absence of God from the Shoah is also His silence in the face of the unremembered dead, an unremembrance that makes of their death a double annihilation.

It is only the victims themselves, in the red flowering of their annonymous, unspeakable deaths, who can rescue God from the void of His silence. Theirs is "the purple word," blood-soaked and royal; theirs is the song over the thorn, the living mystery of the *Niemandsrose* above the lacerating murderousness of "the thorn." The Song of Solomon is present here, as is also, in a tragic, distancing discretion of allusion, that crown of thorns worn by the Nazarene. Celan has written a psalm out of Auschwitz that is simultaneously an "antipsalm," exactly as matter postulates and collides with antimatter. The Jew in the Shoah speaks to and against the nonspeaking, the unspeaking, of God. So long as the Jew addresses God, God must listen. It may be that this compelled listening has, in the Auschwitz world, become the fragile thread—*der Staubfaden*—whereby hangs the existence, the survival, of God in a heaven, in a cosmos, laid waste *(himmelswüst)*. If, in the Christ passion, a divine being, the Son of God and of man, is held to have died *for* man, so in the Shoah, the Jewish people ("Radix, Matrix")—

> (Wurzel
> Wurzel Abrahams. Wurzel Jesse. Niemandes
> Wurzel—o
> unser.)

> (Root
> Root of Abraham, root of Jesse, No-one's
> Root—o
> ours.)

—can be seen, understood, to have died *for* God, to have taken upon itself the inconceivable guilt of God's indifference, or absence, or impotence.

Such concepts are not amenable to rational analysis—even as Celan's Shoah poems are not amenable to critical paraphrase or equalizing interpretation. We move here in the sphere of lived metaphor, of language *beside itself,* which is one of the (wholly insufficient) images or tropes whereby we can come nearer the question with which I began: that of the very possibilities of human discourse in regard to God and to the Shoah—a duality that has, for the Jew, been made an irreparable unison. To ask what, if any, are such possibilities is to ask metaphysically and theologically. It is to recognize the essential inadequacy of pragmatic-positivist levels of argument.

This does not mean that any viable answer will be forthcoming. In Paul Celan's suicide (in Paris, in 1970), at the height of his powers, lies more than a hint of overwhelming desolation. How can a Jew speak of the Shoah in the language of his murderers? How can he speak of it in any other language? How can he speak of it at all? Under stress of ultimate need, but of a need that batters in vain against the outermost confines of the human word, Celan's late poems enter a vocabulary, a syntax, a semantic mode, inaccessible to most of us. They are written in a tongue "north of the future." It may be that the Shoah has eradicated the saving grace, the life-giving mystery of meaningful metaphor in Western speech and, correlatively, in that highest organization of speech which we call poetry and philosophic thought. There would be a just logic and a logic of justice in such eradication. Or it may be that the compulsion to articulacy within Judaism—the commandment of dialogue even with, even against, a mute God—will persist.

It is my belief that such persistence, with all that it implies not only for the precarious survival of Judaism, but for that, no less precarious, of our civilization as a whole, depends on the seminal force, on the haunting tenacity of the metaphysical and the theological presences in our psyche. The question of Auschwitz is far greater than that of the pathology of politics or of economic and social-ethnic conflicts (important as these are). It is a question of the conceivable existence or nonexistence of God, of the "No-one" who made us, who did not speak out of the death wind, and who is now on trial. In that court, which is the court of man in history, how can the language spoken in indictment or defense, in witness or denial, be one from which His absence is absent, be one in which no psalm can be spoken against Him?

Notes

1 · How fascinating, how disconcerting would be a history of modern Judaism with no reference to the Shoah: a history of the immense successes of Jews in the sciences, in Marxism, in psychoanalysis, in the modern philosophies of language from Mauthner and Wittgenstein to Chomsky and Saul Kripke; a recounting of the success story of Jews in America; a chronicle of the often dominant role of Jews and Jewish talent in twentieth-century finance, in the mass media, in humor, and in certain areas of literature. But there is no such book; and we could not bear it if there were.

2 · In his valuable bilingual edition of Paul Celan's poetry, *Paul Celan* (South Hinskey: Carcanet, 1983), Michael Hamburger in his translation of "Psalm" inexplicably renders this line as "conjured out of the dust."

PART III

Fiction as Truth

12 · Irving Howe

Writing and the Holocaust

*O*ur subject resists the usual capacities of mind. We may read the Holocaust as the central event of this century; we may register the pain of its unhealed wounds; but finally we must acknowledge that it leaves us intellectually disarmed, staring helplessly at the reality or, if you prefer, the mystery of mass extermination. There is little likelihood of finding a rational structure of explanation for the Holocaust: it forms a sequence of events without historical or moral precedent. To think about ways in which the literary imagination might "use" the Holocaust is to entangle ourselves with a multitude of problems for which no aesthetic can prepare us. Neither encompassing theory nor religious faith enables us to reach a firm conviction that now, at last, we understand what happened during the "Final Solution."

The Holocaust is continuous with, indeed forms, a sequence of events within Western history, and at the same time it is a unique historical enterprise. To study its genesis within Western history may help us discover its roots in traditional anti-Semitism, fed in turn by Christian myth, German romanticism, and the breakdown of capitalism in twentieth-century Europe between the wars. But it is a grave error to make, or "elevate", the Holocaust into an occurrence outside of history, a sort of diabolic visitation, for then we tacitly absolve its human agents of their responsibility. To do this is a grave error even if, so far and perhaps forever, we lack adequate categories for comprehending how such a sequence of events could occur. The Holocaust was long prepared for in the history of Western civilization, although not all those who engaged in the preparation knew what they were doing or would have welcomed the outcome.

In the concentration camps set up by the Nazis, such as those at Dachau and Buchenwald, there was an endless quantity of cruelty and sadism, some of it the spontaneous doings of psychopaths and thugs given total command of the camps by the Nazi government, and some of it the result of a calculated policy taking into cynical account the consequences of allowing psychopaths and thugs total command. Piles of corpses accumulated in these camps. Yet a thin continuity can be detected between earlier locales of brutality and the "concentrationary universe." In some pitiable sense, the prisoners in these camps still lived—they were starved, broken, tormented, but they still lived. A faint margin of space could sometimes be carved out for the human need to maintain community and personality, even while both were being steadily destroyed. Horrible these camps surely were; but even as they pointed toward, they did not yet constitute the Final Solution.

The Nazis had an idea. To dehumanize systematically both guards and prisoners, torturers and tortured, meant to create a realm of subjugation no longer responsive to the common norms and expectations of human society; and from this process of dehumanization they had themselves set in motion, the Nazis could then "conclude" that, indeed, Jews were not human. This Nazi idea would lead to and draw upon sadism, but at least among the leaders and theoreticians, it was to be distinguished from mere sadism: it was an abstract rage, the most terrible of all rages. This Nazi idea formed a low parody of that messianism which declared that once mankind offered a warrant of faith and conduct, deliverance would come to earth in the shape of a savior bringing the good days—a notion corrupted by false messiahs into a "forcing of days" and by totalitarian movements into the physical elimination of "contaminating" races and classes. There was also in Nazi ideology a low parody of that yearning or mania for "completely" remaking societies and cultures that has marked modern political life.

When the Nazis established their realm of subjection in the concentration camps, they brought the impulse to nihilism, so strong in modern culture, to a point of completion no earlier advocate had supposed possible. The Italian-Jewish writer Primo Levi, soon after arriving at Auschwitz, was told by a Nazi guard: "Hier ist kein warum" ("Here there is no why, here nothing need be explained"). This passing observation by a shrewd thug provides as good an insight into the world of the camps as anything found in the entire scholarly literature. What we may still find difficult to grasp is the peculiar blend of ideology and nihilism—the way these two elements of thought, seemingly in friction, were able to join harmoniously, thereby releasing the satanic energies of Nazism.

By now we have an enormous body of memoirs and studies describing the experience of imprisonment in the concentration camps. Inevitably, there are clashes of remembrance and opinion. For the psychoanalyst Bruno Bettelheim, held captive in Dachau and Buchenwald in 1939, it was apparently still possible to cope with life in the camps, if only through inner moral resistance, a struggle to "understand" that might "safeguard [one's ego] in such a way that, if by any good luck he should regain liberty, [the prisoner] would be approximately the same person he was" before being deprived of liberty. Precisely this seemed impossible to Jean Améry, a gifted Austrian-Jewish writer who had been imprisoned in Auschwitz. No survivor, no one who had ever been tortured by the SS, he later wrote, could be "approximately the same person" as before.

Even to hope for survival meant, in Améry's view, to "capitulate unconditionally in the face of reality," and that reality was neither more nor less than the unlimited power and readiness of the SS to kill. The victim lived under "an absolute sovereign" whose mission—a mission of pleasure—was torture, "in an orgy of unchecked self-expansion." Thereby "the transformation of the person into flesh became complete." As for "the word"—which for Améry signified something akin to what safeguarding the ego meant for Bettelheim—it "always dies when the claim of some reality is total." For then no space remains between thought and everything external to thought.

It would be impudent to choose between the testimonies of Bettelheim and Améry. A partial explanation for their differences of memory and understanding may be that Bettelheim was a prisoner in 1939 and Améry in 1943–1945. Bettelheim's ordeal predated slightly the Final Solution, while Améry was held captive in the Auschwitz that Hannah Arendt quite soberly called a "corpse factory." It is also possible that these writers, in reflecting upon more or less similar experiences, were revealing "natural" differences in human response. We cannot be certain.

By the time the Nazis launched their Final Solution, such differences of testimony had become relatively insignificant. The Holocaust reached its point of culmination as the systematic and impersonal extermination of millions of human beings, denied life (and even death as mankind had traditionally conceived it) simply because they fell under the abstract category of "Jew." It became clear that the sadism before and during the Final Solution, on the trains that brought the Jews to the camps and in the camps themselves, was not incidental or gratuitous; it was a carefully worked-out preparation for the gas chambers. But for the Nazi leaders, originating theoreticians of death, what mattered most was the *program* of extermination. No personal qualities or accomplishments of the victims, no features of character or appearance, mattered. The abstract perversity of categorization declaring Jews to be *Untermenschen* as determined by allegedly biological traits was unconditional.

No absolute division of kind existed between concentration and death camps, and some, like the grouping of camps at Auschwitz, contained quarters for slave laborers *and* gas chambers, with recurrent "selections" from the former feeding the latter. Still, the distinction between the two varieties of camps has some descriptive and analytic value; it enables us to distinguish between what was and was not historically unique about the Holocaust.

Whatever was unique took place in the death camps, forming a sequence of events radically different from all previous butcheries in the history of mankind. Revenge, enslavement, dispersion, large-scale slaughter of enemies, all are a commonplace of the past; but the physical elimination of a categorized segment of mankind was, both as idea and fact, new. "The destruction of Europe's Jews," Claude Lanzmann has written, "cannot be logically deduced from any . . . system of presuppositions. . . . Between the conditions that permitted extermination and the extermination itself—the *fact* of the extermination—there is a break in continuity, a hiatus, an abyss." That abyss forms the essence of the Holocaust.

I cannot think of another area of literary discourse in which a single writer has exerted so strong, if diffused, an influence as Theodor Adorno has on discussions of literature and the Holocaust. What Adorno offered in the early 1950s was not a complete text or even a fully developed argument. Yet his few scattered remarks had an immediate impact, evidently because they brought out feelings held by many people.

"After Auschwitz," wrote Adorno, "to write a poem is barbaric." It means to "squeeze aesthetic pleasure out of artistic representation of the naked bodily pain of those who have been knocked down by rifle butts. . . . Through aesthetic principles or stylization . . . the unimaginable ordeal still appears as if it had some ulterior purpose. It is transfigured and stripped of some of its horror, and with this, injustice is already done to the victims."

Adorno was by no means alone in expressing such sentiments, nor in recognizing that his sentiments, no matter how solemnly approved, were not likely to keep anyone from trying to represent through fictions or to evoke through poetic symbols the concentration and death camps. A Yiddish poet, Aaron Tsaytlin, wrote in a similar vein after the Holocaust: "Were Jeremiah to sit by the ashes of Israel today, he would not cry out a lamentation. . . . The Almighty Himself would be powerless to open his well of tears. He would maintain a deep silence. For even an outcry is now a lie, even tears are mere literature, even prayers are false."

Tsaytlin's concluding sentence anticipated the frequently asserted, but as frequently ignored, claim that all responses to the Holocaust are inadequate, including, and perhaps especially, those made with the most exalted sentiments and language. Here, for instance, is Piotr Rawicz, a Jewish writer born in the Ukraine who after his release from the camps wrote in French. In his novel *Blood from the Sky*, Rawicz put down certain precepts that the very existence of his book seems to violate: "The 'literary manner' is an obscenity. . . . Literature [is] the art, occasionally remunerative, of rummaging in vomit. And yet, it would appear, one has to write. So as to trick loneliness, so as to trick other people." Looking back at such remarks of several decades ago, we may wonder what these writers were struggling to express, what half-formed or hidden feelings prompted their outcries. I will offer a few speculations, confining myself to Adorno.

Adorno was not so naive as to prescribe for writers a line of conduct that would threaten their very future as writers. Through a dramatic outburst he probably meant to focus upon the sheer difficulty—the literary risk, the moral peril—of dealing with the Holocaust in literature. It was as if he were saying, Given the absence of usable norms through which to grasp the meaning (if there is one) of the scientific extermination of millions, given the intolerable gap between the aesthetic conventions and the loathsome realities of the Holocaust, and given the improbability of coming up with images and symbols that might serve as "objective correlatives" for events that the imagination can hardly take in, writers in the post-Holocaust era might be wise to be silent. Silent, at least, about the Holocaust.

This warning, if such it was, had a certain prophetic force. It anticipated, first, the common but mistaken notion that literature somehow has an obligation to encompass (or, as professors say, to "cover") all areas of human experience, no matter how extreme or impenetrable they might be; and, second, the corruptions of the mass medium that would suppose itself equipped to master upon demand any theme or subject. (I think here of a story that I have on the highest authority. The producers of the television serial called *Holocaust* first approached Leo Tolstoy with a tempting offer to write the script, for they had heard he was the author of some good books. After listening to them politely, the Russian writer turned pale and mumbled, "No, no, there are some things that even I cannot do. For what you want, you should turn to Gerald Green.")

Adorno might have been rehearsing a traditional aesthetic idea: that the representation of a horrible event, especially if in drawing upon literary skills it achieves a certain graphic power, could serve to domesticate it, rendering it familiar and in some sense even tolerable, and thereby shearing away part of the horror. The comeliness of even the loosest literary forms is likely to soften the impact of what is being rendered, and in most renderings of imaginary situations we tacitly expect and welcome this. But with an historical event such as the Holocaust—an event regarding which the phrase "such as" cannot really be employed—the chastening aspects of literary mimesis can be felt to be misleading, a questionable way of reconciling us with the irreconcilable or of projecting a symbolic "transcendence" that in actuality is no more than a reflex of our baffled will.

Adorno might have had in mind the possibility of an insidious relation between the represented (or even the merely evoked) Holocaust and the spectator enthralled precisely as, or perhaps even because, he is appalled—a relation carrying a good share of voyeuristic sadomasochism. Can we really say that in reading a memoir or novel about the Holocaust, or in seeing a film such as *Shoah*, we gain the pleasure, or catharsis, that is customarily associated with the aesthetic transaction? More disquieting, can we be sure that we do not gain a sort of illicit pleasure from our pained submission to such works? I do not know how to answer these questions, which threaten many of our usual assumptions about what constitutes an aesthetic experience; but I think that even the most disciplined scholar of the Holocaust ought, every once in a while, to reexamine the nature of his responses.

More speculative still is the thought that Adorno, perhaps with only a partial awareness, was turning back to a "primitive" religious feeling— the feeling that there are some things in our experience, or some aspects of the universe, that are too terrible to be looked at or into directly. In ancient mythologies and religions there are things and beings that are not to be named. They may be the supremely good or supremely bad, but for mortals they are the unutterable, since there is felt to be a limit to what man may see or dare, certainly to what he may meet. Perseus would turn to stone if he were to look directly at the serpent-headed Medusa, though he would be safe if he looked at her only through a reflection in a mirror or a shield (this latter strategy, as I shall argue, being the very one that the cannier writers have adopted in dealing with the Holocaust).

Perhaps dimly, Adorno wished to suggest that the Holocaust might be regarded as a secular equivalent—if there can be such a thing—of that which in the ancient myths could not be gazed at or named directly; that before which men had to avert their eyes; that which in the properly responsive witness would arouse the "holy dread" Freud saw as the essence of taboos. And in such taboos, I suppose, the prohibition was imposed not in order to enforce ignorance, but to regulate, or guard against the consequences of, knowledge.

How this taboo might operate without the sanctions and structure of an organized religion and its linked mythology I cannot grasp: it would require a quantity of shared or communal discipline beyond anything we can suppose. Adorno must have known this as well as anyone else. He must have known that in our culture the concept of limit serves mostly as a barrier or hurdle to be overcome, not as a perimeter of respect. Perhaps his remarks are to be taken as a hopeless admonition, a plea for the improvisation of limit that he knew would not, and indeed could not, be heeded, but which it was nevertheless necessary to make.

Holocaust writings make their primary claim, I would say, through facts recorded or remembered. About this most extreme of human experiences there cannot be too much documentation, and what matters most in such material is exactitude: the sober number, the somber date. Beyond that, Holocaust writings often reveal the helplessness of the mind before an evil that cannot quite be imagined, or the helplessness of the imagination before an evil that cannot quite be understood. This shared helplessness is the major reason for placing so high a value on the memoir, a kind of writing in which the author has no obligation to do anything but, in accurate and sober terms, tell what he experienced and witnessed. To do this, as Isaac Rosenfeld once remarked, is to have the rare "courage . . . to stay near the thing itself and not to cast out for the usual reassurance."

Can we so readily justify our feelings about the primary worth of reliable testimony? Prudential arguments seem increasingly dubious here, since it should by now be clear that remembering does not necessarily forestall repetition. The instinctive respect we accord honest testimony, regardless of whether it is "well written," may in part be due to a persuasion that the aesthetic is not the primary standard for judgments of human experience, and that there can be, indeed often enough have been, situations in which aesthetic and moral standards come into conflict. Our respect for testimony may also be due in part to an unspoken persuasion that we owe something to the survivors who expose themselves to the trauma of recollection: we feel that we should listen to them apart from whether it "does any good." As for the millions who did not survive, it would be mere indulgence to suppose that any ceremonies of recollection could "make up for" or "transcend" their destruction—all such chatter, too frequent in writings about the Holocaust, is at best the futility of eloquence. Still, there are pieties that civilized people want to confirm even if, and sometimes because, these are nothing more than gestures.

Another piety is to be invoked here. We may feel that heeding the survivors' testimony contributes to the fund of shared consciousness, which also means to our own precarious sense of being, whether individual or collective, and that, somehow, this is good. Henry James speaks somewhere of an ideal observer upon whom nothing is lost, who witnesses the entirety of the human lot, and although James in his concerns is about as far from something like the Holocaust as any writer could be, I think it just to borrow his vision of consciousness for our very different ends. The past summoned by Holocaust memoirs not only tells us something unbearable, and therefore unforgettable, about the life of mankind; it is also a crucial part of our own time, if not of our direct experience. To keep the testimony of Holocaust witnesses in the forefront of our consciousness may not make us "better" people, but it may at least bring a touch of accord with our sense of the time we have lived in and of where we have come from.

There is still another use of this testimony, and that is to keep the Holocaust firmly within the bounds of history, so that it will not end up as a preface to Apocalypse or eschatology or, worse still, decline into being the legend of a small people. "Nobody," said the historian Ignacy Schipper in Maidanek, "will *want* to believe us, because our disaster is the disaster of the entire civilized world." Schipper's phrasing merits close attention. He does not say that the disaster was experienced by the entire civilized world, which might entail a sentimental "universalizing" of the Holocaust in the manner of writers such as William Styron; he says that the disaster of the Jews was (or should have been) shared by the entire civilized world, so that what happened to "us" might form a weight upon the consciousness of that world, even as we may recognize that sooner or later the world will seek to transfer it to some realm "beyond" history, a realm at once more exalted and less accusatory. Yet, history is exactly where the Holocaust must remain; and, for that, there can never be enough testimony.

Let us now turn briefly to a few witnesses, invoking them along a slope of destruction. Chaim Kaplan's Warsaw diary, covering a bit less than a year from its opening date of September 1, 1938, is a document still recognizably within the main tradition of Western writing: a man observes crucial events and strives to grasp their significance. Kaplan's diary shows the discipline of a trained observer; his prose is lucid and restrained; he records the effort of Warsaw Jewry to keep a fragment of their culture alive even as they stumble into death; and he reveals a torn soul wondering what premises of faith, or delusion, sustain his "need to record." Barely, precariously, we are still in the world of the human as we have understood it, for nothing can be more human than to keep operating with familiar categories of thought while discovering they will no longer suffice.

Elie Wiesel's first book, *Night*, written simply and without rhetorical indulgence, is a slightly fictionalized record of his sufferings as a boy in Auschwitz and during a forced march together with his father and other prisoners through the frozen countryside to Buchenwald. The father dies of dysentery in Buchenwald, and the boy—or the writer remembering himself as a boy—reveals his guilty relief at feeling that the death of his father has left him "free at last"—not as any son might feel, but in the sense that now he may be able to save himself without the burden of an ailing father. No sensitive reader will feel an impulse to judgment here. Indeed, that is one of the major effects of honest testimony about the Holocaust—it dissolves any impulse to judge what the victims did or did not do, since there are situations so extreme that it seems immoral to make judgments about those who must endure them. We are transported here into a dark subworld, where freedom and moral sensibility may survive in memory but cannot be exercised in practice. Enforced degradation—from which no one, finally, is exempt—forms the penultimate step toward the ovens.

The ovens dominate the camps that the Nazis, not inaccurately, called *anus mundi*. Filip Müller's *Eyewitness Auschwitz* is the artless account of being transported from his native Slovakia in April 1942 to Auschwitz, where he worked for two and a half years as a *Sonderkommando*, or assistant at the gas chambers. Somehow Müller survived. His narrative is free of verbal embellishment or thematic reflection; he indulges neither in self-apology nor self-attack; he writes neither art nor history. His book is simply the story of a simple man who processed many corpses. Even in this book, terrible beyond any that I have ever read, there are still a few touches recalling what we take to be humanity: efforts at theodicy by men who cannot justify their faith, a recital of the Kaddish by doomed prisoners who know that no one else will say it for them. In the world Müller inhabited and served, "the transformation of the person into flesh" and of flesh into dust "became complete." It was a world for which, finally, we have no words.

But is there not, a skeptical voice may interject, a touch of empiricist naïveté in such high claims for Holocaust memoirs? Memory can be treacherous among people who have suffered terribly and who must feel a measure of guilt at being alive at all. Nor can we be sure of the truth supplied by damaged and overwrought witnesses, for whatever knowledge we may claim about these matters is likely to come mainly from the very memoirs we find ourselves submitting, however uneasily, to critical judgment.

The skeptical voice is cogent, and I would only say in reply that we are not helpless before the accumulated mass of recollection. Our awe before the suffering and our respect for the sufferers does not disable us from making discriminations of value, tone, authority. There remain the usual historical tests, both through external check and internal comparison; and there is still that indispensable organ, the reader's ear, bending toward credence or doubt.

The test of the ear is a delicate and perilous one, entailing a shift from testimony to witness—a shift that, except perhaps with regard to the scrappiest of chronicles, seems unavoidable. Reading Holocaust memoirs, we respond not just to their accounts of what happened; we respond also to qualities of being, tremors of sensibility, as these emerge even from the bloodiest pages. We respond to the modesty or boastfulness, the candor or evasiveness, the self-effacement or self-promotion of the writers. We respond, most of all, to a quality that might be called moral poise, by which I mean a readiness to engage in a complete reckoning with the past, insofar as there can be one—a strength of remembrance that leads the writer into despair and then perhaps a little beyond it, so that he does not flinch from anything, neither shame nor degradation, yet refuses to indulge in those outbursts of self-pity, sometimes sliding into self-aggrandizement, that under-standably mar a fair number of Holocaust memoirs.

But is there not something shameful in subjecting the work of survivors to this kind of scrutiny? Perhaps so; yet, in choosing to become writers, they have no choice but to accept this burden.

The Holocaust was structured to destroy the very idea of private being. It was a sequence of events entirely "out there," in the objective world, the world of force and power. Yet, as we read Holocaust memoirs and reaffirm their value as evidence, we find ourselves veering—less by choice than by necessity—from the brute external to the fragile subjec-tive, from matter to voice, from story to storyteller. And this leaves us profoundly uneasy, signifying that our earlier stress upon the value of testimony has now been complicated, perhaps even compromised, by the introduction of aesthetic considerations. We may wish with all our hearts to yield entirely to the demands of memory and evidence; but, simply by virtue of reading, we cannot forget that the diarist was a person formed before and the memoirist a person formed after the Holocaust. We are ensnared in the cruelty of remembering, a compounded cruelty, in which our need for truthful testimony lures us into tests of authenticity.

That, in any case, is how we read. I bring as a "negative" witness a memoirist not to be named: he puts his ordeal at the service of a familiar faith or ideology, and it comes to seem sad, for that faith or ideology cannot bear the explanatory and expiatory burdens he would place upon it. Another memoirist, also not to be named: he suborns his grief to public self-aggrandizement, and the grief he declares, surely sincere, is alloyed by streaks of publicity.

But Chaim Kaplan cares for nothing except the impossible effort to comprehend the incomprehensible; Filip Müller for nothing except to recall happenings even he finds hard to credit; Primo Levi for nothing but to render his days in the camps through a language unadorned and chaste.

We are trapped. Our need for testimony that will forever place the Holocaust squarely within history requires that we respond to voice, nuance, personality. Our desire to see the Holocaust in weightier terms than the merely aesthetic lures us into a shy recognition of the moral reverberations of the aesthetic. This does not make us happy, but the only alternative is the silence we all remember, now and then, to praise.

"We became aware," writes Primo Levi, "that our language lacks words to express this offense, the demolition of man." Every serious writer approaching the Holocaust sooner or later says much the same. If there is a way of coping with this difficulty, it lies in a muted tactfulness recognizing that there are some things that can be said and some that cannot.

Let me cite a few sentences from T. S. Eliot: "Great simplicity is only won by an intense moment or by years of intelligent effort, or by both. It represents one of the most arduous conquests of the human spirit: the triumph of feeling and thought over the natural sin of language." Exactly what Eliot meant by that astonishing phrase, "the natural sin of language," I cannot say with assurance, but that it applies to a fair portion of Holocaust writing, both memoir and fiction, seems to me indisputable. A "natural sin" might here signify the inclination to grow wanton over the deepest griefs, thereby making them the substance of public exploitation. Or it might mean a mistaken effort, sincere or grandiose, to whip language into doing more than it can possibly do, more than thought and imagination and prayer can do—language as it seduces us into the comforting grandiose.

When, by now as a virtual cliché, we say that language cannot deal with the Holocaust, we really have in mind, or perhaps are covering up for, our inadequacies of thought and feeling. We succumb to that "natural sin of language" because anyone who tries seriously to engage with the implications of the Holocaust must come up against a wall of incomprehension. *How could it be?* It is not the behavior, admirable or deplorable, of the victims, nor the ideology the Nazis drew upon that forms the crux of our bewilderment, but how human beings, raised in the center of European civilization, could do such a thing. If we then fall back on intellectual shorthand, invoking the problem of radical evil, what are we really doing but expressing our helplessness in another vocabulary? Not only is this an impassable barrier for the thought of moralists and the recall of memoirists; it is, I think, the greatest thematic and psychological difficulty confronting writers of fiction who try to represent or even to evoke the Holocaust.

For the central question to be asked about these writings, a few of them distinguished and most of them decent failures, is this: what can the literary imagination, traditionally so proud of its self-generating capacities, add to—how can it go beyond—the intolerable matter cast up by memory? What could be the organizing categories, the implicit premises of perception and comprehension, through which the literary imagination might be able to render intelligible the gassing of 12,000 people a day at Auschwitz? If, as Sidra DeKoven Ezrahi remarks, literature has traditionally called upon "the timeless archetypes of human experience" to structure and infer significance from its materials, how can this now be done with a sequence of events that radically breaks from those "timeless archetypes"? A novelist can rehearse what we have learned from the documentation of David Rousset and Filip Müller, from Primo Levi and Eugen Kogon, but apart from some minor smoothing and shaping, what can the novelist *do* with all this? And if, through sheer lack of any other recourse, he does fall back upon the ideological or theological categories of received Western thought, he faces the immediate risk of producing a fiction with a severe fissure between rendered event and imposed category— so that even a sympathetic reader may be inclined to judge the work as resembling a failed allegory in which narrative and moral are, at best, chained together by mere decision.

Let us see all this concretely, as it might affect a novelist's job of work. Yes, the facts are there, fearful and oppressive, piled up endlessly in memoirs and histories. He has studied them, tried to "make sense" of them in his mind, submitted himself to the barrage of horror. But what he needs—and does not have—is something that for most ordinary fictions written about most ordinary themes would come to him spontaneously, without his even being aware that it figures crucially in the act of composition: namely, a structuring set of ethical premises, to which are subordinately linked aesthetic biases, through which he can form (that is, integrate) his materials. These ethical premises and aesthetic biases are likely to obtrude in consciousness only as a felt lack, only when a writer brooding over the endlessness of murder and torment asks how it can be turned or shaped into significant narrative. Nor, if he tries to escape from a confining realism and venture into symbolic or grotesque modes, can he find sufficiently used—you might say, sufficiently "broken in"—myths and metaphors that might serve as workable, publicly recognizable analogues for the Holocaust experience. Before *this* reality, the imagination comes to seem intimidated, overwhelmed, helpless. It can rehearse, but neither enlarge nor escape; it can describe happenings, but not endow them with the autonomy and freedom of a complex fiction; it remains—and perhaps this may even figure as a moral obligation—the captive of its raw material.

The Holocaust memoirist, as writer, is in a far less difficult position, True, he needs to order his materials in the rudimentary sense of minimal chronology and reportorial selectivity (though anything he honestly remembers could prove to be significant, even if not part of his own story). Insofar as he remains a memoirist, he is not obliged to interpret what he remembers. But the novelist, even if he supposes he is merely "telling a story," must—precisely in order to tell a story— "make sense" of his materials, either through explicit theory or, what is usually better, absorbed assumptions. Otherwise, no matter how vivid his style or sincere his feelings, he will finally be at a loss. All he will then be able to do is to present a kind of "fictionalized memoir"—which means not to move very far beyond what the memoirist has already done.

To avoid this difficulty, some novelists have concentrated on those camps which were not just "corpse factories" and that allowed some faint simulacrum of human life; or, like Jorge Semprun in *The Long Voyage*, they have employed flashbacks of life before imprisonment, so as to allow for some of that interplay of character and extension of narrative which is essential to works of imaginative fiction. Once our focus is narrowed, however, to the death camps, the locale of what must be considered the essential Holocaust, the novelist's difficulties come to seem awesome. For then, apart from the lack of cognitive structures, he has to face a number of problems that are specifically, narrowly literary.

The Holocaust is not, essentially, a dramatic subject. Much before, much after, and much surrounding the mass exterminations may be open to dramatic rendering. But the exterminations, in which thousands of dazed and broken people were sent up each day in smoke, hardly knowing and often barely able to respond to their fate, have little of drama in them. Terribleness, yes; drama, no.

Of those conflicts between wills, those inner clashes of belief and wrenchings of desire, those enactments of passion, all of which make up our sense of the dramatic, there can be little in the course of a fiction focused mainly on the mass exterminations. An heroic figure here, a memorable outcry there—that is possible. But those soon to be dead are already half or almost dead; the gas chambers merely finish the job begun in the ghettos and continued on the trains. The basic minimum of freedom to choose and act that is a central postulate of drama had been taken from the victims. The Nazis indulged in a peculiarly vicious parody of this freedom when they sometimes gave Jewish parents the "choice" of which child should be murdered.

The extermination process was so "brilliantly" organized that the life, and thereby the moral energy upon which drama ultimately depends, had largely been snuffed out of the victims before they entered the gas chambers. Here, in the death camps, the pitiful margin of space that had been allowed the human enterprise in the concentration camps was negated. Nor was it exactly death that reigned; it was annihilation. What, then, can the novelist make of this—what great clash or subtle inference—that a Filip Müller has not already shown us?

If the death camps and mass exterminations allow little opening for the dramatic, they also give little space for the tragic in any traditional sense of that term. In classical tragedy, man is defeated; in the Holocaust, man is destroyed. In tragedy, man struggles against forces that overwhelm him, struggles against the gods and against his own nature; and the downfall that follows may have an aspect of grandeur. This struggle allows for the possibility of an enlargement of character through the purgation of suffering, which in turn may bring a measure of understanding and a kind of peace. But except for some religious Jews who were persuaded that the Holocaust was a reenactment of the great tradition of Jewish martyrdom, or for some secular Jews who lived out their ethic by choosing to die in solidarity with their fellows, or for those inmates who undertook doomed rebellions, the Jews destroyed in the camps were not martyrs continuing along the ways of their forefathers. They died, probably most of them, not because they chose at all costs to remain Jews, but because the Nazis chose to believe that being Jewish was an unchangeable, irredeemable condition. They were victims of a destruction that, for many of them, had little or only a fragmentary meaning—few of the victims, it seems, could even grasp the idea of total annihilation, let alone regard it as an act of high martyrdom. All of this does not make their death less terrible; it makes their death more terrible.

So much so that it becomes an almost irresistible temptation for Holocaust writers, whether discursive or fictional, to search for some redemptive token, some cry of retribution, some balancing of judgment against history's evil, some sign of ultimate spiritual triumph. It is as if, through the retrospect of language, they would lend a tragic aura.

Many of the customary resources and conventions of the novel are unavailable to the writer dealing with the Holocaust. Small shifts in tone due to the surprises of freedom or caprice; the slow, rich development of character through testing and overcoming; the exertion of heroic energies by characters granted unexpectedly large opportunities; the slow emergence of moral flaws through an accumulation of seemingly trivial incidents; the withdrawal of characters into the recesses of their selves; the yielding of characters to large social impulses, movements, energies—these may not be entirely impossible in Holocaust fiction, but all must prove to be painfully limited. Even so apparently simple a matter as how a work of fiction is ended takes on a new and problematic aspect, for while a memoirist can just stop at some convenient point, the novelist must think in terms of resolutions and completions. But what, after having surrendered his characters to their fate, can he suppose those resolutions and completions to be? Finally, all such literary problems come down to the single, inclusive problem of freedom. In the past, even those writers most strongly inclined to determinism or naturalism have grasped intuitively that to animate their narratives they must give at least a touch of freedom to their characters. And that, as his characters inexorably approach the ovens, is precisely what the Holocaust writer cannot do.

The Israeli critic Hannah Yaoz, reports Sidra Ezrahi, has "divided Holocaust fiction into historical and transhistorical modes—the first representing a mimetic approach which incorporates the events into the continuum of history and human experience, and the second transfiguring the events into a mythic reality where madness reigns and all historical loci are relinquished." At least with regard to the Holocaust, the notion that there can be a "mythic reality" without "historical loci" seems to me dubious—for where then could the imagination find the materials for its act of "transfiguring"? Still, the division of Holocaust fiction proposed by Yaoz has some uses, if only to persuade us that finally both the writers who submit to and those who rebel against the historical mode must face pretty much the same problems.

The "mimetic approach" incorporating "events into the continuum of history" has been most strongly employed by the Polish writer Tadeusz Borowski in his collection of stories, *This Way for the Gas, Ladies and Gentlemen.* Himself an Auschwitz survivor, Borowski writes in a cold, harsh, even coarse style, heavy with flaunted cynicism, and offering no reliefs of the heroic. Kapo Tadeusz, the narrator, works not only with, but on behalf of, the death system. "Write," he says, "that a portion of the sad fame of Auschwitz belongs to you as well." The wretched truth is that here survival means the complete yielding of self.

Like Filip Müller in his memoir, Borowski's narrator admits that he lives because there is a steady flow of new "material" from the ghettos to the gas chambers: "It is true, others may be dying, but one is somehow still alive, one has enough food, enough strength to work."

Let the transports stop and Kapo Tadeusz together with the other members of "Canada" (the labor gang that unloads the transports) will be liquidated.

Kapo Tadeusz lives in a world where mass murder is normal: it is *there,* it works, and it manages very well without moral justifications. The tone of detachment, which in a naturalistic novel would signal moral revulsion from represented ugliness, has here become a condition of survival. To lapse into what we might regard as human feeling—and sometimes Kapo Tadeusz and his fellow prisoners do that—is to risk not only the ordeal of memory but the loss of life: a pointless loss, without record or rebellion.

Borowski's style conveys the rhythm of a hammering factuality; and, in a way almost too complex to describe, one appreciates his absolute refusal to strike any note of redemptive nobility. Truthful and powerful as they are, Borowski's stories seem very close to those relentless Holocaust memoirs which show that there need be no limit to dehumanization. And that is just the point: for, truthful and powerful as they are, Borowski's stories "work" mainly as testimony. Their authenticity makes us, I would say, all but indifferent to their status as art. We do not, perhaps cannot, read these stories as mediated fictions, imaginative versions of a human milieu in which men and women enter the usual range of relations. In Kapo Tadeusz's barrack, there is simply no space for that complex interplay of action, emotion, dream, ambivalence, generosity, envy, and love that forms the basis of Western literature. The usual norms of human conduct—except for flashes of memory threatening survival—do not operate here. "We are not evoking evil irresponsibly," writes Borowski, "for we have now become part of it." Nor does it really matter whether Borowski was drawing upon personal memories or "making up" some of his stories. Composed in the fumes of destruction, even the stories he might have "made up" are not actually "made up": they are the substance of collective memory. *Hier ist kein warum.*

Inevitably, some Holocaust writers would try to escape from the vise of historical realism, and one of the most talented of these was the Ukrainian Jew Piotr Rawicz. Resting on a very thin narrative base, Rawicz's novel *Blood from the Sky* is a sustained, almost heroic rebellion against the demands of narrative—although in the end those demands reassert themselves, even providing the strongest parts of his wantonly brilliant book. What starts out as a traditional story soon turns into an expressionist phantasmagoria seeking to project imagistic tokens for the Holocaust, or at least for the hallucinations it induces in the minds of witnesses. The story, often pressed far into the background, centers on a rich, highly educated, aristocratic Jew named Boris who saves himself from the Nazis through his expert command of German and Ukrainian—also through a disinclination to indulge in noble gestures. Upon this fragile strand of narrative Rawicz hangs a series of vignettes, excoriations, prose and verse poems, and mordant reflections of varying quality. The most effective are the ones visibly tied to some historical event, as in a brief sketch of a Nazi commander who orders the transport from Boris's town of all women named Goldberg because a woman of that name has infected him with a venereal disease. Symbolically freighted passages achieve their greatest force when they are also renderings of social reality, as in this description of a work party of prisoners sent by the Nazis to tear apart a Jewish cemetery:

> The party was demolishing some old tombstones. The blind, deafening hammer blows were scattering the sacred characters from inscriptions half a millennium old, and composed in praise of some holy man. . . . An *aleph* would go flying off to the left, while a *he* carved on another piece of stone dropped to the right. A *gimel* would bite the dust and a *nun* follow in its wake. . . . Several examples of *shin*, a letter symbolizing the miraculous intervention of God, had just been smashed and trampled on by the hammers and feet of these moribund workmen.

And then, several sentences later:

> Death—that of their fellow men, of the stones, of their own—had become unimportant to them; but hunger hadn't.

The strength of this passage rests upon a fusion of event described and symbol evoked, but that fusion is successfully achieved because the realistic description is immediately persuasive in its own right. Mimesis remains the foundation. When Rawicz, however, abandons story and character in his straining after constructs of language that will in some sense "parallel" the Holocaust theme, the prose cracks under an intolerable pressure. We become aware of an excess of tension between the narrative (pushed into the background but, through its sheer horror, still dominant) and the virtuosity of language (too often willed and literary). Rawicz's outcroppings of expressionist rage and grief, no matter how graphic in their own right, can only seem puny when set against the events looming across the book.

Still, there are passages in which Rawicz succeeds in endowing his language with a kind of hallucinatory fury, and then it lures us into an autonomous realm of the horrifying and the absurd. But when that happens, virtuosity takes command, coming to seem self-sufficient, without fixed points of reference, as if floating off on its own. Losing the causal tie with the Holocaust that the writer evidently hopes to maintain, the language overflows as in a discharge of sheer nausea. At least with regard to Holocaust fiction, I would say that efforts to employ "transhistorical modes" or "mythic reality" are likely to collapse into the very "continuum of history" they seek to escape—or else will come loose from the grounds of their creation.

"M'ken nisht," literally, Yiddish for "one cannot"—so the Israeli writer Aharon Appelfeld once explained to me why, in his fictions about the Holocaust, he did not try to represent it directly, always ending before or starting after the exterminations. He spoke with the intuitive shrewdness of the writer who knows when to stop—a rare and precious gift. But his remark also conveyed a certain ambiguity, as if *m'ken nisht* had a way of becoming *m'tur nisht*, "one must not," so that an acknowledgment of limit might serve as a warning of the forbidden.

In approaching the Holocaust, the canniest writers keep a wary distance. They know or sense that their subject cannot be met full face. It must be taken on a tangent, with extreme wariness, through strategies of indirection and circuitous narratives that leave untouched the central horror—that leave it untouched but always invoke or evoke it as hovering shadow. And this brings us to another of the ironies that recur in discussing this subject. We may begin with a suspicion that it is morally unseemly to submit Holocaust writings to fine critical discriminations, yet once we speak, as we must, about ways of approaching or apprehending this subject, we find ourselves going back to a fundamental concern of literary criticism: namely, how a writer validates his material.

Before. Aharon Appelfeld's *Badenheim 1939* is a novella that, at first glance, contains little more than a series of banal incidents in a Jewish resort near Vienna at the start of the Second World War. Each trivial event brings with it a vague drift of anxiety. A character feels "haunted by a hidden fear, not her own." Posters go up in the town: "The Air Is Fresher in Poland." Guests in the hotel fear that "some alien spirit [has] descended." A musician explains deportations of Jews as if he were the very spirit of the century: it is "Historical Necessity." Appelfeld keeps accumulating nervous detail; the writing flows seamlessly, enticingly, until one notices that the logic of this quiet narrative is a logic of hallucination and its quietness mounts into a thick cloud of foreboding. At the end, the guests are being packed into "four filthy freight cars"— but here Appelfeld abruptly stops, as if recognizing a limit to the sovereignty of words. Nothing is said or shown of what is to follow: the narrative is as furtive as the history it evokes; the unspeakable is not to be named.

During. Pierre Gascar, a Frenchman, not Jewish, who was a POW during the Second World War, has written in his long story "The Seasons of the Dead" one of the very few masterpieces of Holocaust fiction. Again, no accounts of torture or portrayal of concentration camps or imaginings of the gas chambers. All is evoked obliquely, through a haze of fearfulness and disbelief. The narrator makes no effort to hide his Parisian sophistication, but what he sees as a prisoner sent to a remote camp in Poland breaks down his categories of thought and leaves him almost beyond speech.

Gascar's narrator is assigned to a detail that takes care of a little cemetery molded with pick and shovel for French soldiers who have died: "We were a team of ghosts returning every morning to a green peaceful place, we were workers in death's garden." In a small way "death's garden" is also life's, for with solemn attentiveness the men who work there preserve the civilizing rituals of burial through which mankind has traditionally tried to give some dignity to the death of its members. Gradually signs of another kind of death assault these men, death cut off from either natural process or social ritual. The French prisoners working in their little graveyard cannot help seeing imprisoned Jews of a nearby village go about their wretched tasks. One morning they find "a man lying dead by the roadside on the way to the graveyard," a man who has "no distinguishing mark, save the armlet with the star of David"; and as they dig new graves for their French comrades, they discover "the arm of [a] corpse . . . pink . . . like certain roots." Their cemetery, with its carefully "idealized dead," is actually in "the middle of a charnel, a heap of corpses lying side by side." And then the trains come, with their stifled cries, "the human voice, hovering over the infinite expanse of suffering like a bird over the infinite sea." As in Claude Lanzmann's great film *Shoah*, the trains go back and forth, endlessly, in one direction filled with broken human creatures, and in the other empty. Death without coffins, without reasons, without rituals, without witnesses: the realization floods into the consciousness of the narrator and a few other prisoners. "Death can never appease this pain; this stream of black grief will flow forever"—so the narrator tells himself. No explanation follows, no consolation. There is only the enlarging grief of discovery, with the concluding sentence, "I went back to my dead"—both kinds, surely. And nothing else.

After. In a long story, "A Plaque on Via Mazzini," the Italian-Jewish writer Giorgio Bassani adopts as his narrative voice the amiable coarseness of a commonplace citizen of Ferrara, the north Italian town that before the war had 400 Jews, 183 of whom were deported. One of them comes back, in August 1945: Geo Josz, bloated with the edematous fat of starvation, with hands "callused beyond all belief, but with white backs where a registration number, tattooed a bit over the right wrist . . . could be read distinctly, all five numbers, preceded by the letter J." Not unsympathetic, but intent upon going about their business, the citizens of Ferrara speak through the narrator, "What did he want, now?" Ferrara does not know what to make of this survivor, unnerving in his initial quiet, with his "obsessive, ill-omened face" and his bursts of sarcasm. In his attic room, Josz papers all four walls with pictures of his family, who were destroyed in Buchenwald. When he meets an uncle who had fawned upon the fascists, he lets out "a shrill cry, ridiculously, hysterically passionate, almost savage." Encountering a broken-down old count who had spied for the fascist police, he slaps him twice—it is not so much his presence that Josz finds unbearable as his whistling "Lili Marlene."

As if intent upon making everyone uncomfortable, Josz resumes "wearing the same clothes he had been wearing when he came back from Germany . . . fur hat and leather jerkin included." Even the warmhearted conclude that "it was impossible . . . to converse with a man in costume! And on the other hand, if they let him do the talking, he immediately started telling about . . . the end of all his relatives; and he went on like that for whole hours, until you didn't know how to get away from him.''

A few years later Josz disappears, forever, "leaving not the slightest trace after him." The Ferrarese, remembering him for a little while, "would shake their heads good-naturedly," saying, "If he had only been a bit more patient." What Geo Josz thinks or feels, what he remembers or wants, what boils up within him after returning to his town, Bassani never tells. There is no need to. Bassani sees this bit of human wreckage from a cool distance, charting the gap between Josz and those who encounter him on the street or at a café, no doubt wishing him well, but naturally, in their self-preoccupation, unable to enter his memories or obsessions. His very presence is a reproach, and what, if anything, they can do to reply or assuage they do not know. For they are ordinary people, and he. . . . The rest seeps up between the words.

Aftermath. On the face of it, "My Quarrel with Hersh Rasseyner," by the Yiddish writer Chaim Grade, is an ideological dialogue between a badly shaken skeptic, evidently the writer himself, and a zealous believer, Hersh Rasseyner, who belongs to the Mussarist sect, "a movement that gives special importance to ethical and ascetic elements in Judaism." But the voices of the two speakers—as they meet across a span of years from 1937 to 1948—are so charged with passion and sincerity that we come to feel close to both of them.

Like Grade himself, the narrator had been a Mussarist in his youth, only to abandon the yeshiva for a career as a secular writer. Yet, something of the yeshiva's training in dialectic has stuck to the narrator, although Grade is shrewd enough to give the stronger voice to Hersh Rasseyner, his Orthodox antagonist. What they are arguing about, presumably, are eternal questions of faith and skepticism—the possibility of divine benevolence in the evil of His creation, the value of clinging to faith after a Holocaust that His hand did not stop. In another setting, all this might seem an intellectual exercise, but here, as these two men confront one another, their dispute signifies nothing less than the terms upon which they might justify their lives. For Rasseyner, the gas chambers are the inevitable outcome of a trivialized wordliness and an enfeebled morality that lacks the foundation of faith. For the narrator, the gas chambers provoke unanswerable questions about the place of a God who has remained silent. Back and forth the argument rocks, with Rasseyner usually on the attack, for he is untroubled by doubt, while the narrator can only say, "You have a ready answer, while we have not silenced our doubts, and perhaps we will never be able to silence them." With "a cry of impotent anger against heaven"—a heaven in which he does not believe, but to which he continues to speak—the narrator finally offers his hand to Rasseyner in a gesture of forlorn comradeship: "We are the remnant."

In its oppressive intensity and refusal to rest with any fixed "position," Grade's story makes us realize that even the most dreadful event in history has brought little change in the thought of mankind. History may spring endless surprises, but our responses are very limited. In the years after the Holocaust, there was a certain amount of speculation that human consciousness could no longer be what it had previously been (a consoling thought—but for the likelihood that it is not true). Exactly what it might mean to say that after the Holocaust consciousness has been transformed is very hard to say. Neither of Grade's figures—nor, to be honest, the rest of us—shows any significant sign of such a transformation. For good and bad, we remain the commonplace human stock, and whatever it is that we may do about the Holocaust we shall have to do with the worn historical consciousness received from mankind's past. In Grade's story, as in other serious fictions touching upon the Holocaust, there is neither throb of consolation nor peal of redemption, nothing but an anxious turning toward and away from what our century has left us.

The mind rebels against such conclusions. It yearns for compensations it knows cannot be found; it yearns for tokens of transcendence in the midst of torment. To suppose that some redemptive salvage can be eked out of the Holocaust is, as we like to say, only human. And that is one source of the falsity that seeps through a good many accounts of the Holocaust, whether fiction or memoir—as it seeps through the language of many high-minded commentators. "To talk of despair," writes Albert Camus, "is to conquer it." Is it now? "The destiny of the Jewish people, whom no earthly power has ever been able to defeat"—so speaks a character in Jean-François Steiner's novel about a revolt in Treblinka. Perhaps appropriate for someone urging fellow prisoners into a doomed action, such sentiments, if allowed to determine the moral scheme of Holocaust writing, lead to a posture of self-delusion. The plain and bitter truth is that while Hitler did not manage to complete the Final Solution, he did manage to destroy an entire Jewish world.

"It is foolish," writes Primo Levi, "to think that human justice can eradicate" the crimes of Auschwitz. Or that the human imagination can encompass and transfigure them. Some losses cannot be made up, neither in time nor eternity. They can only be mourned. In a poem entitled "Written in Pencil in the Sealed Freight Car," the Israeli poet Don Pagis writes:

> Here in this transport
> I Eve
> and Abel my son
> if you should see my older son
> Cain son of man
> tell him that I

Cry to heaven or cry to earth: that sentence will never be completed.

13 · James E. Young

Holocaust Documentary Fiction:
The Novelist as Eyewitness

> Imagination and memory are but one thing, which for divers considerations
> hath divers names.
> —Thomas Hobbes

> There is no fiction or nonfiction as we commonly understand the distinction:
> there is only narrative.
> —E. L. Doctorow

> That is what the survivors are afraid of, the tricks of art.
> —Arnold Wesker

The impulse in Holocaust writers to insist on a documentary link
between their texts and the events inspiring them has not been limited
to diarists and memoirists: it extends to the novelists of the Holocaust,
as well. Where the diarists and memoirists have struggled to preserve or
reconstruct the eyewitness authority displaced by their narrative, however, the "docu-novelists" of the Holocaust work as hard at manufacturing their own testimonial authority as part of their fictional discourse. In
many cases, their reasons for reinforcing the factual authority in narrative are similar: all of these writers seem to share the fear that the
essential rhetoricity of their literary medium inadvertently confers a
certain fictionality onto events themselves. But in many other cases, the
novelists' reasons for fabricating an eyewitness authority in their fiction
stem more from traditional aesthetic and dramatic motives than from

documentary interests. In addition to exploring the ways in which documentary authority is constructed within Holocaust fiction, this essay will look at how testimony is adopted rhetorically as a narrative strategy in such fiction.

On the one hand, it is difficult to argue with the spirit of Hana Wirth-Nesher's suggestion that "while all narratives are imaginative reconstructions, when it comes to those of mass suffering, we should be particularly vigilant about honoring the line between fact and fiction."[1] On the other hand, it may be just as difficult to delineate this border between fact and fiction in the first place; for as long as facts are presented to us in fictionalizing media, and fiction is presented as fact, the categories themselves remain all too fuzzily defined. If there is a line between fact and fiction, it may by necessity be a winding border that tends to bind these two categories as much as it separates them, allowing each side to dissolve occasionally into the other.

In an article about William Styron's *Sophie's Choice*, Arnold Wesker also wants to know both "where we [are] dealing with fact and where with fiction" and "why, in this novel more than any other, do I want to know?"[2] Even though she is not referring specifically to Styron's novel, Barbara Foley answers this question in part, in reference to a semifictional character in another of the "docu-novels," Gerald Green's *Holocaust*:

> By claiming for Dorf a status halfway between history and myth . . . and by grafting this hybrid creature onto a fictive tale that purports to encompass the enormity of the Holocaust in a single tale of victimization and villainy—Green at once reduces agony to the status of melodrama and distorts the locus of historical responsibility. *Holocaust* is not a fraudulent work simply because it aspires to make history accessible in a popular format . . .; it is fraudulent because it both proposes a shallow resolution and catharsis and performs a frivolous reshuffling of historical facts.[3]

That is, the problem with this and other "documentary fictions" of the Holocaust is that by mixing actual events with completely fictional characters, a writer simultaneously relieves himself of an obligation to historical accuracy (invoking poetic license), even as he imbues his fiction with the historical authority of real events. By inviting this ambiguity, the author of documentary fiction would thus move the reader with the pathos created in the rhetoric of historically authentic characters, even as he suggests the possibility that both his events and those in the world are fictional.

Several other questions arise at this point. First, why is the writer of Holocaust fiction so forcefully compelled to assert the factual basis underlying his work? That is, why is it so important for novelists such as D. M. Thomas, Jean-François Steiner, Gerald Green, and Anatoly Kuznetsov (among others) to establish an authoritative link between their fictions and the Holocaust experiences they represent? Second, to what extent are this literature's dramatic interests, and its supposed documentary interests, served in such claims to historical authority? And how does the perception of authority in the Holocaust novel affect the way readers approach and respond to Holocaust fiction? That is, can Holocaust documentary fiction ever really document events, or will it always fictionalize them?

Having explored already the process of making witness in the diaries and memoirs, I turn here to the ways authentic testimony is incorporated into the fictional text by novelists and used as a figure and literary device in Holocaust fiction.[4] In this context, we will examine the rhetorical trope of eyewitness in Holocaust fiction and some of the narrative methods by which it is generated. For even as many novelists would claim on ethical grounds that they have had no "right" to imagine such suffering, and must therefore rely on actual witnesses' voices, I find that these claims may in themselves also be part of their novelistic discourse. Whether a writer is attempting to retain an eyewitness authority in his diary or memoir, or to fabricate it altogether in his documentary novel, testimony continues to function as the preeminent rhetorical trope underlying the very possibility of a "documentary narrative."

This question of "documentary authority" in Holocaust fiction was brought into particularly sharp relief in the pages of the *Times Literary Supplement,* when letter writer D. A. Kenrick called readers' attention to the rather pronounced debt D. M. Thomas's novel *The White Hotel* owed to Anatoly Kuznetsov's "document in the form of a novel," *Babi Yar.*[5] As Kenrick and other indignant letter writers pointed out, Thomas has not merely paraphrased Kuznetsov, but has actually quoted directly from the text of Kuznetsov's work, in what seems to be an attempt to infuse the most violent scenes in his Holocaust fiction with what he perceives to be their "documentary authority." The following are passages from both novels, the first from *Babi Yar:*

> It began to grow dark.
> Suddenly an open car drove up, carrying a tall, well-knit, elegant officer carrying a riding crop. . . . His [Russian] interpreter stood at his side.
> "Who are these?" he asked a *Polizei* through his interpreter. There were about 50 people sitting on the hillock now.
> "These are our people [Ukrainians]," replied the *Polizei*. "We weren't sure whether to release them."
> "Shoot them! Shoot them right away!" stormed the officer. "If just one of them gets away and spreads the story, not a single Jew will come here tomorrow."
> . . . "Get going! Move! Get up!" shouted the *Polizei*.
> They staggered to their feet as though drunk. It was already late, and this was perhaps why nothing was done to undress this group. Instead, they were led through the passage in the sand wall just as they were.
> . . . Coming through the passage, they emerged on the brow of a deep sand quarry with almost sheer walls. All were herded to the left, single file, along a very narrow ledge.
> The wall rose on the left, and the quarry fell away on the right. The ledge, evidently cut specially for the executions, was so narrow that the victims instinctively leaned against the sand wall so as not to fall in.
> Dina glanced down and grew dizzy. The quarry was fearfully deep. Below lay a sea of bloody bodies. She caught sight of light machine guns strung out on the opposite side of the quarry, and also of German soldiers. They had lit a campfire and seemed to be cooking something.
> When the file of victims had occupied the ledge, one of the Germans moved away from the fire, took his place at a machine gun and began shooting.[6]

And then from *The White Hotel*, where Thomas's omniscient narrator describes his heroine's fate at Babi Yar:

> . . . it started to get dark.
> Suddenly an open car drew up and in it was a tall, well-built, smartly turned-out officer with a riding crop in his hand. At his side was a Russian prisoner.
> "Who are these?" the officer asked the policeman, through the interpreter: pointing to the hillock, where there were about fifty people sitting by this time.
> "They are our people, Ukrainians. They were seeing people off; they ought to be let out."

Lisa heard the officer shout: "Shoot the lot at once! If even one of them gets out of here and starts talking in the city, not a single Jew will turn up tomorrow."

. . . "Come on then! Let's go! Get yourselves up!" the policeman shouted. The people stood up as if they were drunk. . . . Maybe because it was already late the Germans did not bother to undress this group, but led them through the gap in their clothes.

. . . They went through the gap and came out into a sand quarry with sides practically overhanging. It was already half dark, and she could not see the quarry properly. One after the other, they were hurried on to the left, along a very narrow ledge.

On their left was the side of the quarry, to the right a deep drop; the ledge had apparently been specially cut out for the purposes of the execution, and it was so narrow that as they went along it people instinctively leaned towards the wall of sandstone, so as not to fall in.

. . . Lisa looked down and her head swam, she seemed so high up. Beneath her was a sea of bodies covered in blood. On the other side of the quarry she could just see the machine guns and a few soldiers. The German soldiers had lit a bonfire and it looked as though they were making coffee on it.

. . . A German finished his coffee and strolled to a machine gun. . . .[7]

Kenrick notes that many such resemblances might be found, and he then follows by alleging not plagiarism, but rather a more subtle failing on Thomas's part. "It can be argued," Kenrick writes, "that Mr. Thomas has made moving use of the Babi Yar material. But should the author of a fiction choose as his proper subject events which are not only outside his own experience but also, evidently, beyond his own resources of imaginative re-creation?"

Kenrick neglects to mention, however, that Kuznetsov's own novel was also based upon the verbatim transcription of yet another testimonial source. By relying upon the remembrances of a Babi Yar survivor, Dina Pronicheva, as the basis for his narrative, Kuznetsov may also have been "beyond his own resources" of imagination. Because he was not a victim and was too young to remember the surrounding details properly—that is, with appropriate meaning—he has deferred to an actual survivor's testimony and to the authority it carries. If anything, Thomas and Kuznetsov thus seem to share similar motivations in their narrative technique, both believing that in some areas of their own fiction they have neither the right nor the requisite experience to reimagine such suffering.

In his reply to Kenrick, however, Thomas reminds readers that he had, in fact, declared his indebtedness to *Babi Yar* both in the book's acknowledgments and in many interviews. And then, after noting that since his account of Babi Yar is three times the length of Dina Pronicheva's testimony in Kuznetsov's novel, and "equally spare in style," he goes on to offer his own critical interpretation—*qua* justification—of this passage:

> This section is where my heroine, Lisa Erdman, changes from being Lisa an individual to Lisa in history—an anonymous victim. It is this transition, reflected in style as well as content, which has moved and disturbed many readers. From individual self-expression she moves to the common fate. From the infinitely varied world of narrative fiction we move to a world in which fiction is not only severely constrained but irrelevant.
>
> At the outset of Part V, the narrative voice is still largely authorial (though affected by Pronicheva's tone) because there is still room for fiction; Lisa is still a person. But gradually her individuality is taken from her on that road to the ravine; and gradually the only appropriate voice becomes the voice which is like a recording camera: the voice of one who was there. It would have been perfectly easy for me to have avoided the possibility of such attacks as Kenrick's, through some spurious "imaginative re-creation"; but it would have been wrong. The witness's testimony was the truthful voice of the narrative at that point: "It started to get dark," etc. This is how it was—for all the victims. It could not be altered. The time for imagination was before; and, in my novel, after. Imagination, at the point quoted by Kenrick, is exhausted in the effort to take in the unimaginable which happened.[8]

In fact, Thomas had even tried to make this point clear in the text of the novel itself, when his narrator explicitly attributes the authority for Lisa's experiences to Dina Pronicheva's testimony. As part of his fictional narrative, the author thus informs the reader that "Dina [Pronicheva] survived to be the only witness, the sole authority for what Lisa [that is, Thomas's fictional heroine] saw and felt," adding: "Nor can the living ever speak for the dead" (p. 251).

Several issues pertinent to the question of literary testimony and authority emerge in this exchange. In noting that the most stunning passages of *The White Hotel* depend for their power on "the moving use" Thomas has made of the *Babi Yar* material, Kenrick suggests that the order of Thomas's fiction has been less "historical" than aesthetic, intended to excite the emotions and merely to move the reader. Sensitive to this charge and to the implication that he has used an authentic resource merely to heighten the horror in his account, in order to exploit it further at the aesthetic level, Thomas answers that it is precisely because he was not there that he must constrain his fiction, that there are some events one has no right to imagine. The only legitimate voice, he implies, is the authentic, genuine voice of one who was there, who is empirically—not imaginatively—linked to these experiences.

At the same time, however, Thomas concedes somewhat ingenuously that he has affected an "equally spare" style because the "only appropriate voice becomes the voice which is like a recording camera: the voice of one who was there." But here he loses track, it seems, of whose voice is whose. For is the "appropriate voice" here that of Dina, the eyewitness, or is it the more figurative "voice" of his eyewitness style? If it is a voice that is like a recording camera, it is a style; if it is the literal voice of a person who was there, it is Dina's. For Thomas, however, this voice is both a style *and* Dina's actual voice, for Thomas has appropriated Dina's voice *as a style,* a rhetorical move by which he would impute to his fiction the authority of testimony, without the authenticity of actual testimony.

Seemingly torn between presenting Babi Yar as a fictional construct and simultaneously asserting that Babi Yar was not a fiction, Thomas has thus labored to create the authority of an authentic witness within the realm of his text. To do otherwise, he suggests, "through some spurious . . . 're-creation,'" would be to violate the factual integrity of real events, which are now "unimaginable" (that is, not to be imagined) because they happened. The supreme irony in all of this, of course, is that by invoking Dina Pronicheva's testimony for his authority, Thomas is actually relying on Kuznetsov's own novelistic reconstruction of her account. Kuznetsov's declarations of his work's explicit factuality notwithstanding, Thomas, by relying on Kuznetsov's novel for his factual authority, is ultimately invoking a secondhand rendering of a third party's memory, which had been massively censored in the Russian, then rewritten (that is, "un-censored") by Kuznetsov on his immigration to the West, and then translated: hardly the stuff of "authentic" or unmediated testimony. The point here is that no matter how strenuously Thomas defends his debt to Kuznetsov, as a fiction writer, even one so beholden to certain horrific facts, he is still a maker of illusions, which in this case become all the more persuasive because he imputes to them a testimonial authority. In fact, by so dutifully acknowledging both his debt to Kuznetsov and Lisa's debt to Dina, thereby establishing an apparent link between his text and a past fact, Thomas may be reinforcing the illusion of factual authority precisely in order to absolve himself of responsibility for making such an illusion.

The further irony here is that Thomas is ultimately at no more ethical risk than Kuznetsov himself; in fact, Kuznetsov has gone to much greater lengths than Thomas to reinforce his own rhetoric of fact. In his preface to *Babi Yar,* Kuznetsov frames all that follows: "The word 'documentary' in the subtitle of this novel means that I am presenting only authenticated facts and documents and that here you will find not the slightest literary invention—that is, not 'how it might have happened' or 'how it should have been'" (p. xv). He invokes Aristotle's distinction between history and poetry precisely to disclaim all poetic license, to distinguish between poetry and history in order to deny anything but historical quality to his narrative. "The result," he has said in an interview, "is not a novel in the conventional sense, but a photographically accurate picture of actual events."9 As did Thomas, Kuznetsov would also invoke the most persuasive of all documentary representations—the photograph—as a figure for his narrative.

Although the sense of eyewitness is fabricated here, rather than retained as it is in the diaries and memoirs, this quality of witness in testimony thus functions as the operative trope underpinning the factual authority generated in "documentary literature." In this context, we might note further that Thomas's invocation of the "recording camera" as a stylistic model even has a quite literal, if unintentional, dimension. For, although he has not acknowledged any other authentic sources, Thomas seems in several instances to have based many of his most "graphic" descriptions not just on Dina Pronicheva's novelized testimony, but also on the witness of several well-known photographs of the Riga massacres of Jews by the SS *Einsatzgruppen,* taken in December 1941 by the SS.10 In this way, photographs become his surrogate experiences of events, which then function both as his own "eyewitness" memory of events and as the source of further authority in his narrative when the reader's own memory of these images is awakened by Thomas's recollection of them. In effect, however, by recalling in narrative the photographs of the SS, Thomas has ironically depended for his testimonial authority on the *Nazis'* "witness" of their deeds; that is, part of the factual authority in Thomas's "victim-based" narrative may ultimately be deriving not just from the testimony of the

victims, but from that of the photographs taken by the killers themselves.

As Barthes, Sontag, and many others have demonstrated, however,
photographs are as constructed and as mediated as any other kind of
representation.[11] In fact, as a figure for documentary narrative, the
photograph may even be more appropriate than documentary writers
imagine: for the photograph operates rhetorically on precisely the same
assumption at work in documentary narrative. That is to say, as a
seeming trace or fragment of its referent that appeals to the eye for its
proof, the photograph is able to invoke the authority of its empirical link
to events, which in turn seems to reinforce the sense of its own
unmediated factuality. As a metonymic trope of witness, the photograph persuades the viewer of its testimonial and factual authority in
ways that are unavailable to narrative. One of the reasons that narrative
and photographs are so convincing together is that they seem to represent a combination of pure object and commentary on the object, each
seeming to complete the other by reinforcing a sense of contrasting
functions.[12]

As others have done, Kuznetsov distinguishes between authentic
documents in his work and his own voice. By including "A Chapter of
Documents" and several short sections entitled "The Author's Voice,"
Kuznetsov attempts to create an intertext, in which a hierarchy of
speakers' authority is generated. In another example of this tendency,
the prizewinning novel, *Efraim's Book* ("part diary, part documentary,
part interior history," according to the dust jacket), the author Alfred
Andersch thus incorporates into his text courtroom testimony from the
Treblinka and Auschwitz trials in Germany in 1965, even as he suggests
that such testimony may be phenomenologically unincorporable:

> But there was no explanation for Auschwitz. *On at least one occasion SS-Man
> Küttner, known as Kiewe, flung a baby into the air and Franz killed it with two shots.*
> No one has been able to explain Auschwitz. *We saw an enormous fire and men
> were throwing things into it. I saw a man who was holding something that moved its
> head. I said: 'For the love of God, Marusha, he's throwing a live dog into it.' But my
> companion said: 'That's not a dog, it's a baby.'* I am suspicious of anyone who tries
> to explain Auschwitz.[13]

By citing the source of these lines in a prefatory note and setting them
off in italics within the text itself, Andersch disclaims both authorship

and authority for them, and in so doing suggests to the reader that the ontological status of these lines differs fundamentally from that of the surrounding "fictional" text. Because these things actually happened, Andersch (like Thomas and Kuznetsov) would claim not to re-create them imaginatively, thereby keeping "facts" separate from "fiction," and absolving himself of responsibility for imagining—and thereby reperpetrating somehow—the most violent scenes in his novel.

Where Andersch separates testimony from fiction in order to privilege it over his surrounding fiction, others seem to make the distinction in order to privilege the surrounding text as well. And where Thomas would indicate this distinction in relatively subtle ways (in his speaker's asides and in preliminary acknowledgments), other novelists assert the difference much more graphically. By separating "documents" from his own narrative in *Babi Yar,* Kuznetsov simultaneously heightens the distinction between reimagined narrative and authentic documents, even as he allows his narrative to draw its authority from the documents he cites. As do photographs and narrative in photojournalistic media, each kind of representation seems to demand and to fulfill the other, providing either the necessary photographic proof or narrative meaning that comes in captions.

Although Kuznetsov's *Babi Yar* is probably the most celebrated work of Holocaust "documentary fiction" (it was also one of the first to call itself a "documentary novel"), there are dozens of others no less insistent in their documentary authority. Among them, we might note that in the preface to Pierre Julitte's *Block 26: Sabotage at Buchenwald,* Joseph Kessel assures the reader that "nothing of the work derives of fiction, and that everything is true, even so to speak, the commas."[14] But, as we find in so many other "documentary novels," the facts of this revolt are necessarily shaped, edited, and explained by both the writer's and his witnesses' linguistic, cultural, and religious perceptions of them. In this vein, Ezrahi has shown us that even though Jean-François Steiner insists repeatedly on the absolute facticity of his documentary novel based on the revolt at Treblinka, the story he writes is ultimately so couched in biblical language and archetypes as to render all of its participants either Jewish martyrs or heroes—a presentation that conflicts markedly with other accounts of the same revolt.[15] As commentary on the events at Treblinka and as representation of how survivors of the revolt have apprehended their experiences, this novel succeeds.

But as Ezrahi observes, even though "this fiction is grounded in reality, it is sustained more by the spiritual authority of authentic testimony than by accurate documentary" (p. 25). That is to say, it becomes the illusion of documentary authority generated by authentic eyewitnesses that sustains the putative factuality of these texts and, by extension, the power of this fiction.

In a further twist, recalling the cases of Thomas and Kuznetsov, the discrepancies between events as they are represented in Steiner's *Treblinka* and as narrated by Vasily Grossman in his version take on an irony of their own. As Thomas drew upon Kuznetsov, and Kuznetsov upon Pronicheva, Steiner seems to have relied heavily on Vasily Grossman's *L'Enfer de Treblinka* for his witness—even though Grossman himself came to Treblinka as a Soviet journalist after the camp was destroyed. Unlike the other authors, however, Steiner does not make direct attribution to Grossman's work. Instead, he acknowledges that three books on Treblinka exist, one of which (*The Hell of Treblinka*) "is by a war correspondent in the Soviet army who interviewed the first witnesses."[16]

In a related case, Cythia Haft notes that the historian Vidal-Nacquet discovered that another novel, *Et la terre sera pure* by Sylvain Reiner, lifted passages directly from Miklos Nyisli's *Médecin a Auschwitz (Auschwitz: A Doctor's Eye-witness Account)*, without making any acknowledgment.[17] In the cases of both Reiner and Steiner, where full acknowledgments of source material were not made, the writers seem to have assumed that these other works retained a witness quality their narrative could not have—but that, even if it went uncited, might still infuse the surrounding text with the authority of witness.

By interweaving into fictional narrative the words of actual witnesses, perhaps written at the time, these novelists would create the texture of fact, suffusing the surrounding text with the privilege and authority of witness. At a crucial place near the end of *Treblinka*, Steiner thus cites directly Yankel Wiernik's memoir, not only trusting the eyewitness to tell the story better but, by seeming to yield to the authority of an actual eyewitness, incorporating that same authority into his text. As Thomas and Kuznetsov have done, Steiner now distinguishes between his mere reconstruction and an authentic witness's memoir—now quoted verbatim—precisely to lend testimonial authority to his own surrounding narrative. And as so often happens in Holocaust fiction, it comes at a particularly dramatic moment, partly to heighten the drama and, it seems, partly to shore up the authoritative integrity of the text at its most vulnerable moment: "Everything seems threatened. Only one man can still save the situation: Wiernik. Let us listen to his testimony" (p. 289). As part of the transition from his words to Wiernik's, Steiner turns to both present tense and first person at this moment and indents the testimony, setting it apart from his own. It is, in fact, first-rate storytelling, precisely because it is purportedly verified now by the witness to events just when we needed his authority most.

The interspersing of authentic witness with less authentic finds its place as a narrative technique in all kinds of Holocaust documentary literature, especially in the memoirs. Even the most authentic memoirs, such as Leon W. Wells's *The Death Brigade*, incorporate the witness of diary into memoir: the narrative written within events would now suffuse that written after events with an even more privileged authority. Just as photographs are used to authenticate and to increase the authority in actual witness accounts, such as Erich Kulka's *Escape from Auschwitz* or Filip Müller's *Eyewitness Auschwitz*, Leon Wells incorporates fragments of his diary into his own memoir precisely at the moment when the killing process begins.[18]

From invoking the "spiritual authority of authentic testimony," however, it is only a short step to fabricating it altogether within a text, whether it is called "fictional" or "nonfictional." Alvin Rosenfeld has noted in this regard that two other writers—John Hersey and Leon Uris—have, as part of their fictions, actually created their own documentary sources. In the editor's prologue to Hersey's *The Wall*, based on Emanuel Ringelblum's *Notes from the Warsaw Ghetto*, the author exclaims of his own novel, "What a wonder of documentation!" and then goes on to tell the reader that the narrator, Levinson, "was too scrupulous to imagine *anything*," although Rosenfeld reminds us that the writer has actually had to imagine *everything*.[19] Rosenfeld also suggests that if documentary evidence is the aim, the reader might prefer to turn directly to the "actual historical testimonies we do have."

But this is to imply that the primary difference between fabricated and "actual" testimony is a matter of actual documentary evidence—when, in fact, *neither* may actually be evidence, but only the persuasively constructed illusion of evidence. Where the nonfiction account attempts to retrieve its authentic connection to events in order to reinforce its documentary authority, fiction necessarily fabricates its link to events in order to reinforce its documentary authority. The difference between fictional and nonfictional "documentary narratives" of the Holocaust may not be between degrees of actual evidential authority, but between the ontological sources of this sense of authority: one is retrieved and one is constructed wholly within the text as part of the text's fiction. As it was for the diaries and memoirs, the operative trope underpinning the documentary character of Holocaust fiction is the rhetorical principle of testimony or witness, not its actuality.

At the end of his study of "literary non-fiction," Ronald Weber concludes that "the first task of the writer of literary non-fiction is always *to convince the reader that his work is adequate as history.*"[20] That is to say, the aim is not to write factual history, but merely to persuade the reader that it is factual. If Holocaust documentary fiction depends on the concept of testimony as a rhetorical trope only in order to provide an "unusually compelling experience for the reader," however, then these writers' narrative methods remain a matter of style. For documentary narratives are in this view compelling as "reading experience" precisely because they claim to be so much more than mere "reading experience."

In this way, the literary documentarist draws on the same sort of ambiguity between factual and fictional narrative that the novelist has always generated. Indeed, much of the force of novelistic discourse seems to derive precisely from the ambiguity its dual claims of fact and fiction stimulate in the reader, as Lennard Davis has noted in his study of the origins of the English novel.[21] And just as earlier novelists dissembled, veiling their authorial presence in order to create the illusion of the text's autonomy, contemporary documentary novelists now conflate their narratives with such rhetorically factual materials as photographs, newspaper articles, and eyewitness testimony in order to lend them a certain factual authority.

As fundamental to the nature of the novel as this ambiguity might be, however, without keeping in mind the distinction between the novelist's claims to fact and the actual fabulative character of his narrative, the reader risks a certain phenomenological beguilement at the hands of the novelist—and now at the hands of the documentary novelist. By allowing himself to be moved to the willing suspension of disbelief by the documentary novel's contrived historical authority, the reader risks becoming ensnared in the all-encompassing fiction of the discourse itself, mistaking the historical *force* of this discourse for the historical facts it purports to document.

In the case of Holocaust documentary narrative, this "rhetoric of fact" is invoked toward a number of different ends; and among them, it seems, is also an emotional response to the "sense of the real," a reinforcement of a work's supposed factuality, and the establishment of the authentic link between writer, text, and events. That is why the documentary authority in the works of writers such as Thomas, Kuznetsov, Steiner, and Andersch begins to assume critical importance. If this "rhetoric of fact" is intended to provide an unusually compelling reading experience, merely to move the reader, then Adorno's objections to poetry out of Auschwitz retain a certain validity. For, in this case, the authors would indeed be wringing pleasure from the naked pain of the victims. If, on the other hand, these works want only to refrain from conferring an essential fictionality on actual historical events, then we might take into account both the legitimate impulse to document events and the manner in which "real past events" are inevitably fictionalized by any narrative that gives them form. Insofar as it works to authenticate—and thereby naturalize—its particular interpretation of events, documentary narrative might even be considered an expressly ideological mode of discourse in both its means and its ends.

After Hayden White's description of what he calls "figurative historicists" as those writers of history who "remain unaware of the extent to which what they say about their subject is inextricably bound, if not identical with, how they say it," we might henceforth refer to the writers of documentary narrative as "figurative documentarists," who write—and then ask us to accept—their work as if it were documentary.[22] This distinction is an important one, for without distinguishing the work's effectiveness in presenting itself as documentary fact from its reflexive interpretation of fact, the ingenuous reader risks confusing a work in the documentary style for the documentary evidence it purports to be. And by mistaking the figurative appeal to fact for reality itself, and then acting on behalf of what amounts to figurative fact, there is a sense in which we thereby accomplish—or reify—the rhetorical figures of fiction. In effect, by looking beyond the factual nature of Holocaust documentary fiction and focusing instead on the fabulative character of these facts, critical readers can sustain the constitutive ambiguity of "literary testimony," even as they relieve themselves of critical ambivalence; in this way, we might continue to learn from Holocaust documentary fiction without being drawn intractably into its essential rhetoric.

Notes

1 · Hana Wirth-Nesher, "The Ethics of Narration in D. M. Thomas's *The White Hotel,*" *The Journal of Narrative Technique* 15 (Winter 1985): 17.

2 · Arnold Wesker, "Art between Truth and Fiction: Thoughts on William Styron's Novel," *Encounter* 72 (January 1980): 52.

3 · Barbara Foley, "Fact, Fiction, Fascism: Testimony and Mimesis in Holocaust Narratives," *Comparative Literature* 34 (Fall 1982): 337.

4 · See James E. Young, "Interpreting Literary Testimony: A Preface to Rereading Holocaust Diaries and Memoirs," *New Literary History* 18 (Winter 1987): 403–423.

5 · "The White Hotel," *Times Literary Supplement*, March 26, 1982, p. 355.

6 · Anatoly Kuznetsov, *Babi Yar: A Documentary Novel* (New York: Dial Press, 1967), pp. 74–75. All further references to this work will be noted in the text.

7 · D. M. Thomas, *The White Hotel* (New York: Viking Press, 1981), pp. 246–247. All further references to this work will be noted in the text.

8 · "The White Hotel," *Times Literary Supplement*, April 2, 1982, p. 24.

9 · "The Memories," *New York Times Book Review*, April 9, 1967, p. 45.

10 · Cf. the descriptions on p. 243 of *The White Hotel* (see note 7, above) and the photographs of massacres in Lijepaja, Latvia, and Sniadowa, Poland, in Gerhard Schoenberner, *The Yellow Star* (New York: Bantam Books, 1969), pp. 92–97.

11 · See Roland Barthes, *Camera Lucida: Reflections on Photography* (New York: Hill & Wang, 1981) and *Image-Music-Text* (New York: Hill & Wang, 1977), pp. 15–51. See, too, Susan Sontag, *On Photography* (New York: Farrar, Straus, and Giroux, 1973). It is worth noting here that Sontag writes specifically of Holocaust photographs she saw when she was twelve years old. "Nothing I had seen—in photographs or in real life—ever cut me as sharply, deeply, instantaneously," suggesting the sheer "power" of referential evidence in the photograph.

Also see Joel Snyder and Neil Walsh Allen, "Photography, Vision, and Representation," *Critical Inquiry* 2 (Autumn 1975): 145; John Berger, *About Looking* (New York: Pantheon, 1980); and Kendall L. Walton, "Transparent Pictures: On the Nature of Photographic Realism," *Critical Inquiry* 11 (December 1984): 246–277.

12 · This is one reason newspapers and other forms of photojournalism are so effective in conveying this sense of factual authority. In the interaction between

written texts and photographs, the photograph seems to demand a caption for its meaning (even though it also makes meaning in the events it represents); and the accompanying narrative demands a photograph as proof not only that "the story" really happened, but that it happened as it has been told.

13 · Alfred Andersch, *Efraim's Book* (New York: Viking/Penguin, 1984), p. 143.

14 · Pierre Julitte, *Block 26: Sabotage at Buchenwald* (New York: Doubleday, 1971), p. xi; also quoted in Sidra Ezrahi, *By Words Alone: The Holocaust in Literature* (Chicago: University of Chicago Press, 1980), p. 25, as part of an excellent discussion, "Documentation as Art."

15 · Ezrahi suggests we compare Steiner's account, for example, with Yankel Wiernik's diary, *A Year in Treblinka*, and Vasily Grossman's *L'Enfer de Treblinka* (Ezrahi, *By Words Alone*, p. 32).

16 · Jean-François Steiner, *Treblinka* (New York: New American Library, 1979), p. 304. In the afterword to the original French edition, Steiner's reference is exactly the same: "*L'Enfer de Treblinka*, par un correspondant de guerre de l'armée sovietique qui interrogea les premiers témoins" (*Treblinka* [Paris: Librairie Artheme Fayand, 1966], p. 394).

17 · In her study *The Theme of Nazi Concentration Camps in French Literature* (The Hague: Mouton & Company, 1973), Cynthia Haft cites Steiner and Reiner as instances of dishonest fiction, "part of a trend which we abhor," and notes that after legal proceedings, Reiner reedited his book to include acknowledgments where they were due (p. 191).

18 · Leon W. Wells, *The Death Brigade* (New York: Holocaust Library, 1978), p. 133. See, among many other excellent memoirs, Erich Kulka, *Escape from Auschwitz* (South Hadley, Mass.: Bergin & Garvey Publishers, 1986); and Filip Müller, *Eyewitness Auschwitz: Three Years in the Gas Chambers* (New York: Stein & Day, 1979).

19 · Alvin Rosenfeld, *A Double Dying: Reflections on Holocaust Literature* (Bloomington: Indiana University Press, 1980), p. 66; John Hersey, *The Wall* (New York: Knopf, 1950); Leon Uris, *Mila 18* (New York: Doubleday, 1961).

20 · Ronald Weber, *The Literature of Fact* (Athens: Ohio University Press, 1980), p. 163, emphasis added.

21 · Lennard Davis, *Factual Fictions: The Origins of the English Novel* (New York: Columbia University Press, 1983), pp. 212–213.

22 · Hayden White, "Historicism, History, and the Figurative Imagination," *History and Theory* 14 (1975): 53.

14 · Terrence Des Pres

Holocaust *Laughter?*

Writing about the Holocaust is like any other writing insofar as the field of Holocaust study requires unproved, and usually undeclared, principles to generate order and authorize perspective. At one time, the critical term for a writer's unverified assumptions was *myth*. More recently, the notion of informing *fictions* has come to the fore, although the term *ideology* is also used, as when in their study of Bakhtin, Clark and Holquist write: "Ideology in this sense is locatable in all that texts take for granted, the preconditions held to be so certain by their authors that they need not be stated."[1] In every case, we recognize that texts and fields cannot go forward without grounding in attitudes that are themselves groundless. And it is not only ideas that function in this way; as Foucault has pointed out, any body of knowledge depends on methods that are officially prescribed, in particular "the techniques and procedures accorded value in the acquisition of truth [and] the status of those who are charged with saying what counts as truth."[2] Some system of practice and belief, some format of permission and taboo, must be accepted before knowledge becomes possible—a "regime of truth" from which discourse takes its bearing and legitimacy.

That writing depends on fictions, on principles of organization that cannot be proved or even accounted for, is perhaps apparent; it is also, with the agony of Auschwitz in mind, a little shocking. For as soon as we ask if the field of Holocaust studies is, like other fields, ordered by

This is the last complete version of Terrence Des Pres's essay, which was still being revised by the author at the time of his death in November 1987—B.L.

216

an uncertified set of assumptions and procedures, we have to concede that it is. The artists among us go forward in any way obsession compels or invention points. But those of us who interpret these things, if we want our ideas accepted by a community of peers, conform to the fictions that underwrite our enterprise. It is true, of course, that fields reconstitute themselves. Newer fictions supplant others no longer helpful or exciting. It seems possible that the field of Holocaust studies might modify itself in this way—or even, at this distance from the event, that a change is under way. My concern, however, is less to chart new directions than to establish the fact that fictions shape discourse generally; and that, in writing about the Holocaust, we are at every moment governed by rulings of this fictional kind. At present, the following prescriptions set limits to respectable study.

1. The Holocaust shall be represented, in its totality, as a unique event, as a special case and kingdom of its own, above or below or apart from history.

2. Representations of the Holocaust shall be as accurate and faithful as possible to the facts and conditions of the event, without change or manipulation for any reason—artistic reasons included.

3. The Holocaust shall be approached as a solemn or even a sacred event, with a seriousness admitting no response that might obscure its enormity or dishonor its dead.

These fictions are not tyrannical; but, even so, they foster strong restrictions. They function as regulatory agencies to influence how we conceive of, and write about, matters of the Holocaust. Because they are fundamental and widely shared, we are convinced of their authority and accept them without question. The third of these is my concern— the attitude of solemnity, as we might call it—but I have cited three to establish the notion of a class. We might see, moreover, that any of these is enforced by the others: the Holocaust is unique, its data cannot be trifled with, and we respect these conditions by staying within the bounds of high seriousness.

In the opening essay in this volume, Raul Hilberg says that the Holocaust remains "a novel event" and "a new marker in history," something "new in the history of the world, something almost out of this world." Professor Hilberg goes on to point out that our deepest responsibility is to bear witness by rigorous attention to what happened, as if, perhaps, the integrity of the facts were absolute. So fierce an obligation, in any case, rules out imagination and looks upon the artist's creative response with distrust. There is, however, a problem. If the event cannot be seen within the long continuum of human experience, while at the same time the facts are self-sufficient, how shall the Holocaust be written about at all—assuming that representations of the world are necessarily different from the world in itself? In terms of literary response, moreover, are some genres useful while others are not? Tragedy, perhaps, but not comedy? When Elie Wiesel says that a novel about Auschwitz is either not a novel or not about Auschwitz, does he mean that, in this special case, fiction cannot cope? Or does he mean—as Hilberg implies—that in the presence of this awful godlike thing, no graven image is permitted?

A set of fictions controls the field of Holocaust studies and requires of us a definite decorum, a sort of Holocaust etiquette that encourages some, rather than other, kinds of response. One of these fictions dictates that anything pertaining to the Holocaust must be serious, must be reverential in a manner that acknowledges the sacredness of its occasion. This imperative is natural, or so at first we feel. But when we come to questions of literary treatment, especially to the disposition of literary modes, difficulties arise. In particular, the *problem of response* is surrounded by questions. To begin with, is laughter possible in literary treatment of the Holocaust? If possible, is it permitted? Is the general absence of humor a function of the event in itself, or the result of Holocaust etiquette—or both? Laughter may or may not be possible; but it is not too much to say that most of us take a dim view of jokes or playfulness in matters so painful.

Since the time of Hippocrates, on the other hand, laughter's medicinal power has been recognized, and most of us would agree that humor heals. Even so, can laughter be restorative in a case as extreme as the Holocaust? That something so slight should alleviate the burden of something so gigantic might, on the face of it, be a joke in itself. But then, humor counts most in precisely those situations where more decisive remedies fail. The situation, in this case, is our helplessness facing our knowledge of the Holocaust. The question is whether or not, on occasion, laughter can be helpful. We know the ready answer because we know what has been said, namely, that toward matters of the Holocaust the comic attitude is irreverent, a mode that belittles or cheapens the moral severity of its subject. At the same time, no one disputes its survival value. In dark times, laughter lightens the burden. Possibly this accounts for the fact—to which I will return—that in his *Notes from the Warsaw Ghetto* Emanuel Ringelblum included the many jokes that kept people going in the ghetto.

I would like, at this point, to cite three works of fiction that span the duration of literary reaction to the Holocaust, all of which are comic in degree, though by no means alike or even similar. The books I have in mind are Tadeusz Borowski's *This Way for the Gas, Ladies and Gentlemen*,[3] first published in story format in 1948; then Leslie Epstein's *King of the Jews*,[4] which appeared in 1979; and, most recently, published in book form in 1986, Art Spiegelman's *Maus*.[5]

Whereas *King of the Jews* is comic in a multitude of ways, including play of language as well as management of plot, the other works are comic mainly in conception. The literary conceit at the heart of *This Way for the Gas* is the narrator's pretense of normality. In *Maus* the governing conceit is the cartoon itself, the comic-book pretense that Jews are mice and Nazis cats. In all three cases, however, the world depicted is grotesque and exaggerated by virtue of its comic perspective. Of course, the actuality of the Holocaust is already exaggerated and grotesque. Here, however, actuality is displaced by a fiction—by a *what if*—that is durable enough, and skillfully enough imposed, to inform the narrative with its own invented principle.

Displacement is the goal of any story, in degree; all fiction aims to usurp the real world with a world that is imagined. In comedy, however, the revolt is more pronounced, and we might suppose that without Borowski's pretense of normality, or Epstein's larger-than-life figure of the trickster, or Spiegelman's game of cat and mouse, the books I have cited would be as grim as the world they refer to. It is largely for this reason, moreover, that realistic fiction so often fails. In its homage to fact, high seriousness is governed by a compulsion to reproduce, by the need to create a convincing likeness that never quite succeeds, never feels complete, just as earnestness feels inadequate to best intentions. Comic works, on the contrary, escape such liabilities; laughter is hostile to the world it depicts and subverts the respect on which representation depends.

The crucial distinction, in this case, has much to do with the different ways the world of actuality is accepted (and blessed) or rejected (and cursed) by different literary modes. Whereas tragedy and lamentation affirm the authority of existence, and proceed in a mimetic mode that elevates *what is*, the comic spirit proceeds in an antimimetic mode that mocks *what is*, that deflates or even cancels the authority of its object. Tragic seriousness, with its endorsement of terror and pity, accepts the terrible weight of what happens. There is thus a connection between solemnity and reverent regard for the burden of the past, a sense of responsibility, perhaps also of guilt, that unites us with the scene of suffering and quiets us with awe.

Of the many imperatives informing Holocaust studies, none is so potent as the need to affirm historical authority—in this case, a strict fidelity to the memory of the camps and the ghettos. Our way of saying Never Again is to insist that the Holocaust took place, and then to ensure—through the act of bearing witness—that this unique evil and pain are wholly with us even now. We preserve the truth of the event by saying yes to the authority of the Holocaust over our spiritual lives, allowing its shadow to darken our judgment generally. We guard the future by bondage to the past. This seems a noble posture, reassuring, but perhaps also debilitating.

The tradition of high seriousness will not be abandoned, but at this point in time—a certain weariness having settled upon us—I want to consider the energies of laughter as a further resource. We know, to begin with, that a comic response to calamity is often more resilient, more effectively equal to terror and the sources of terror than a response that is solemn or tragic. Why this should be so takes us again to the difference in genres (genres considered as frames of reception in terms of which we settle our relation to the world). The mimetic mode is proper to high seriousness because tragedy celebrates the mystery of what comes to pass. The antimimetic mode is proper to comedy because the comic spirit ridicules what comes to pass. Laughter revolts (and from the perspective of lament appears revolting). The works I have cited enact this resistance; they refuse to take the Holocaust on its own crushing terms, even though all three depend for their foundation upon sharp memory of actual events. In each case, however, what survives is the integrity of an imagined world that is similar to, but deliberately different from, the actual world of the Holocaust. Our knowledge of history is not denied but displaced, and we discover the capacity to go forward with, so to speak, a foot in both worlds. A margin of self-possession is thereby gained, a small priceless liberty, urging us to take heart.

Of the books cited, *This Way for the Gas* affords the least amount of breathing space, the least distance between actuality and comic displacement. Tadek, the principal character, tells us that "having, so to say, broken bread with the beast,"[6] he has become one with the world of Auschwitz. The horror of the camp, for such as himself, becomes normal. He and his fellows speak with easy familiarity about "the ramp," "the Cremo," and "the puff." When things are going well they say, "Keine Angst" ("No problem"). The perversity of the German phrase resides in the comic incongruity of superficial meaning (as in "No problem") with meaning truly horrible (as in *Todesangst*, a term for "mortal fear"). In *This Way for the Gas*, ordinary behavior mocks and is mocked by simultaneous behavior entirely inhuman, as when, on the ramp, Tadek and his comrades take pleasure in eating while they shove children and whole families to their deaths.

In Borowski's narrative, horror and banality join, and a central ludicrous moment emerges to repeat itself each time the main character slips, each time he loses his ironic grip and falls back into his humanity. In one instance, a prisoner in the women's barracks, Mirka, has hidden a baby she is trying to save. Of course, the child will not be saved and, seeing the stupidity of the attempt, Tadek is suddenly possessed by "a wild thought" and says to himself: "I too would like to have a child with rose-coloured cheeks and light blond hair. I laugh aloud at such a ridiculous notion."[7] It is not that his laughter is comic, but that an elementary human response is out of place, has become ridiculous and wild. Possibly only those *too* familiar with the camps will appreciate Borowski's point—as if laughter were, in this case, a curse upon us all.

This Way for the Gas is a ferociously ironic book, and nothing so genteel as humor can be said to exist within its pages. The kind of laughter that confers charity and saving grace is altogether absent. Not distance but violent proximity is its aim. Borowski sets his comic energies against the world of Auschwitz, but also against the world that allowed Auschwitz to happen, and then against the self's helpless decency as well; thus, in the end, his laughter is set against life altogether. Back home, having survived the camp and the war, Tadek feels "full of irreverence bordering almost on contempt."[8] That is *one* kind of Holocaust laughter. Almost wholly negative, it can be called demonic, a kind of self-conscious ridicule devoid of redemptive power except for the vigor of mockery itself. The comic spirit is often ambivalent, cursing and blessing at once, but in *This Way for the Gas* the curse is nearly total. Reviling that which overwhelms him, Borowski is in hopeless revolt; hence his inflexible stance and grim disregard for the reader.

By contrast, in Leslie Epstein's *King of the Jews* the narrator's voice promotes a wonderful civility, a sweet insistence on decorum in a world where decorum sounds out of place and quaint. The narrator addresses us as "ladies and gentlemen," and assumes that those to whom he speaks (the readers) are an extension of the community he speaks about (the imaginary ghetto). This emphasis on community is part of the fiction and a cardinal point to keep in mind. Even in its zany naming, the novel assigns a communal as well as a private identity to its characters—for example, Phelia Lubliver, the Ghetto Queen, or Urinstein, Minister of Vital Statistics, and of course Chaim, who is the ghetto's Elder. For the most part, behavior among the Ghettoites of Suburb Balut is bizarre, frenetic, but almost always shared. In this way, Epstein's novel presents a comic spectacle that is larger than life (which seems, on reflection, to be a paradox of the Holocaust itself, at once much larger—yet greatly lesser—than life). But the goings-on in Epstein's novel are large in a more comprehensive way, as well, and take their gross size and shape from a kind of folk or communal laughter that Mikhail Bakhtin, in his book on Rabelais, calls "carnivalesque."[9]

I do not mean to say that the Holocaust becomes a carnival, but rather that in a world of death the spectacle of life defending itself is open to unusual perspectives. In Bakhtin's view, carnival laughter draws its authority from utopian hunger in general. It attacks all rules, regulations, and hierarchies, and revolts against any order that claims to be preeminent or fixed. Things lofty, grand, and solemn are degraded, pulled down to earth, officialdom and worldly power first of all. At the same time, carnival laughter celebrates the regenerative powers of human community as such, life and the plenitude of life, and proceeds by way of vulgarity and excess. Food and sex take on exaggerated value as the functions of the belly and genitals are magnified. Lower forms of humor—jokes, puns, slapstick, and clowning—prevail in an endless spectacle of humble becoming. Here, then, is an appalling feast of fools. Here is neither terror nor pity but, rather, a fearless affirmation of life against death.

Such is the sense of carnival laughter in Bakhtin's definition. To connect it with the Holocaust, let us go back for a moment to Ringelblum's *Notes,* in particular to the jokes he recorded as he observed them circulating in the Warsaw ghetto. Here are three:

> A Jew alternately laughs and yells in his sleep. His wife wakes him up. He is mad at her. "I was dreaming someone had scribbled on the wall: 'Beat the Jews! Down with ritual slaughter!'" "So what were you so happy about!" "Don't you understand? That means the good old days have come back! The Poles are running things again!"

> Horowitz [Hitler] asked the local Governor General [Hans Frank] what he has been doing to the Jews. The Governor mentioned a number of calamities, but none of them sufficed for Horowitz. Finally, the Governor mentioned ten points. He began: "I have set up a Jewish Self-Aid Organization." "That's enough; you need go no further!"

> H[itler] is trying to imitate Napoleon. He began the war with Russia on the 22d of July *[sic]*, the same day Napoleon invaded Russia. But H. is already late. . . . They say that at the beginning of his Russian campaign Napoleon put on a red shirt, to hide the blood if he should be wounded. H. put on a pair of brown drawers.[10]

In examples one and two, the community laughs at itself. In the third case, the community laughs at its enemy, exploding its fear with a punch line. These jokes are part of the historical record and are significant in the following ways: (1) they are the property of the ghetto community; (2) they are examples of carnival humor, in which bodily existence is emphasized and disaster is absorbed by the community at large; and (3) these jokes reappear, along with others from Ringelblum, in *King of the Jews,* in which Hitler is called the Big Man and is often referred to as Horowitz. I take it that Epstein sees what Ringelblum sees, an entrance to the hidden spirit of the ghetto through its jokes, a view of communal underlife that opens the possibility for a comic enactment of life against death, and thus for a representation of the Holocaust that includes laughter.

As I suggested earlier, the major scenes and episodes in the novel are communal, often with the entire ghetto population involved. There is, however, one exception. In the part of the novel entitled "The Yellow Bus," a single citizen of the ghetto—the boy Lipiczany—follows the route of the resettlement trains to see where the deportees are being transported. They are sent to their death, of course: first to be gassed in a bus, then disposed of in a nearby ravine. Here the community is absent, and so is the lively spirit of carnival laughter. Insofar as comedy survives, it is the muted laughter of last blessing. In a situation where the victims are often condemned for going to their deaths "like sheep," Epstein's humor commiserates with the frail humanity of those who perish.

The rest of the narrative takes place in Suburb Balut, in an embattled situation where the social order of the ghetto, organized in fluid ways to promote life, is set upon by the inflexible order of Hitler's "death's-head" regiment, organized to maximize destruction. All survivors of the camps remember the intense necessity referred to by the term "to organize," the need to steal and improvise and trade in order to support collective life, a kind of fluid organization distinct from the infamous "organization" of Hitler's killing-machine. In the world of the Holocaust, moreover, the organization of death is the official order; the organization of life is unofficial, against the law, and exists as an undersurge of renegade energies supporting the community in a multitude of spontaneous ways. Between these contrary orders is a no-man's-land occupied by the *Judenrat* and even more, of course, by the Elder himself. The ambiguity of these border positions is extreme, undecidable. Ghetto leaders are forced to preserve a hidden order of life by accommodating the official order of death; and, inevitably, the realms of life and of death begin to be fused.

Epstein's characterization of the ghetto's leadership thrives on the inherent ambiguity of power's position. Twice the goings-on of the *Judenrat* are presented, each time as dramatic, highly comic dilemmas. The first of these episodes enacts the formation of the Council's initial membership. Notables gather at the ghetto's grand café, the Astoria, to appoint a Council of Elders. The sixteen slots are grabbed by the ghetto's rich and influential citizens, who expect their official position to save them. But in fact they were tricked, and in the street they find themselves trapped: "There, between the gutters, in their underclothes, or wearing no clothes at all, were the Council of Elders, hopping like frogs over each other's backs. On either side, holding a pistol, stood a Totenkopfer. Laughing. Joking. Puffing a cigarette."[11]

One of the novel's grander debacles, the demise of the first *Judenrat* is horrific and ludicrous alike—a scene outrageous to readers unused to comic mediation in literature of the Holocaust. That the SS did sometimes force captive Jews into the "game" of leapfrog would seem to rule out any response except the sternest lament. Yet what can lament, or any mode of high seriousness, do with behavior so bizarre? Vigorous ambivalence is perhaps a better, more capable response in cases so appalling and funny at once, a kind of ambivalence that is the especial domain of carnival laughter.

In the later *Judenrat* episode, the members must produce the first list of victims for deportation, a list that the decency of the Ghettoites forbids them to draw up. In despair, they collectively decide to commit suicide, and everyone on the Council takes poison. They appear to be dead, but then Trumpelman arrives to resurrect them, and in gratitude for a second life they compose, pell-mell and in a frenzy, the list required of them. Their death was a hoax brought on by poison that was "just sleeping pills." The scene is certainly funny, perhaps also outrageous, but in it we see the activity of actual ghetto councils in all their ambiguity, the sort of sad, insufficient endeavor that makes action in extremity difficult to judge—and not so easily dismissed by the kind of condemnation in hindsight that surrounds the historical record of *Judenrat* behavior.

The great point—without which there could be no comedy—is that in *King of the Jews* the characters assert themselves as members of a community. In one of the novel's central episodes, the communal character of events takes political form and results in an energetic, if short-lived, surge of festival triumph during the period of the General Strike, led by the "fecalists"—those whose humble job is the removal of the ghetto's waste. The artist Klapholtz has been shot for painting the Jacobin tricolor on the ceiling of the Church of the Virgin Mary for the Elder's Jewish wedding. The martyrdom of Klapholz provokes an uprising among the Citizens of the Balut, and thus they proceed:

Hundreds of workers broke ranks and raced across the street. Even the shirtwaist girls were coming. They surrounded the excrement wagons and turned them around. Then they began to march behind them out of Jakuba Street. Their voices rang out: "Food! Fuel! A better life!" Their fists were in the air. . . .

What a spectacle it was. A procession of resolute Jews! They seemed to themselves to consist of an irresistible force. The world, which had been snatched from them, would be seized once again. . . .

The broken body of Klapholtz draped over the wooden staves of the leading wagon, rocked back and forth. His arms and legs and the head on his neck seemed full of energy. Someone ran up and attached a flower to his trousers. He was their martyr, their hero. Ladies and gentlemen, what other artist—not even Victor Hugo, not Michelangelo—has moved men so greatly, or filled them with the conviction that they could change the course of their lives?

So began the first day of the Five Day General Strike.[12]

The foregoing passage stands as an illustration for the carnival form of Epstein's novel overall. Pouring into the street, the citizens of the ghetto join forces behind the "excrement wagon" on which their hero—"full of energy"—flops along at their head. In these lowly circumstances they feel possessed by "an irresistible force," which is the power of imagination summoning the power of life in its collective thrust, a force magnified by the community acting as a whole. This is the same power that they, the Ghettoites, invest in I. C. Trumpelman, in the ghetto's view a figure messianic and immortal. In fact, Trumpelman is a monstrous benefactor; he is a medicine man and a quack, a savior and a betrayer who destroys the ghetto in order to save it. His behavior, like that of the *Judenrat*, is radically ambivalent, a blessing and a curse together. Precisely this ambivalence, pointing to life and death at once, is the carnivalesque element and the sign of laughter in *King of the Jews*.

That the General Strike is festive as well as grotesque is plain enough. But, in their lesser way, so are the episodes depicting the *Judenrat*, and so, finally, is every communal scene in the novel. We cannot convincingly imagine such goings-on in a realistic mode, even though events similar to these did actually occur. Nothing that takes place in the novel is impossible, but only exaggerated and exploited for its life/death ambiguity. In its historical enactments, carnival is a actual event made possible by art—by the deliberate suspension of actual order in favor of an imagined order faithfully mimicked. Festival is the dramatic representation of a utopian order that exists nowhere but that follows from the logic of community and finds embodiment through artifice. For a specific allotment of time, carnival reigns and the "real" world is turned upside down; the antimimetic order cancels, for a time, official reality. Bakhtin would say that realism and respect for the status quo go hand in hand with oppression; whereas the antiworld of carnival, with its gross rejection of *what is,* is integral to freedom.

In Epstein's novel, carnival excess frees the citizens of Suburb Balut from bondage to an order of death. At another level, the highly artificial style of the novel—its play with polite formalities, its mockery of programs, its patent delight in distortion—frees us from the hegemony of terror in the spectacle we behold. We are facing the Holocaust, but at a liberating distance, a point Epstein makes over and over by deriving the novel's central episodes from actual records of the Holocaust. Real events are recalled, reminding us that all of this happened. Examples include the rule of M. C. Rumkowski, head of the *Judenrat* at Lodz (mimicked in the novel by Trumpelman's career); the betrayal and failed escape in disguise of Itzak Wittenberg, leader of the resistance at Vilna (mimicked by the fate of Lipsky, the leader of the Edmund Trilling Brigade); and, at the end, the Soviet army's refusal, on the far bank of the Vistula, to come to the aid of the Polish uprising in Warsaw (mimicked by the fate of the ghetto fighters at the King Ladislaus Bridge). Like the other books, *King of the Jews* derives its urgency from faithful attention to actual experience—but then goes on to displace it in grotesque and exaggerated ways.

Ringed round by its destroyers, caught up in a perfect net of death, the community of Epstein's novel conducts itself with frantic energy, the better to resist the darkness closing in. They know what is in store for them, and so do we. But carnival laughter admits no fear, and against their fate the Ghettoites embrace an antimimetic counterworld that shuts out terror and pity together. During the European Middle Ages, this kind of festive revolt was permitted only on feast days and other occasions—births, marriages, funerals—separating carnival time from the structures of daily life. If it occurred at all during the Holocaust, it could only take rise in the ghettos, where a degree of community was still intact. Ringelblum's collection of jokes suggests that the spirit of carnival laughter was fitful and appeared in small ways only. From this modicum of evidence, Epstein has taken his cue and gone on to create, *inside* the historical world alluded to, an antiworld, the communal space of Baluty Suburb. This secondary world resists the reality principle. Actuality is recognized, but not accepted as final—even when, of course, its finality is obvious. But human beings do not live by reality alone, or even chiefly. And it is this willful displacement, this shrewd mockery of the real in serious works of art, that we might call "Holocaust laughter."

The idea of a cartoon about the Holocaust is more or less upsetting. At least I thought so when I first encountered *Maus*. But, in fact, the notion of victims as mice and assailants as cats opens a wholly unexpected perspective that feels—*this* is what upsets—remarkably apt. Art Spiegelman portrays two stories side by side—his own with his father in Queens, then his father's in Poland through the war—and both are faithful to actual circumstance. It appears, moreover, that Spiegelman manages this double story only so long as the fairy-tale element intervenes; he requires a comic shield against knowledge too starkly hideous and weighted with guilt to face apart from laughter's mitigation.

At the request of his son, Vladek recalls his story of flight and final capture as he, his wife, and their family scramble to survive in Poland under the Nazi occupation. This part of *Maus* is too grim, perhaps, to be credited in normal human imagery; but it is also accurate, indeed obsessively attentive to the ordeal in Poland at that time. There is nothing funny about Vladek's story as a whole, although details and moments of the narrative are comic for the fantastic slapstick horror, the incongruities and sharp reversals, that he and his wife undergo day by day, sometimes hour by hour, as they struggle to survive. In Artie's story, on the other hand, there is a good deal of humor. His father, for example, has picked up the survivor's scavenger habits and saves useless items (a piece of phone wire found in the street) to no purpose beyond the son's exasperation. Vladek and his second wife, Mala, bicker endlessly, he has a tricky heart condition, and at one point he sneaks Artie's favorite coat into the trash the better to force a new one— a cheap, vinyl ski jacket—upon his son. This is almost situation comedy, the sort of thing that, apart from its terrible background, we expect on television. The two stories are linked by a network of historical and psychological connections, and then by a pathos too deep, perhaps, for words—but not for Spiegelman's mouse-and-cat iconography. In one example (Fig. 1), helplessness is palpable as the family in Poland struggles to save its small son Richieu.[13]

Figure 1

The moment of tension in the top frames replays itself as, in the lower frame, the outcome is known and defeat is acknowledged. Vladek pedals his exercise bike at a furious pace, all the while getting nowhere. The speed of his pedaling corresponds to the effort to save Richieu, the brother Artie never saw; and with the confession—the renewed recognition?—of failure, the pedaling stops. The agony of the earlier predicament, and Vladek's pain as he remembers, yield a pathos that would be excessive except for the iconography through which suffering is displaced. By portraying the victims as mice, we see them at a distance, and they, in turn, are able to say things that were long ago clichés in Holocaust writing of the standard sort—for example, "synagogues burned, Jews beaten with no reason, whole towns pushing out all Jews."[14] It seems clear that the cat-and-mouse fable, together with its comic-book format, work in a Brechtian manner to alienate, provoke, and compel new attention to an old story.

The testimony of survivors often requires a detachment that keeps

Figure 2

them at a distance from self-pity, whereas for us the pathos of their stories, and sometimes the mere telling of such stories, is nearly overwhelming. In flight from the Nazis, Vladek and Anja strain themselves to the utmost; they manage to escape a dozen deaths, but in the end comes arrest and transport to Auschwitz. Their life, their entire being, is part of a vast inescapable agony that must simply be endured. Much the same, in its lesser way, is true for the attempt Artie and Vladek make to improve father-son relations between them; there is a great deal of maneuvering that comes, pretty much, to nothing. Both stories are steeped in futility. The path of destiny (see Fig. 2) is governed by the swastika, while the priority of loss makes belated measures—the safety box—quixotic and sadly humorous.[15]

In *Maus* the spectacle of pathos is complete, a seamless world of pain except for the comic energies at work. What is needed is a representation that will not swamp us and the story together, and this Spiegelman provides by conceiving of Jews as mice, Germans as cats, Poles as pigs, and all others as dogs. This single displacement allows us to reimagine the terror of events in images that are often horrible but usually humorous, as well. The iconography of the mouse is perhaps the perfect sign for this amalgam of lightness and weight. And at every moment, finally, the separate stories of Vladek and Artie turn out to be inseparable—a point confirmed by the comic-book format, by the way the two worlds interlock on the page. In yet another example (Fig. 3), the children were thought to be safe, and Artie, too, as a son of survivors, is one of "our" children.[16]

At the heart of *Maus* is the family romance, replete with guilt and

Figure 3

232 • *Terrence Des Pres*

unresolved complexities caused by the hold of the past upon the present, a kind of knowledge-as-suffering that cannot be dismissed, but only shared in the "survivor's tale" before us. The best-laid plans of mice and men come to nothing—except, in this case, a remarkable work of art. In Spiegelman's book, laughter is used to dispel and to embrace, a kind of comic ambiguity that diffuses hostility, on the one hand, and on the other prompts charity toward those who suffered, those who remember, and also those who might simply wish to know. Humanity at large is at fault in a world where no one is a hero, and therefore a world in which to laugh is as good as, and possibly wiser than to weep.

In *Maus*, as in the other books I have cited, pity and terror are held at a distance, and this is not, finally, a bad thing. To be mired still deeper in angst and lament is hardly what is needed. The value of the comic approach is that by setting things at a distance it permits us a tougher, more active response. We are not wholly, as in tragedy's serious style, compelled to a standstill by the matter we behold. At the same time, however, the books I have cited manage to respect the "fictions" with which I began. They take the Holocaust seriously. They allow for its particularity and even for the historical record. All this they assume and point to. But they would not, as I said, lie down in darkness. As comic works of art, or works of art including a comic element, they afford us laughter's benefit without betraying convictions. In these ways they foster resilience and are life-reclaiming.

The Albany conference, "Writing and the Holocaust," ended with a sense that our struggle to derive value from the Holocaust has exhausted itself. If so, the most powerful sign of our time is without, at the moment, shared significance or common ground for understanding. Some of our best commentators—Raul Hilberg, Cynthia Ozick, and Saul Friedländer among them—have declared outright that the Holocaust is without meaning, that it allows for no redeeming grace, that the years of Hitler's death-sweep remain a time unique to history and with no hope of mediation apart from the heroism of sheer remembrance.

Possibly they are right. But is writing about the Holocaust at an impasse by necessity? The works I have cited suggest that it is not. Then again, Borowski, Epstein, and Spiegelman have taken peculiar directions, difficult to judge, still more difficult to follow. Creative artists, moreover, are quicker to break taboos than critics like ourselves who must, to perpetuate discourse, accept *some* degree of protocol. How to come to terms with the Holocaust is still our foremost problem. Meanwhile, the prevailing etiquette has limits, or so it would seem from laughter's prospect.

Notes

1 · Katerina Clark and Michael Holquist, *Mikhail Bakhtin* (Cambridge: Harvard University Press, 1984), p. 299.

2 · Michel Foucault, *Power/Knowledge: Selected Interviews and Other Writings, 1972–1977*, ed. Colin Gordon (New York: Pantheon, 1980), p. 131.

3 · Tadeusz Borowski, *This Way for the Gas, Ladies and Gentlemen* (New York: Penguin Books, 1976).

4 · Leslie Epstein, *King of the Jews* (New York: Coward, McCann & Geoghegan, 1979).

5 · Art Spiegelman, *Maus: A Survivor's Tale* (New York: Pantheon, 1986).

6 · Borowski, *This Way for the Gas*, pp. 111–112.

7 · Ibid., pp. 89–90.

8 · Ibid., p.179.

9 · Mikhail Bakhtin, *Rabelais and His World*, trans. Helene Iswolsky (Cambridge: MIT Press, 1968).

10 · Emmanuel Ringelblum, *Notes from the Warsaw Ghetto*, ed. and trans. Jacob Sloan (New York: Schocken Books, 1974). The three citations come, respectively, from pages 79, 55, and 216.

11 · Epstein, *King of the Jews*, p. 70.

12 · Ibid., pp. 148–149.

13 · Spiegelman, *Maus*, p. 81.

14 · Ibid., p. 33.

15 · Ibid., p. 125.

16 · Ibid., p. 108.

15 · *Howard Needler*

Red Fire upon Black Fire: Hebrew in the Holocaust Novels of K. Tsetnik

*H*ebrew fiction about the Shoah has some distinctive features that give it a unique character; and in the case of the particular writer I shall discuss in this essay, K. Tsetnik, these features are also such as to give the work a highly unusual setting among established literary genres. The issues raised by such a term as "Holocaust fiction" are in themselves complex, especially in the light of periodic assertions that the Shoah was itself a fiction, something that never occurred at all. The writers of such fiction are likely to feel responsibility toward the historical events to which its readers may relate it, as well as to their own artistic principles. The kinds of fiction I am alluding to all base their claims to authenticity upon the truth of the horrors to which, however obliquely or symbolically, they refer; and when the fiction in question is the work of a survivor of the Nazi terror, the issue is more than the age-old question of how poetic fictions realize truth—it is also a matter of testimony, and of how and to what that testimony is rendered through the medium of fiction.

Harry Preleshnik, the hero of K. Tsetnik's first novel, *Salamandra*, expresses one view of the intimate relation of survivorship to the presentation of testimony. Harry, at a camp "selection," is standing naked in the line of "Mussulmen" before the camp doctor who uses his finger to designate those to be sent to immediate annihilation. At this moment, "it was not for the world that he yearned; rather, there pulsed suddenly in him a strange will to come among human beings once more, and to tell them what death looked like."[1] The very neutrality and generality of Harry's goal—not to tell the world what Nazis were doing to Jews, but to visit human beings, and describe to them the face of death—intensifies the reader's awareness of his author's testimony to the utter dehumanization achieved by the death camps. If testimony, as it seems here, is concerned with the stimulation of feeling and awareness in those to whom it is offered, narrative fiction is not only an appropriate vehicle, but one that may well be as effective as documentary prose, if not more so. But in this case, as in most others, in the giving of testimony more is at stake. The woman who, in a long queue of Russian women waiting for news of men who had disappeared in Stalin's purges, asked Anna Akhmatova if she could describe that scene was presumably not just interested in knowing whether the poet could convey to her readers the patience, desperation, and mental anguish of the waiting women: she must have wanted her to inculcate in her readers a belief that the unbelievable, outrageous scene was *true*. So testimony wrestles with the unspeakable and the unbearable, seeking ways to realize it for those who did not experience it. Harry Preleshnik, if he survives, will be a Lazarus returned from among the dead: his writing, like his person, will be an attestation of the incredible. And for this reason, Harry's testimony acquires a weight and a significance far transcending his own modest aspirations, intimating for the reader the difference between two vitally important objectives: reconstruction of the experience of a human being caught up in a web of monstrous evil, and level-headed communication to "disinterested" readers of what actually happened.

Reflection on this difference necessarily raises the question of language. Books about the Shoah have been written in virtually all the languages spoken by the Jews sent to the death camps (including German which, despite Steiner's strictures in *Language and Silence*, has proved capable of bearing such a burden). Among these languages, one might reasonably expect Yiddish to hold a privileged position, since it was the language of the European Jewish culture that the Nazis sought to destroy. To write about the Shoah in Yiddish would therefore be to testify to the survival of Yiddish culture while attesting its destruction through that of the Jews who sustained it. It would be an act of piety toward the slaughtered through the restoration of speech to them in their own tongue. And in this way, it would demonstrate the power of language to perform acts of piety available to neither the dead nor the living. If writing about the Shoah constitutes a special category within the literature of testimony, Yiddish writing about the Shoah is a special case within this special category, as more particularly calculated to redeem and restore the murdered past.

Insofar as it achieves such effects as these, Yiddish writing about the Shoah necessarily looks backward. It cannot hope for the degree of neutrality provided by any of the various other languages of Europe. But neither can Hebrew, the other major Jewish language of the twentieth century. Indeed, for many centuries, Hebrew was the backward-looking language of lamentation and consolation, the necessary vehicle of Jewish response to catastrophe, as illustrated by the Lamentations of Jeremiah, the medieval *qinot* over the destruction of Jerusalem, the poetry of Rabbi Ephraim of Bonn, the chronicles of Shabbetai ben-Meir Ha-Kohen and Nathan of Hannover, and so on. But the restoration of Hebrew as a spoken tongue, and the establishment of the State of Israel with Hebrew as its official language, changed all that, making Hebrew, for the first time in more than two millennia, the language of the Jewish future. Such a dramatic change could not fail to be reflected in the new role available to Hebrew, both as language of testimony and as vehicle of response to the Nazi terror. Some of the positive and negative aspects of the assumption of this role by the Hebrew language are suggested by analogy with the condition in which K. Tsetnik represents the protagonists of his various novels at the conclusion of the war. Harry Preleshnik, the hero of *Salamandra*, confronts the peace in a serious crisis of identity. In the short novel *Naqam* [Revenge], which recounts his return to the town of his youth before the war, he is so lacking in purpose that even his thirst for revenge dries up when, armed with a machine gun given him by a Russian soldier, he finds an SS man cowering in a ruined house. In this respect, he seems like the characters of Aharon Appelfeld who wander aimlessly through nameless and featureless landscapes. In another short novel, *Hasha 'on 'asher me 'al laro'sh* [The Clock Overhead]—whose last chapter, ironically titled with the German word *Wiedergutmachung*, deals with the subject of reparations—the unnamed and barely present protagonist finds it impossible to resume life as it was before the war, and is appalled by the accounting approach to reparation for the annihilation of his parents and sister.

These Hebrew novels powerfully image the barrenness and hopelessness of looking back. But the identification of Hebrew with Palestine, the only place in the world where it was spoken, only too readily suggests in what direction Hebrew looks forward.

Despite the much-discussed uneasiness of any presumed relation between the destruction of the European Jews and the establishment of the State of Israel, the logic of such an association is reflected in the idea of Israel as a place of rebirth for survivors of the Shoah, and of Hebrew, the language of Israel, as the forward-looking language for accounts of their survival. Other novels of K. Tsetnik (*Ha 'imut* [The Confrontation] and *Kehol me'efer* [Phoenix over the Galilee]) deal with this aspect of the situation, but make the effort to build a new life in Israel highly problematical. The setting of these novels is too fraught with commerce, business, and obsessive day-to-day routines to offer much space for the working-out of problems of identity or deep ontological questions. As the language of these soul-destroying transactions is Hebrew, it is apparently—and paradoxically—more expressive of the difficulties encountered by survivors in Israel than of what sustains them. In *Ha 'imut*, K. Tsetnik shows this through the roughly parallel careers of Harry and his friend Abrasha, another survivor. Harry, severely traumatized as he is, has emerged from the years of terror physically intact, Abrasha turns out to have a weak heart; in the difficult housing conditions of overcrowded Tel Aviv, Harry finds a room in which he takes great personal pride and readily establishes himself there, but Abrasha seems unable to settle in a permanent dwelling. Both Abrasha and Harry write about their horrific experiences, but whereas Harry has little difficulty in finding a publisher for his first book (entitled *Salamandra!*), Abrasha dies before his work can be published, to be buried in a pauper's grave without even Harry, who has not heard of his death, to escort his coffin to burial—and subsequently Harry, trudging determinedly from publisher to publisher with Abrasha's manuscript, is unable to find anyone willing to accept it.

Harry does find a publisher for his own work. But in what language is the book published? In what language is it written? We are not told. But K. Tsetnik's first book, entitled, like Harry's, *Salamandra*, was published in Hebrew. Since, in this essay, I propose to discuss some aspects of the language of K. Tsetnik's novels and to offer a line of interpretation arising from my discussion, it might seem critically important to determine at the outset whether he composed these novels in Hebrew, or whether they were translated from Yiddish or another language. (I have in fact heard it said that at least the first one or two of his novels were secretly translated from Yiddish into Hebrew, although no mention of translation has appeared in any printing known to me.) But I intend to argue on the ground that the peculiar features of K. Tsetnik's Holocaust fiction (and, by extension, of other writers in Hebrew on such themes, although they form no part of my present subject) are due in large part to the particular historical development of the Hebrew language and to its specific identification with Jewish religion and cultural tradition. In what follows, I will be assuming that if it was not the writer who calls himself K. Tsetnik, it was his unpublicized translator who consciously exploited the specific characteristics of Hebrew for the achievement of the effects I shall seek to define.

Hebrew is *lashon-haqodesh,* essentially a scriptural language, whose astoundingly rapid modernization has done little to obscure its biblical roots. In the history of modern Hebrew literature, one can readily distinguish between writers who have sought to exploit and emphasize this aspect of Hebrew, such as S. Y. Agnon, and those who have wished to minimize it, such as S. Yizhar. (However, the ease with which Hebrew vocabulary invokes the age of the Patriarchs, for example, is richly exploited by Yizhar in the opening pages of his famous story "The Prisoner," although for the purpose of identifying that age with Arabs, rather than with Jews.) In general, Israeli writers have found a real challenge in the development of a Hebrew literary language adapted to the expression not only of Jewish but of universal human concerns. But the difficulties of achieving that objective, arising from the enormous range of local reference in the vocabulary and structure of the holy language, and constituting a potentially serious obstacle for Israeli writers aspiring to see their work as part of the mainstream of world literature, sometimes function as advantages for the writer on themes connected with the Shoah.

The tenth chapter of *Salamandra* describes the arrival at Auschwitz of a train full of Jews. The opening sentence is: "Harakavet nikhnesah 'el hapla'netah ha-ḥadashah" ("The train entered the new planet," p. 139). The word *pla'neṭah,* which according to Hannah Yaoz is a code word, not only for K. Tsetnik but for other Holocaust novelists,[2] serves to denote the absolute strangeness of the place, like nothing else on the familiar planet Earth. It is night: "Ka'n shaltah dumiyah. Hakol damam, 'afilu hahamon hazorem mitokh haqeronot. Muhash hayah ki ka'n shorerim huqim 'aherim. . . . Happenasim hadolqim naghu ka'n benogah 'aher" ("Here silence reigned. All was silent, even the multitudes streaming out of the cars. You could feel that different laws ruled here. . . . The platform lights burning here had a different radiance," p. 139). The word *nogah* stands out in this sentence because of its occurrences in prophetic literature (e.g., Joel 2:10 and, metaphorically, Isaiah 60:3), where it is used to designate the divine splendor reflected in the shining of the heavenly bodies, and from which it has found its way into traditional liturgical Hebrew. At this point in K. Tsetnik's narrative, where the description of Auschwitz is still neutral, the use of the words *naghu* (shone) and *nogah* (radiance) might almost seem designed to prompt such an exclamation as Jacob's, "Surely the Lord is in this place" (Genesis 28:16). But the arousal of any such notion by the word *nogah* is immediately quelled by words suggesting that the ruler of this place is an intimate of night and darkness, not of light or day: "Murgash hayah behush shehalaylah 'omed ka'n le-sheiruto shel shalit 'adir, kol-yakhol, hashofekh memshalto 'al pla'netah zu" ("He was stirred by the feeling that here night stood at the service of a powerful, indeed omnipotent ruler, who had poured his dominion out over this planet," p. 139). In the next paragraph: "Mal'akhei hahabbalah 'akh he'ifu behka 'ayin" ("The angels of destruction passed their eyes over you," p. 139). The "angels of destruction" suggests the supernatural beings that visit and afflict the souls of the wicked: it opens a second possibility that the "new planet" is the world to come; the bewildered newcomers, souls that have died to the world without even knowing it. Moreover, these disoriented Jews appear to have landed in a Christian afterlife, since "nigash 'ehad mimal'akhei-hahabbalah vehehel maheveh be'etsba'o yaminah usmo'lah" ("one of the angels of destruction approached and began to motion with his finger, to the right and to the left," p. 139). After these two false intimations—the first, of arrival in the radiance of the Lord of the Creation; the second, of arrival in the Christian afterlife, where a demonic figure like Jesus in judgment uses his finger to separate the "sheep" from the "goats"—there comes a third, with the breaking of the silence that has dominated the scene up to this point: "Ribbono-shel-'olam! Ma holekh poh? Yiddish, leshon-'am peshuttah, ka'n, "al hapla'netah hamufla'ah? Kelomar, shehameddaber hu' me'aḥeinu benei yisra'el?. . . . Le'an hitgalgalnu? ("Lord of the world! What's going on here? Yiddish, plain 'mamaloshen,' here, on this amazing planet? Surely the one speaking it is one of our brothers, the children of Israel?. . . . Where have we got to?" p. 149). Finally, with the sound of human language, the scene takes on a human face, but the ironic inversion produced by the familiar sound of Yiddish in the mouths of the enemies of the Jews (or, perhaps better, of the Jewish servants of the enemy) is obvious, and is seen to extend from the conventions of the strange new planet to its overlords.

As the "processing" of the new arrivals continues, the chimneys of the crematorium are glimpsed from afar for the first time, "metamrot 'avkhei-"ashan" ("sending up spires of knotted smoke," p. 141). These words recall, beyond any doubt, the "blood and fire and spires of smoke" ("dam ve'esh vetimrot-'ashan") of the Passover Haggadah. Ironically, the expression denoting the powers with which the Lord contrives the Exodus of the Jews from Egypt is inverted into a phrase connoting the final "absorption" of the Jews into the death camp Auschwitz, where the other two components of the tripartite phrase (blood and fire), though dreadfully present, are still hidden from view, and only the smoke is seen. In place of divine power and guidance, leading the Israelites to the Promised Land, we find chimneys bringing Jews to "heaven" (in the words of a "kapo": "By way of these chimneys you'll all go up to heaven" ["Derekh ha'arubot ha'eleh ta'alu kulkhem lashamayim," p. 141]. In sum, the language of this short opening scene, within two pages, not only assigns the unique strangeness of the death camp a provisional place among the ontological possibilities allowed by the existing cosmos; it also represents its functioning, by way of the smoking chimney, its central symbol, as an ironic reversal of the scriptural progress of the Israelite nation toward freedom and independence under the guidance of its God.

Language of this kind is abundantly distributed throughout the books of K. Tsetnik, and of others writing in Hebrew about the Shoah. As already noted, Hannah Yoaz argues that their books build a network of codes out of such words as *ashan* (smoke), *mishloah* (consignment), and *qaron* (railcar). On the subject of *"ashan,"* perhaps the most important example in her discussion, Yaoz writes: "The physical phenomenon called 'smoke,' before the Second World War, had no connection with the tragic burning of masses of people (for example, one spoke rather of 'smoke of campfires'—a sign of vacations, camping skills, the transmission of signs and information—or of cigarette smoke . . .)"[3] But there is a more profound and sinister association to be drawn with the smoke of Auschwitz: the smoke of industry, whose factories and warehouses, which had sprouted all over the face of Europe during the nineteenth century, constituted a significant model for the organization of the Nazi extermination camps, and whose smokestacks were the unmistakable archetypes of the crematorium chimneys. Not only the novels of K. Tsetnik, but extensive documentation, make it clear that the death camps were giant factories of atrocity: of soap manufactured from the fat of human bodies, Jewish bodies; textiles woven from human hair, Jewish hair; smoke produced by the burning of human flesh and bone, Jewish flesh and bone. This is a matter that passes beyond the boundaries of encoding, amounting rather to the attestation of a new, bizarre, and terrible creation on the foundation of the one we know—the creation of what is called "another planet."

This dreadful re-creation—miscreation—extends also to the creation of man and woman. In Genesis 1:27, we read: "In the image of God created He them." In contrast to this, the deformed creation of the lords of the death camps is not man, but "Mussulman"—what K. Tsetnik, in *Salamandra*, ironically terms "the flower of the twentieth century" ("perakh hame'ah ha"esrim," p. 151). Again, there is an ironic reversal of the divine creative process: instead of a being "in the image of God," we have a creature from whom the image of man has been all but effaced. A more graphic image of the Nazi transmogrification of the "image of God" occurs at least three times in K. Tsetnik's works: in *Salamandra*, in *Qar'u lo pipel* [They Called Him "Pipel"], and in *Hasha'on 'asher me'al loro'sh* [The Clock Overhead]. To cite the last of these: "Suddenly, the blade of the shovel flashed in the air, to descend with full force right inside his mouth. And again, and again. . . . They lifted up from the ground a monstrous creature *(yitsur-mifletset)*. Two unsocketed eyes of a no-man hung from the rim of a fountain of blood. The hacked wreck of a man, who could not bring out from within him even a murmur" (trans. Nina DiNur). A "monstrous creature," a "no-man"—this is a clear negation of the divine creation of man, with its play on the word *yitsur/yatsar,* and adds a critically important element to the literary reconstitution of the world, *sui generis*, of the death camps, while completing the framework for a preliminary understanding of how the Hebrew language serves this literary purpose of K. Tsetnik.

It has been pointed out above that K. Tsetnik's books, whatever else they are, are works of testimony. *Salamandra* is subtitled *Chronicle of a Jewish Family in the Twentieth Century*, and its opening pages establish an historical grounding that persists through the surreal material that follows it. But, in a review of *Qar'u lo pipel*, published in *Davar* in 1961, Immanuel Ben-Gurion wrote: "It is not merely a book of testimony, and certainly not a novel." Some of K. Tsetnik's books, such as *Ha 'imut* [The Confrontation], or *Keḥol me'efer* [Phoenix over the Galilee], seem beyond any possibility of serious doubt to be novels, but the answer to Ben-Gurion's implied question (What, beyond a book of testimony, is it? or, perhaps, What, in order to be a book of testimony, did it have to be?) seems to come most plausibly from a region outside the limits of conventional literary genres. The few instances offered above, admittedly sketchy but hardly unrepresentative, suggest that K. Tsetnik's work amounts to a sort of revisionist scripture, the scripture of a grotesque "other" creation by a monstrous parody of the Deity who created light and found it good—a demon who creates darkness and finds *that* praiseworthy; creates death instead of life; deforms men and women hideously, rather than forming them in the image of God; in short, does everything as an absolute denial and mockery of the divine Creation.

"Where have we got to (*le'an hitgalgalnu*)?" the bewildered prisoners ask themselves at the moment of their arrival in Auschwitz, and the metaphor of cyclicity *(gilgul)* implied by the word *hitgalgalnu* is indeed appropriate to the situation that has brought them to the setting of this new and atrocious creation. In another wordplay deriving from the same root, Gilgal is the name of the place where the prophet Samuel executed the Amalekite king Agag, whom Saul had spared after his defeat in battle: "And Samuel cut Agag to pieces before the Lord in Gilgal" (I Samuel 15:33). After Auschwitz, we may be tempted to rewrite: "And Agag cut Samuel to pieces before the Lord in Gilgal." The place-name Gilgal now has sinister reason for identification with cycle and revolution—*gilgul*—after the epoch that witnessed the world turned upside down in the bitterest, most widespread, and most protracted resurgence of Amalekitish savagery against Israel. And in light of these considerations, the specific outrages that K. Tsetnik's books have to attest are subsumed by the utterly bleak, all-encompassing vision of a world designed, formed, and governed by diabolical powers of unmitigable evil. The draining of all goodness out of the world of the survivor is reflected in the scripture that he writes, or that writes itself through him.

A particular function of the Hebrew language in the work of K. Tsetnik, then, is to establish scriptural archetypes, however fleetingly, that will be ironically inverted or distorted by the narrative. But that is not all it achieves, and not necessarily the most important thing. Harry Preleshnik, the hero of these books, survives and arrives in the Promised Land, not, like the Patriarchs and sons of the Covenant, conveyed by divine power and sustained by divine assurance, but deprived of hope, promise, faith, family—of everything but memory, hatred, and lust for revenge. And here Hebrew serves him in another way, for the language itself, in its vocabulary and idiom, incorporates covenant and faith, promise and its fulfillment, without imposing upon this ravaged hero the necessity of faith in anything whatsoever. It bestows *voice* upon one who has lost, or feels impotent to use, the power to speak.

"And the Lord passed, and a great and powerful wind shook the mountains and smashed the rocks before the Lord, but the Lord was not in the wind; after the wind was an earthquake, but the Lord was not in the earthquake; after the earthquake was fire, but the Lord was not in the fire; and after the fire, a still, small voice" (I Kings 19:11–12). Something like this voice rises now from the depths of the Hebrew language, and bestows upon the writer of the twentieth century the possibility of speaking with the voices of prophecy and vision, even though he lacks vision and cannot prophesy—voices that in themselves express reproof, forgiveness, and lamentation. Ben-Gurion, who saw in another place a source of vision for K. Tsetnik's books, has paraphrased Scripture to give his own eloquent expression to the particularity of the power that these narratives enfold: "He revealed what he had seen in the vision of his flesh and bones. It is a scroll of fire—red fire upon black fire, that no man shall behold, and live."

244 · *Howard Needler*

Notes

· K. Tsetnik, *Salamandra* (Modan, 1975), p. 159. All further references to this work will be noted in the text.

2 · Hannah Yaoz, *Sipporet hashoah be 'ivrit ke-sipporet hisṭorit vetranshisṭorit* (Tel Aviv: Eked, 1980), pp. 119 ff.

3 · Ibid., p. 157.

16 · *Berel Lang*

Writing-the-Holocaust: Jabès and the Measure of History

Edmond Jabès is right, but for the wrong reasons. Jewish life and history *are* tied to the life and history of the letter, the word, the book—but not because of the alien and driven presence he claims in common for those histories, challenged wherever they would settle, contingent, permanently in exile. For each of them—Jew and writing—the will to exist follows a different and direct route, much less tenuous (indeed, not tenuous at all) than the one Jabès traces and then exemplifies in his own writing. The convergence between the history of a people and the life of discourse is still there: this much of Jabès's claim, startling, ironic as it is, survives. But the convergence is in affirmation and assertion, in a common and extraordinary will to exist—not in hesitation or doubt or anxiety. One would never recognize this order of history from what Jabès discloses to his reader; and the reason for the failure, first of author and then, as he submits, of reader, attends one question that is not uttered in *The Book of Questions*[1] but that must have been presupposed for that book to exist at all. It is thus, unhappily, repressed—this question of whether writing centered in the Holocaust, the Nazi genocide against the Jews, is even possible: literarily and morally *possible*.

To direct that question at Jabès, only one of many writers to whom it could be addressed, may seem mischievous: *The Book of Questions* is so unremittingly self-conscious, so deliberate, so firmly attuned to the principle of equity and to the reasons of language and of history. And surely one part of the answer implied by Jabès is worth holding to. Far from being an instrument, a neutral means, writing is itself an action with moral design—and, just as other persons are obliged to take responsibility for such acts, the writer, too, will stand moral inspection for the relation between what he does and what he does it *to:* his writing is a judgment on the *character* of his subject as well as a portrayal of it. What writing is about, in other words, ought to make a difference in the writing itself, on moral no less than on aesthetic grounds; here, indeed, is a point at which those two categories, usually separated by literary taboo, converge. Why *not* write a traditional novel with the Holocaust as subject? And we learn, in response, from *The Book of Questions*—from its repeated disruption in the narrative texture, the continuing dislocation and relocation of anything like the authorial point of view, the incessant putting of questions that remain unrequited—that the steady temper and domestication of family history that traditionally govern the novel will not suffice. A genre committed to life or even death in the bosom of the nineteenth-century middle class would simply fail as the vehicle for a subject that challenged the very possibility of social existence.

One consequence of this infringement by ethics on literary convention is to make explicit the possibility of potential literary subjects that cannot be written about at all. For if the subject of discourse is to have a voice in determining the character of that discourse, then there may be subjects that prove intractable for *any* of the available literary forms—indeed, if "literariness" is intrinsically bound to the doubling and thus mediating effect of representation, that cannot be embodied in any *possible* form. An example of the latter effect is, indeed, quickly evident, fixed in the question that Jabès represses. For if an ostensive subject of literary discourse demanded to "speak for itself"—as "the facts"—then to interpose another (even an artistic) voice would inevitably be to mute that first one, to blunt or avert its force and so to diminish it. This is, in fact, very much the objection that Theodor Adorno was to direct at the possibility of Holocaust poetry; so, for him, Paul Celan's "Todesfuge" would be immoral—in what it *attempted* to do, not for its failure or success in the attempt.

To be sure, Jabès has decided this same issue differently: Holocaust writing *is*, for him, possible. But the question of justification, the necessity of a defense for the word against the alternative of silence, is evidently an issue for him, as well. Moreover: Jabès acknowledges the unusual requirements posed by the Holocaust as a literary subject, not only by the unsettled genre of *The Book of Questions* but by structural perplexities within that means. The continuing indirection and obliqueness in his writing is identifiable by none of the standard literary figures of indirection, such as allegory or irony; these, we infer, are not *sufficiently* indirect or oblique. He seems, in fact, to devise here a new literary figure by which the Unspeakable or Unwritable is hinted at, alluded to, implied—supported by a premise which asserts that for any such Unmentionable, nothing *could* be spoken or written that did more than ascribe the "name." The Nazi genocide against the Jews, disclosing itself in the lives of the two main characters, Sarah and Yukel, provides a frame for *The Book of Questions*. The "questions" asked or implied within the text, the events related, the knots resolved or retied by aphorism verge continually on this background; it is itself one of the *dramatis personae*. But never is the Holocaust, or any of the pieces of history that make it up, given by name or identified in those terms. This is true for quite specific items as well as for the framework within which they appear. The SS man, the number tatooed on an arm, the yellow star—each of these appears in Jabès's text, but without preface and without elaboration. The reader who did not already know what they were or who did not otherwise have a lexicon available would find no understanding in Jabès's words; he would recognize only that he was meant to be pained by them (the words and the things). If anything more than this monitory sense is required in his response, the reader must supply it himself; it is he, then, the reader, who must write the circumstances within which the questions of *The Book* are raised, the circumstances not only of fact, but of the emotional and moral force that the facts carry with them.

Jabès's strategy here may be surmised. The enormity of the Holocaust is evident, goes without saying. Because of this, the Holocaust cannot be represented by the usual poetic or fictional devices that would, if they worked as they usually do, "epitomize" it, exhibit features by which the reader might more fully imagine or realize it. At best, the writer would belabor the obvious: what artifice could more fully "realize" the facts of the Holocaust? At worst, what he wrote would fail even to match the intensity of those facts. Let us write, then, in the assumed presence of the events, take the existence and enormity for granted—even if this means that the reader must be left to provide on his own the texture of historical detail and evocation of imagined responses that the representations of the text, individually or together, do not. In one sense, to be sure, there is nothing unusual in this Jabèsian strategy: a reader is always required to bring *something* to a text, even if this is only an understanding of grammar and vocabulary. But once we move beyond the first requirements of literary competence, the question of literary propriety—of when the writer is requiring the reader to do the *writer's* work—becomes more pressing. Is there not a warranted division of labor between writer and reader? Or is the reader obliged to supply *whatever* the author (for whatever reasons) chooses to leave out? We can reasonably doubt that if an author fails to give a literary account of the character—in literary fact, emotion, value—of events that have significant consequences within his work, the burden of doing so is simply transferred to the reader.

We understand here the dilemma that Jabès—and any writer who takes the Holocaust as subject—confronts. On the one hand, it is difficult, perhaps impossible, for a writer to meet the Holocaust face-to-face, to re-present it. The events themselves are too large for the selective mirror of fiction, too transparent for the unavoidable conceits of literary figuration; linguistic representation is in any case redundant—thus an impediment—when the events that converge on a subject speak directly and clearly for themselves. On the other hand, to write about the Holocaust obliquely, by assumption, leaves the task that had been declined by the author to the reader, who can hardly—if the *writer* will not—hope to find a path from personal emotion and imagery to artifice. Where, then, is the work of literary representation to be done?

This dilemma, it will be recognized, does not affect Jabès alone; it has in fact affected and been acknowledged, tacitly or explicitly and in much the same terms, by other serious writers on the Holocaust, many of whom also, as it happens, choose the alternative within the dilemma that Jabès follows—the way of indirection, of assumption. D. M. Thomas, Aharon Appelfeld, Jakov Lind: each demands that the reader provide a supporting ground and literary frame of fact and expression—detailing the face and aura of horror—that more usually, for less extravagant and painful subjects, the writer himself would accept responsibility for enacting. And the converse also seems to hold—that, among the writers on the Holocaust who fail, many fail precisely because they would directly impose an artistic hand: fictionalize, epitomize, give figures to the events of the Holocaust, as they might write about any other subject, heedful only of literary conventions and techniques rembered from another and easier life.

Against the formulation of this dilemma, it might be objected that it obtains its force only by begging an important question; this is the question of whether Holocaust writing (or, for that matter, any writing) is, or need be, representational—whether it is characteristically "about" something at all. For if that archaism (as the objection has gone), that "nostalgia for a presence," were be avoided, the dilemma it serves as a presupposition would also disappear. If writing were not, or did not need to be, representational, the issue of commensurability between literary appearance and historical or even moral reality would not arise. There might be other obstacles that a writer would have to face—in any event, the standard literary problem of persuasion, of the author's need to overcome the will of the reader; but the contest then would be between will and will—not between them (singly or together) and an external means of measurement.

This objection, it may be recalled, marks the beginning of a recent theory of writing that was first proposed in a broader context than the writing of extreme situations; and when Jabès attempts in *The Book of Questions* to revise the conventions of literary balance or equity, it is evidently the germ of this recent theory that moves the design of his work, that is meant to impel the reader away from the possible worlds of fictional artifice to an insistence on a single and unmediated reality. The conclusion drawn by this theory—for example, in Roland Barthes's conception of "intransitive" writing, according to which the writer does not represent or reflect on an object but "writes himself"—is directed specifically against that theory of writing which fosters the dilemma of the Holocaust writer. For intransitive writing means precisely writing that is nonreferential, nonrepresentational; not even the existence of a world external to the literary work, let alone the properties of that world, are to affect the *writing* about it (or, then, its reading). Thus, the subject of discourse is problematic even so far as concerns its existence—and here we also see the price exacted by this first step in the reaction against representationalism. For if the reference of discourse is now internalized in the writer himself, it is reasonable to wonder what happens to the event—or, subsequently, the fact—that would otherwise have existed independently as the reference of discourse. The most evident possibility here, of course, is that event and fact, together with the terms of discourse, should simply be bracketed, suspended—that the facts of history should be excluded from their customary role as a basis for the writing of history. This possibility, obviously, is more than an abstraction; it means that the individual items otherwise assumed to comprise history are themselves liable to suspension—and this, by implication, means for Holocaust writing a suspension or bracketing of the events of the Holocaust itself.

Any such consequence might be viewed as refuting the theory from which it follows, although that has not, in fact, seemed to curtail the appearances of the theory. The need to consider this objection, however, is itself curtailed because of a *third* formulation of the relationship between writing and representation—a theory of writing that moves beyond the conception of writing as intransitive, that Jabès himself evidently *means* to go beyond the second account, and that he almost makes good on. The systematic progression here is exemplary. For if representational writing is incommensurable with the events of the Holocaust, and if the step beyond that, intransitive writing, escapes the tyranny of representation only at the expense of denying historical reference, still another step remains that is also not relational, not "about" something, but one-sidedly *with* or *in* the object: not, then, writing *about* the Holocaust; and not, beyond that, writing the writer—but writing-the-Holocaust. Here, in contrast to intransitive writing, it is the object, not the author, that is written: in effect, the object writes itself. The narrative voice—insofar as we refer at all to what is now quite clearly an anthropomorphism—is the voice of history; the object itself takes over, construing the form and the means in addition to the literary content.

Like the two other conceptions of writing, this one, too, revises the relation among the syntactic "elements" of a text; thus, in *The Book of Questions,* Jabès, writing now not *about* a subject but writing the subject, proposes for the reader, both by assertion and example, that substantive issues—moral, cognitive—turn into, indeed *are*, literary form. Thus, for Jabès, writing is not detachable from that which is written about, but is an immediate function or appearance of it. Only so, it seems, can we understand the strain that Jabès's writing puts on the conventions of the text, and then on the expectations of the reader; only so does the indirection, the constant blurring of a "subject" come into focus for the reader: there *is* no subject distinct from the medium; there is only the event, the span of history itself.

This turn or trope has important general consequences at the level of the theory of discourse, but its more immediate consequences are also more dramatic, at least for the claim that it is at this juncture that Jabès goes astray. For if Jabès—the author now as medium or vehicle—means to have his subject write itself, to have the "voice" of the event speak, then the reader is entitled, even obliged, to measure the discourse he hears as he would any voice that claims reality for itself, without allowance for the insulation or distancing that "fiction" commonly claims in pleading its case for divergence from fact. If it is the Holocaust that allegedly speaks (and, behind it, the character of Jewish history) in other words, then the reader is responsible on *his* side for deciding whether the voice is authentic. And if Jewish history, as it expresses itself, is linked in *The Book of Questions* to a conception or even a theory of the word that *provides* the voice—then the two of them together, not simply the analogy but also its content, must be recognizable, must persuade the reader that it is indeed he who is present. And it is here that *The Book of Questions*—now the event of writing the Holocaust— misleads the reader; and that Jabès, as medium, if not as author, fails.

On the evidence of his writing, we infer that the Holocaust came as no surprise to Jabès, that it only confirmed what he had already, perhaps always, known. It was, after all, just another moment, larger but not otherwise distinguished, in the persistent counterpoint of Jewish history: the threat of an imminent end to that history. "Being Jewish," *The Book of Questions* answers itself, "means having to justify your existence. It means having the same sleepless nights in common, suffering the same insults. It means desperately looking for the same buoy, the same helping hand. It means swimming, swimming, swimming, in order not to sink" (p. 68). Genocide, in other words, was for the Jew no twentieth-century invention. He had long lived under its shadow; it had, in fact, been part of his original conception of self, a measure of the way he defined and saw himself. To take these terms even at face value is also to infer that the Holocaust is no more than an instance of "holocaust"— holocaust being the pattern that has given shape to Jewish history as a whole. We know, then, why *The Book of Questions* moves so freely between events of the mid-twentieth century and the centuries of Jewish history before it: together they occupy a single, virtual present.

Nor, again, is it accidental that it is the Jews, as Jabès asserts, whom history has embedded in language and books; that with the Jews, the Word becomes something more than a mere instrument or means, revealing itself as physiognomic, as the spirit and ethos of the speaker. For language, too, we are supposed to understand, is symptomatic—an *instance*—of holocaust, of life on the abyss. "The world exists because the book exists," Jabès first notes, placing reality inside language—and then: "The wings of the word are questions." And so to the conclusion: "For Judaism and writing are but the same waiting, the same hope, the same wearing out" (pp. 31, 132). It is absence, privation, from which language sets out and which then constantly shapes—and threatens—it. Language *starts* with the question, the recognition of incompleteness; otherwise, why (with this question Jabès might hope to provide evidence for his own claim) would language have come into existence at all?

Even read as fiction, this remarkable conjunction of the history of a people and the nature of language—is it simile? metaphor? a *literal* joining?—might well move Jabès's reader to silence. That two independently evolved artifacts should turn out to be mirror images would be startling if the two were small and rudimentary objects; and here, where it is, on one side, the extraordinary human invention of language and, on the other, the causally overdetermined history of the Jews that are matched, the effect is stunning, an intimation of the possibility that history, even as a *whole*, may turn out to represent in its apparently innumerable pieces, traces, and reversals, only one thing: a single character.

But a striking possibility is all, in the end, that Jabès can make of his analogy, since the content of the analogy is what he would have it judged by—and what, finally, is also open to question, and, beyond that, to objection. The reader's questions here may well in fact usurp the questions of the text. *Is* there reason to admit the description of the Jew as alien, as outsider, as continually beset—what the historian Salo Baron labeled, with a noticeable edge, the "lachrymose conception of Jewish history?" Is there evidence (on the other hand) for thinking of language itself as a divisive or alien presence, as intrinsically endangered? To be sure, Jabès is not alone in entering these claims. In his view of the Jew as wanderer, in fact, he may speak with the voice of the majority, at least of a recent majority. One important line of such thinking, ironically opposed to Jabès in its conclusions, is evident in Zionist writers who, from Harzl on, take as their starting point the Jew as exiled, deracinated, estranged. For these writers, the redemption of Jewish history—a latter-day Messianism—will come only as that historical exile is brought to an end, when the Jew "finds himself." Even the remarkable analogy between Jew and writing, moreover, has echoes elsewhere. Jacques Derrida epitomizes this background by locating the "differance" in writing at the juncture between the Jew and the Letter: "the situation of the Jew," Derrida complements Jabès's theme, "is exemplary of the situation of the poet, the man of speech, and of writing."[2]

But corroboration requires more than repetition and, in the end, the analogy thus asserted is historically unbalanced; it may, beyond this, be simply mistaken. The dissonance here comes from several directions—historical, moral and, not least, psychological. If we ask, for instance, with respect to its conceptual development, from whose point of view the designation of alien or outsider is *first* made, at least one account would find that title first ascribed from a point of view that is not *itself* alien. It is the person who is at home and is then obtruded on who reacts most immediately to the stranger, to whatever or whomever disturbs the familiar network of relations and expectations within which he lives. As self-consciousness assumes a (prior) consciousness of others, so will the consciousness of self-as-alien follow the consciousness of other-as-alien. Certainly this genealogy is no less plausible an opinion than its alternative; and, according to it, the representation of the Jew as alien would not, could not, have come from the Jew himself, but from the outside, joining itself to whatever identity the Jew had first chosen—or found—for himself. But then the *latter* identity, by implication, would not initially have the character of alienation or estrangement at all.

Even the possibility of this order of development, however, has been ignored in the many accounts according to which Jewish identity is engendered primarily by conflict, by the antagonism of anti-Semitism, by the imposed awareness of the contingency of Jewish existence—in short, by holocaust. Here, the threat of extinction from the outside is held responsible for the internal will to survive and, before that, for the will to exist. This is a premise, we recall, of Sartre's *The Anti-Semite and the Jew*, in which the designation "Jew"—like the designation "Dirty Jew"—is alleged to come mainly from without; once remove the external pressure exerted by either of these, and the internal commitment to Jewish identity also disappears. To be sure, Jews writing about themselves have often, with varying degrees of emphasis, repeated a similar view; but even this proves only that an individual may *come* to know no more about himself than what is imposed from the outside. No one doubts that an external view can be adopted as his own by the person viewed, but this assimilation serves as little more than an indicator of individual biography; certainly it does not—*could* not—account for the persistence of the Jews as a community or group. The designation of outsider or alien may be a *consequence* of survival—it can hardly be its motive or purpose. The contradiction threatened here, moreover, is finally as much logical as it is psychological: can one first deny (oneself or anybody else) in order to affirm? The role of alien or exile could not disclose itself first as assertion or affirmation—and it is to the latter that we must look for explanation of, first, the life and, then, the persistence of Jewish history.

The measure of confidence required here is at once as basic and as general as that expressed by Spinoza, met on all sides as an alien, cut off from non-Jew and Jew alike—who would yet write in the *Ethics* that "the effort by which each thing endeavors to persevere in its own being is nothing but the actual essence of the thing itself" (Bk. III, Prop. 7). And surely, if one feature stands out in Jewish history that might account first for the origins of the Jew and then later for his continuing history (even in opposition), we find it intimated here, in the singular desire of the Jew to exist, and to exist *as* Jew. This impulse, moreover, is not the familiar-but-secondary version of desire as inspired by anxiety or fear, by a sense of mortality; it is, rather, the desire for an object where the object is known and directly willed. Is it so difficult for the modern consciousness to admit that the idea of the divided self, of a spirit alienated from itself, is itself a recent artifact—that the image of the Jew as congenitally alien is not *itself* congenital, but rather an historical contrivance, nourished conscientiously in the romantic notion of alienation by volunteer poets and philosophers from nineteenth-century Germany, France, and England? As Zionism was moved by the nationalism of that century, so the conception of the Jew as wanderer and alien was also nourished externally, by the same currents, at the same time; it is itself, in good measure, alien.

The contrast between the instructions of this overheated and recent past and those of older—and longer—periods of Jewish history makes the parochialism of the recent view evident. Even searched randomly, for example, the pages of the Hebrew Bible disclose not simply the absence of an alienated consciousness—of self or other—but its opposite. Certainly we cannot think of the Psalmist as estranged when he sings that "the earth is the Lord's, and the fullness thereof." Nor is Amos divided in himself when, scolding Israel, he holds out to them a future in which they will yet "walk humbly with their God." Job, in anger and despair, still "knows that his redeemer liveth"—and the Hebrews at Sinai, as a people and with one voice, respond confidently, willingly, that "they shall do and they shall listen." From Abraham to Koheleth, there is assurance, not doubt, resolve rather than temporizing. When Israel backslides or sins, even then this is not because of inner torment or doubt; its sins are those of self-assertion, pride, appetite. These are, after all, a "stiff-necked" people. The prose style of the Hebrew Bible is itself as far removed from tentativeness or from the anxiety of a contingent existence (and from Jabès's prose) as any text in the history of writing.

To be sure, the biblical Jew is, even if central, not the only indicator of a long history: exile begins as the biblical narrative ends—and with it a new factor of physical distance and separation. But to say even *then* that it is this later phenomenon of estrangement that becomes the moving force for the Jew—that it is the physical separation, internalized, turned into consciousness, that then dominates the subsequent history and work of the Jews—is so partial a view as, by itself, to be false. Rabbinic Judaism and the Talmud, the migrations and settlement in North Africa and France, even the walls set up around the medieval ghetto: the sense of dislocation and separation that undoubtedly accompanies these institutions does not impede the purposeful and unproblematic consciousness required (and forthcoming) to maintain the strong and living communities that express themselves here. In the literature of the Jews, the most explicit formulation of the idea of alienation, of the spirit in exile, comes in the kabbalist and later the Hasidic writings; but it is important to remember that when these traditions emphasize the doctrines of loss and separation, of "Zimzum," they are speaking finally about *mankind and the world* as alien from God, not restrictively about the Jew. And again, more than this: these traditions are themselves contested from within, eddies in a broader and more potent—and quite differently directed—stream. When Jabès writes that "every Jew drags behind himself a scrap of the ghetto," (p. 82), he openly concedes that he does not speak of Jewish history *before* the ghetto; he fails to suggest altogether what else the Jew may be "dragging" behind him.

What is it, then, that Jabès is right about, albeit for the wrong reasons? There remains the form of the analogy between the Jew and language—an analogy that can stand on grounds other than, even opposed to, those that he offers. Think, for example, of the requirements of affirmation, in persons as with language. Is it too much to claim that, with the Covenant that first linked the Jews and the one God, defining the Jews as Jews, language also took on a new identity? We do not know historically when language first found itself adequate to the making of promises; difficult as it is to know what are the logical and then the moral requirements for the act of promising, it is clear that both these norms are tied closely to the verbal expression of the promise itself. But it also seems clear that at the moment when promises become possible—simultaneously with the negative counterpart of that event, the discovery of the lie, or the *un*making of the past or present—language and the consciousness it represents assume an identity they had not had before. Nietzsche's version of this change cannot be ignored: that promise-making nourishes *ressentiment*, placing the will in thrall to the future. But on the latter account, no less than on the former, the promise or covenant transforms language as a whole, turns it from mere description or expression—the response to a stimulus—to a claim on time, embodying not only expectation, but the will. Here, language itself becomes selfconscious.

The biblical God is only heard, never seen. He challenges everything palpable. The written word is the one "graven" image exempted from the many biblical interdictions against idolatry; as an image, it, too, has a palpable appearance, but what matters nonetheless is that part of it which does not appear. Language is also, after all, a way of dispelling the alien, of opening passages among persons and between them and the world. Admittedly there is a risk in the venture of a word, even a menace—as the speaker or writer chances himself, substitutes assertion for privation. The word itself, moreover, is mute: once spoken or written, it cannot answer *for* itself—it, too, becomes an historical object. And if we were to look only at these dangers, then we might indeed think first of the precariousness of language, of its contingency, of the challenge it offers to silence with the odds of success heavily against it. (The efficacy of language, John Dewey remarked, is a miracle beside which the wonder of transubstantiation pales.) But all these threats seem slight indeed as we compare them to the menace of a world *without* language: surely it is there, in silence, that isolation and contingency—the *truly* alien existence—would be met. Thus, the bonds among the word, its utterer, and its witness together shape an affirmation—in the identity of the Jew, on one side, and in the character of language, on the other; this analogon and radical change also brings the two together, marks them commonly in history.

But, against such a view of writing and Jew, *The Book of Questions* insists that The Book—every book—*is* questions, tacitly if not openly, in its origins if not in the present: language and the word, we are supposed to understand, begin life as interrogatives. This version of linguistic origins is undoubtedly a useful corrective, morally and historically, to the pseudo-anthropology that for so long represented those origins as exclamatory or phatic. But should not history itself be observed here, meager and fragmentary though its evidence is? The oldest writings of which we have record are more prosaic than either exclamations *or* interrogatives. They consist mainly of items that are not often subsumed under a grammatical category or literary genre at all. They comprise, rather, catalogs or lists: of supplies, possessions, battles, ancestors. The List is, in fact, a revealing literary "kind": more openly than almost any other, it reveals the elements of writing, its natural history, re-creating the act of memory with one foot in the past and the other in the present. The list, moreover, becomes likely—even possible—not in a moment of privation, but in one of surfeit: together with everything else that the speaker or writer has, sees, knows (these are the items *on* the list), there is also room for a list (this is not itself on the list). Abundant, even self-indulgent, the list is a means of creating a home, of *being* at home. And that, it turns out, is only a prelude or intimation of what language can do in the way of affirmation, of securing a foothold where before there was none. To be sure, none of these features solves the possible objection that the list, so far as literary invention is concerned, is a primitive device, that we learn nothing from it about discourse, about tense and connective, about *form*. But there is nothing natural or necessary about narrative form; it is itself an invention. And one might, in fact, looking backward, see the list as a premonition of literary structure, as well—as narration manqué: it is only the connectives that remain to be, and later would be, supplied.

Is it enough to say, then, of Jabès's contrary view of character in the Jew and in language that it is simply mistaken? The matter seems more one of inequity than of error, but an inequity that turns easily into error. Jabès, himself a Jew in exile, sees all Jews as exiles. (Forced in adult life to find a new homeland, he would choose France, not the State of Israel; he could imagine no resolution in Israel, since exile for him was ontological not geographical. Would this choice also reflect the alien *language* of Israel? Thus, alien beyond the already alien. . . .) And even then, the language *he* uses—in his own terms, necessarily a stepmother tongue—becomes chancy, problematic, also in exile, never at home with the norms of representation or with an affirmation of the present: writing, following life itself, turns into questioning. The plea cannot be made here that we owe Jabès, as we do other writers and artists, the "benefit of clergy"—the license of poetry and art to imagine his own worlds and to be tested only by his own premises, by the quality of his individual invitation to suspend disbelief. There *cannot* be too "literal" a reading of Jabès; for, in proposing to write-the-Holocaust, he has himself agreed—*stipulated*—that no distinction should be made between facts and literary facts, between facts and fiction. Moral discourse—and it is this character that he would realize in his writing—has but one face. Thus, unlike aesthetic discourse, it has no disguise by means of which it can conceal itself.

We might say, then, that we learn from *The Book of Questions* more about Jabès than we do about the Jew, more about Jabès's life as a Jew than about the Jew's life as Jew. And this brings us back, a long way round, to the problem of the writer in the aftermath of the Holocaust. The author for whom memory forces attentiveness, it turns out, can not assume the existence of the Holocaust in his writing; nor can he, with the history of domestication that has shaped the instrument of writing, simply write *about* the Holocaust. He may perhaps, as we have found the attempt in Jabès, write-the-Holocaust—but that possibility makes extraordinary demands on the writer: in serving as medium, calling his subject to speak for itself, the author must himself be willing to be measured by that subject. And it is there, as the Holocaust turns out for Jabès not to be one event, or set of events, but a universal history— universal history of notable disproportions—that the Holocaust *fails* to write itself, the responsibility for that failure falling on Jabès, if only as scribe.

Jabès, in a way that few writers of "imagined literature" have dared, takes as a subject for literature the life and consciousness of the Jew. He thus ventures much more than the many recent writers for whom the Jew serves only to provide an idiom or dialect (the *parole*), with life itself and its universal moments—loves, partings, sorrows, pleasures— supplying the *langue*. This boldness represents an unusual will for literary particularity: it ought to remain a challenge for writers and writing, in whatever direction they turn, whatever they choose to write about or to write. But it does not by itself settle the question of other, even much lesser particularities. One objection to the very possibility of writing about the Holocaust is that, where the facts speak for themselves, anything a writer might then add by artifice or literary figuration is likely to be a conceit, an obtrusion, a diminution. It would be difficult to deny, moreover—within this thesis or independent of it—that the Holocaust is not something to be dissolved in generalization, not to be woven in its one text through many others. But this, in the end, is just what Jabès does—and the fact that he would act here in the name of principle, honoring the convergence of moral justice and literary means, does not by itself redeem his view of the Holocaust or make it more than a piece of the more general pattern of holocaust. Moreover, because the larger particularity, the general pattern presented as a model of Jewish history, is mistaken, the lesser one—the Holocaust itself—also comes to be misrepresented: imaginatively and consistently, but nonetheless, misrepresented. Thus, Jabès is right: the history of the Jew and the life of language *are* closely linked. But Jabès is wrong— for to see either the one or the other as symbolized or epitomized in the Holocaust would be to fail all three: Jew, language, Holocaust.

Notes

1 · Edmond Jabès, *The Book of Questions,* trans. R. Waldorp (Middletown: Wesleyan University Press, 1976). All further references to this work will be noted in the text.

2 · Jacques Derrida, "Edmond Jabès and the Question of the Book," in *Writing and Difference,* trans. Alan Bass (Chicago: University of Chicago Press, 1978), p. 65.

17 · Leslie Epstein

Writing about the Holocaust

*I*n a review I wrote more than ten years ago, a review of books by Terrence Des Pres and Lawrence Langer, I said the following: "I have come, finally and reluctantly, to the conclusion that almost any honest eye-witness testimony of the Holocaust is more moving and more successful at creating a sense of what it must have been like in the ghettos and the camps than *almost* any fictional account of the same events." This was not a very smart remark for one engaged in writing a Holocaust novel of his own: indeed, that stick of a sentence was used to bang me over the head more than once after the book in question actually appeared. Perhaps this is the time for me to say that the mandate of our discussions—to wit, to examine the difficulties we face when writing about the Holocaust— applies to me only obliquely, since researching and writing *King of the Jews* proved to be remarkably problem-free, and my troubles indeed began only after the book was published. Hence, what I want to think about here are the real issues raised by the sentence just quoted.

In 1976 I followed that remark, first, by immediately adding, "I am not sure why this should be so" and, then, by lamely concluding, "More time, it seems, will have to pass before we are free enough to imagine the facts." Well, a little more time has passed—enough perhaps for me to offer a different thesis: not that fiction, or the imaginative rendering of the Holocaust, flourishes or has even revived, but that, lest those who destroyed European Jewry remain in a crucial sense victorious, it *must* flourish.

I have argued in another forum that the war against the Jews was in some sense a war against certain qualities of the Jewish imagination, and to make my case here I must repeat a bit of what I said there. The books the Germans burned, the paintings they mocked in their Exhibition of Degenerate Art, the music banned from the concert halls, even the humorous sketches they removed from the radio, were in the main the work of Jews or representative of what they called the "destructive Jewish spirit." We all know the culture of "Blood and *Kitsch*" with which they filled the void: the aesthetics of violence and the exaltation of joy; the frisson of murder, together with the idolization of family life, the folk, the state, the leader; the inevitable joining of the saccharine and the grotesque, the most modern technology with the most primitive rituals and pagan rhythms.

Behind this aesthetic lies the repudiation of the idea that all men are connected each to each, the denial of the symbolic and metaphoric power of words, and the pathological dissociation of image from import, act from consequence. Thus the famous example of Mussolini's son, leaning from his aircraft and watching the bombs burst below him, "come fiori." Everywhere, always, violence, war, destructiveness, death itself, is turned into something beautiful. If to some degree civilization began when a man settled for screaming at his enemy instead of stoning him to death, then the task for the Third Reich was to turn words back into rocks; that is to say, to drain them of their imagistic and metaphoric properties. This was most nearly accomplished by the Horst Wessel song, in which the language of Jewish blood spurting under the knife was all too often, all too soon, followed by actual Jewish blood spilled on the streets. George Steiner and Hannah Arendt have noted that Auschwitz is in some manner the literal replication on earth of what Western man had banished to, and nourished in, the underground, that is, the deep, unconscious sources of the imagination. because many, perhaps most, in our century seem to have lost the faculty of belief, and with it the ability to symbolize and sublimate, their chief recourse has been to realize metaphors as fact—in this instance, to turn the images of sulfur and flame and tortured human masses into actual stone, concrete ovens and palpable bone and flesh.

I have suggested that the Jews, who after all did not cling to a vision of hell or tortured afterlife, were consigned to it precisely because they took the greatest imaginative leap of all, that of comprehending, out of nothingness, a burning bush, an empty whirlwind, the "I am that I am." In an age when that belief was no longer tenable, when the supreme fiction, *which is that we matter,* became a rebuke to the counter-vailing belief, *which was that everything is possible,* then the extermination of the Jews, who in their finite minds conceived of the infinite, becomes an attack on the imagination itself.

We return to our original question: why did works of the imagination, and specifically works of fiction, the novel, seem in the generation following the Holocaust so much less successful in comprehending it than the plain words of those who had lived through the events them-selves. First, we are bound to point out that such a situation is not so remarkable. Wordsworth said that poetry, and by extension all work of the imagination, is emotion recollected in tranquillity. Tolstoy did not write *War and Peace* until all those who participated in the Napoleonic Wars were dead. It should not surprise us if it takes even longer to regain anything resembling tranquillity after the Holocaust—indeed, it is astonishing to contemplate the idea of tranquillity at all. Moreover, good books, much less a novel by Tolstoy, are always rare. We should be grateful for those—a Rachmil Briks, a Wiesel, a Borowski, an Ap-pelfeld—who did emerge from the maelstrom with the power of mem-ory intact, even as we must wonder how many artists of the very first rank might have written about the Holocaust had they not perished in it—or, like Mandelstam and Babel, within the crushing coils of another totalitarian state.

Still, there seemed to be something about the Holocaust, the degree of suffering it caused, its meaning, its implications, that threatened to numb the imagination, not only for a single generation but for all time. "No poetry after Auschwitz" was Adorno's slogan. And, seen from a number of angles, it made a certain sense. Language, as George Steiner argued, particularly the German language, had been corrupted, perhaps irreparably. Moreover, the very act of writing, the exercise of the will of the poet, the shape and form of his poem, implied a kind of meaning, and gave a degree of pleasure, that tended to mitigate if not contradict the very horror, the chaos, that he wished to depict. What other solution, then, but silence?

But what irony in this call! For this numbness, muteness, oblivion not only seemed to confirm the destruction of the imagination, but mirrored the most enduring quality of the fascist aesthetic, the dissociated sensibility, a disease that persisted long after the war itself was done and whose symptoms manifested themselves as amnesia, as a fog of forgetfulness that seemed to engulf an entire population, so that millions might claim with something like sincerity that they had no idea of what was going on.

Moreover, there were, and are, other demands made on the Jewish sensibility and upon Jewish writers who are essentially hostile to the practice of fiction—namely, those of history and religion. The goal (altogether illusory) of history is, of course, the determination of facts. Imagination, the reordering of experience, the emphasis upon emotion, the recombining and splitting and turning upside down and inside out of events, so that—to use examples from my own work—a river from Warsaw should run through Lodz, that horses which froze in Finland should have their manes crystallized in Poland, and that babies whose birth was outlawed in Vilna should nonetheless howl in the ghetto of the Balut: all this of course is anathema to the historian. So, too, is the exercise of humor and irony and personality and point of view, as well as fits of anger, disgust, giving way to despair, to manic laughter, or to an overarching sense of wryness—even though, oddly, every single one of these qualities shines through the work of those historians, the archivists of Lodz, the Ringelblum group in Warsaw, who had to work in secret and in danger and on the spot.

Because the catastrophes of this century are no less momentous than the Exodus or the destruction of the Temple, there can be little doubt that, over time, or perhaps I should say, given time, they will find their way into the liturgy. But these accounts, whether in the form of prayers or ceremonies or simple lamentations, will be emblematic, mythical, and, insofar as they shape the identity of the Jewish people, will serve also to sever that people from all others and from the flow of time itself. They will bear the same relation to history that the statue of the idealized soldiers at the Vietnam Monument bears to the plain stone slab that carries the names of the 50,000 dead—or, for that matter, that the image of the flag raisers at Iwo Jima bears to the actual men in the famous photograph, or that the Tomb of the Unknown Soldier bears to the remains, the embodiment of history's failure, buried below.

What these disciplines, hostile both to fiction and to each other, cannot do is what Holocaust fiction has by and large failed at, as well: to show what life in the ghettos and camps was really like—that is, reproducing, re-creating, restoring to life, in such a way that the reader feels a sense of connectedness, not dispassion and distance, least of all horror and repugnance, to the events and the characters that, Lazarus-like, are called back from the dead. Indeed, if I might anticipate my final argument, I would go so far as to say that while the historians and rabbis surely seek, and often find, meaning and understanding, they cannot instill the peculiar sense of responsibility that the novelist can— the sort of responsibility for creation that might alone (and here you must forgive me for a vision of pie in the sky) bring about the kind of political change that would make another Holocaust less certain, more unlikely.

But, many among you might rightly ask, have there not been plenty of novels, and some very good ones, too, about the Holocaust all along? Well, yes (I have named some authors and will leave it for each of you to recall others, though I want to mention Schwartz-Bart myself)—and no. What concerns me is the manifest inability, both in the popular imagination and in the work of serious artists, to endure even minimal amounts of the reality of the Holocaust. I do not mean so much the depiction of stage villains and noble heroes, of sadistic torturers and suffering children, so much as the creation of an entirely separate universe, unique, in which the world as we know it is hardly recognizable and literature as we have always experienced it can have nothing to say. This discrete and hermetic world is what Larry Langer (in *The Holocaust and the Literary Imagination*, the same book I reviewed ten years ago) calls "l'univers concentrationnaire." The rationale for such work, of course, is that the Holocaust was itself unique, outside of history—indeed, the end of history—and foreign not only to everyday life, but to the normal functioning of the human psyche, as depicted by the realistic novel. Langer's book is important precisely because it is a powerful manifesto, a call for an art equal to a world in which agony and suffering were the only norm, one that, in his words, can "evoke the atmosphere of monstrous fantasy" and "reconstitute reality in shapes and images that reflect a fundamental distortion in human nature."[1]

Obviously such a doctrine runs directly contrary to what I said was the novelist's deepest task: to create a bond, a sense of connectedness between the reader and every aspect of the world that has been salvaged through imagination. In Langer's words, the literature of the Holocaust "is not the transfiguration of empirical reality . . . but its disfiguration, the conscious and deliberate alienation of the reader's sensibilities from the world of the usual and familiar, with an accompanying infiltration into the work of the grotesque, the senseless, and the unimaginable" (pp. 2–3). What this vision of the Holocaust has led to is the sort of novel in which people hop from graves, dwarfs beat tin drums, giants carry alter egos on their backs, rats gnaw on corpses, and so forth and so on. The example Langer cites most approvingly is from *The Painted Bird* and reads in part:

> The massive body of the carpenter was only partly visible. His face and half of his arms were lost under the surface of the sea of rats, and wave after wave of rats were scrambling over his belly and legs. . . . The animals now fought for access to the body—panting, twitching their tails, their teeth gleaming under their half-open snouts, their eyes reflecting the daylight as if they were the beads of a rosary. . . . Suddenly the shifting sea of rats parted and slowly, unhurrying, with the stroke of a swimmer, a bony hand with bony spreading-eagled fingers rose, followed by the man's entire arm. . . . In between the ribs, under the armpits, and in the place where the belly was, gaunt rodents fiercely struggled for the remaining scraps of dangling muscle and intestine. Mad with greed, they tore from one another scraps of clothing, skin, and formless chunks of the trunk [pp. 186–7].

I thought, when first reading Kosinsky, and upon reviewing the excerpt here, that this kind of writing in no way brought us closer to what happened to Jewish men and women and children, but was a kind of *grand guignol*, a horror show, meant to divert us from what the actual atrocity—most unbearable in its monotony, its regularity, its unobtrusiveness—was like. I now have two related and more serious criticisms. First: what Professor Langer and other critics, what the artists themselves, fail to see, the bitter and ironic joke they fail to get, is how this literature reflects, all unknowingly, in sheer innocence, the culture of the oppressor. For what else is this mixture of rats gnawing the flesh from living victims and the sentimental descriptions of the suffering victims—this "atmosphere of monstrous fantasy," on the one hand, commingled with a kind of sacred awe, on the other—than a form of the very "Blood and *Kitsch*" that so marked the culture of the Third Reich?

Second, and worst of all: this sort of fiction, instead of increasing our capacity to suffer and to bear the unbearable, diminishes our ability to see and to feel and to think. For, just as the Germans painted the Jews as less than human, as animals, indeed as microbes, so here the Germans are made into larger-than-life, giant, superhuman monsters. What is being denied is the one crucial fact: that those who suffered, and those who inflicted suffering, were men, and that the Holocaust did not occur in a fantasyland, or outside of history, or in a "univers concentrationnaire," but in the only world we can hope to know, the only one we can experience and be responsible for—our own.

And that, I suspect, is what accounts for the power of the eyewitnesses. They do not, perhaps because they cannot, deny the world from which they came and their connectedness to it. What is most remarkable in their testimony is the utter absence of any of the posturing, the hysteria, the fevered fantasies of so much Holocaust fiction. Their suffering has, as in the Aeschylean formula, brought knowledge, and the secret they possess is this—that just as the Holocaust did not take place in a special universe, so did it not "reflect a fundamental distortion in human nature" but, in fact, was both inflicted and borne by those who were *all too human*. The best account of that steady accrual of insight, and of humanity, too, by the witnesses is of course Terrence Des Pres's book, *The Survivor*. "Under dehumanizing pressure," he writes, struggling himself to explain the extraordinary power of their testimony, "men and women tend to preserve themselves in ways recognizably human."[2]

Seeking an example of such testimony in my original review, I chose, seemingly at random, without really knowing why, this simple sentence by Mary Berg, as she described a rickshaw driver beaten into the Warsaw snow: "The blood was so horribly red the sight of it completely shattered me." I can say more now. There is the intense, even poetic, contrast of the blood and snow, the red, the white, the colors of the Polish flag. There is the full humanity of her ability—in a numbed world, in which corpses were daily swept off the street, or *not* swept off the street—to be shocked, to be shattered. And, of course, there is the implied bond of vulnerability, of humanness, created by the element that flows through the veins of reader, writer, the rickshaw driver, and of those whom the driver had pulled through the ghetto streets, and finally even of those who beat him, warm, still living, into the cold snow. I now feel able to answer half of my original question. The survivors, by their knowledge, by remaining, as Des Pres says, "steady in their humanness," that is to say, by their unified and unifying sensibility, are more effective than the novelists because *they have become nothing less than the novelists themselves*.

But if such speculations help explain the power of the survivors' testimony, nothing I have said here fully accounts for the failure of the imaginative artist. Let me add two final points. First, if it is true that suffering brings knowledge, it is no less the case that knowledge brings suffering. Think of the case of Tadeusz Borowski's collection of stories—perhaps the finest imaginative rendering of the Holocaust in literature—*This Way for the Gas, Ladies and Gentlemen*. What distinguishes it, apart from any number of traditional literary values, is its ability to accept without flinching what is commonplace in horror, its remarkable tone of wry humor and, above all, the stance, at once empathetically connected to the camp inmates and ironically detached from them, a point of view uncannily appropriate for one who was in life, as well as in fiction, a "Kapo." We cannot say for sure why Borowski committed suicide so shortly after he wrote his account, but the way in which he did, with his head in an oven, might well indicate that the burden of responsibility—actual and imaginative—might have proved more than he, or the increasingly inhumane society of which he once again, willy-nilly, found himself an official, could bear.

That the artists' society, his culture, the world of his readers, might be incapable of assimilating his vision, or indeed might be actively hostile to it, is perhaps the most decisive of all the factors I have been discussing. Readers in some sense get the books they deserve, or desire. If they want good ones (an *Age of Wonders*, by Aharon Appelfeld, for example), they will have to be as brave, almost, as the authors— brave enough to accept, as in Appelfeld's case, the clear demonstration that the worst that evil can do is to make its victims resemble the victimizers. That takes not only courage but imagination, a special grace, a psychic confidence, what Coleridge called a suspension of disbelief—that is, of one's preconceived notions, prejudices, even one's worldliness; a suspension, in brief, of that power of repression which allows the reader to keep his own unconscious unavailable to himself, disconnected from the vision of the author, and permits him to say, like a "Good German" or an indifferent Pole: *none of that has anything to do with me.*

Alas! For the first generation after the Holocaust, just the opposite has happened. Instead of becoming, as the survivors became, artists themselves, the readers, the bystanders, have suffered a failure of nerve. They, and the authors of all too much Holocaust fiction, have engaged in what amounts to a conspiracy of denial. None of this would matter, perhaps, if our very idea of what the Holocaust was did not depend upon what artists make of it, and if the failure of imagination did not entail what I have called a crucial failure of responsibility. That failure, for example, is *precisely* what Hannah Arendt meant by the "banality" of evil—a shallowness, a thoughtlessness, an inability to realize what one is doing, a remoteness from reality and, above all, a denial of one's connectedness to others. The outrage, the frenzy, the panic even, that greeted Arendt's thesis when applied to Adolf Eichmann indicates the depth of our need to think of that bureaucrat as different from ourselves, to respond to him, indeed, as a typical character in Holocaust fiction—a beast, a pervert, a monster. The *New York Times Magazine* even published an article that demonstrated from Eichmann's doodlings, notably the suspect way the chimneys on his houses leaned this way or that, that he suffered clinically from that famous "fundamental distortion of human nature." It is almost as if the glass booth erected around him at his trial was there not to protect him from our wrath, but us from the contagion of his disease, his demonic power.

I remember how surprised I was to read in Raul Hilberg how the Nazis most probably did *not* manufacture soap from human fat. Those brown bars, some of which are actually in museums, must have been brought into existence by a universally felt need: first, for an explanation, for surely the rendering of humans for soap and the flaying of their skin for lamp shades revealed to perfection the barbarians' contempt for, and parody of, their own civilization—with its love of cleanliness and quest for technological perfection, for light; and, second, for that horror and the grotesquerie which permits us to distance ourselves from what is all too common—indeed, in this century even commonplace—about the fate of the Jews.

I want to conclude by reminding you of what I said at the beginning: how crucial it is that this distance, this gap, be closed if that fate, or something worse, is not to be repeated. My thesis all along has been that the sense of responsibility and connectedness can be achieved only by the creative artist—and by creative readers, as well. Only those who have the imagination to recognize what they share with the force of evil—what Arendt called "the shame of being human . . . the inescapable guilt of the human race"—can fight fearlessly against it. And only this fight, this fearlessness, can give meaning to the suffering of the Jewish people and, in that sense, bring our millions of dead back to life.

Notes

1 · Lawrence Langer, *The Holocaust and the Literary Imagination* (New Haven: Yale University Press, 1975), p. 30. All further references to this work will be noted in the text.
2 · Terrence Des Pres, *The Survivor: Anatomy of Life in the Death Camps* (New York: Oxford University Press, 1976), p. 6.

Roundtable Discussion

Raul Hilberg
Cynthia Ozick
Aharon Appelfeld
Saul Friedländer

Raul Hilberg

I believe you will receive four different crystallizations in this conference. It goes without saying that we not only say different things, we
listen to different things, and I'm one of you in that respect, having
listened much more, fortunately, than I spoke. One of the perennial
questions in my mind surfaced in the very nature of the structure of this
conference, an old problem to many of you—you might call it a fact-
fiction dichotomy or the business of footnote writers, social scientists on
the one hand, and those who produce the imaginative literature on the
other.

There is, to be sure, a certain arrogance that is sometimes assumed
by the social scientists. It consists of the supposition, which is not even
a matter for debate among historians or political scientists, that quite
naturally the novelists depend upon us for the facts. How could they
write anything if we had not done the research? But as I listened to
various statements I heard a dictum to the effect that when all is said
and done, historiography itself is a kind of fiction, it is a kind of
representation or model, whatever you wish to call it. I was reminded of
what Heinrich Heine once said, that to write prose one should first learn
how to write poetry. And if I might extend this advice, it would seem
that to write about the Holocaust one should perhaps first, even if one
happens to be a historian or a footnote writer, know how to write a story.
I listened with close attention to my colleague Saul Friedländer this
morning, who pointed to something that I was thinking all along: the
story, and how very difficult it is to write this story simply, intelligibly—
how to write about the destruction of the Jews.

The conference has focused on the victims. It came through in every
talk, or most of them. It is as if the history of the Holocaust were the

273

history of its victims, save, again, for Saul Friedländer's reminder that it is also and very significantly German history.

There was for a long time a quarrel, one in which I was involved to some extent, whether one ought to write this history from the standpoint of how the destruction was carried out by the perpetrator or how it happened to the victims. And I chose the perpetrator as the actor, the victim as the reactor. But today at this conference it became clear to me, as never before, that even when one writes as I did about the perpetrators, one does so with an impetus that comes from the victims. For the perpetrator has only very seldom voluntarily described his perpetration.

Saul Friedländer also said something very briefly at the end of his paper to which one or two questioners called attention, something about a central riddle or mystery or enigma. It goes by an old name: Why? Why? I sometimes, though never answering that question myself, ask it, especially of Germans—I ask the Germans, what do you think? And, of course, I never get an answer at all, It seems as though here is an entire nation that is utterly incapable, despite the fact that there are still eighty million Germans on this earth, of explaining its own actions.

If I may offer a variation on Friedrich Nietzsche, this is a problem beyond rationality and irrationality; it is useless to ask what they got out of it. It's useless even to ask what impelled them. I heard the word this past month from one very articulate German, "Ein Rausch," something that just took hold. It's almost untranslatable. I believe very strongly that the attack upon the Soviet Union, and the attack upon Jewry which occurred simultanously, sprang from that same source beyond rationality, for its own sake, for the experience of it, for the making of this history.

Now, as we look at this event which appears in history and yet apart from it, disturbing so many historians, we quite naturally are exposed to multiple demands, but these are not new. How well I recall, having listened to a lecture as an undergraduate student home from the wars in 1947, when the most eminent specialist on the subject of bureaucratic history in Europe remarked, oh, just as an aside, an obiter dictum, that the atrocities committed in the Napoleonic wars were greater than those of World War II. And how well I recall a visitor to Columbia University two years later who said, well, five million Jews were killed and five million Germans, that's the equation, now let's bury it. When I began, against all advice save that of one personal friend, to embark upon this project of mine, I was, of course, engaged in an active protest. To be told year after year, well, that's your funeral, you're ending your career, you'll never publish this thing—is not what I would call the best environment in which to pursue such work. But I'm reminded that today there is on German soil a man like Uwe Adam who wrote a path-breaking book, needless to say not translated into English and not much read in Germany, who has no university position; or Hans-Heinrich Wilhelm, the co-author with Helmut Krausnick of an important book on the Einsatzgruppen, who has no university position, or Götz Aly, another young German who has written a book about identification, census-taking and the like, who has no academic position. I realize there are a few protesters like me who walk the streets of Germany today.

Of course, there are nowadays, precisely because the Holocaust has surfaced as a center of attention, those who demand that other subjects be recognized or brought into the context or umbrella of this term, this ill-defined, cloudy term, Holocaust. There are people who say the Holocaust was visited on a large number of groups. That's counter-revolution of sorts. There are other protests, you heard about them also this morning from Saul Friedländer—on the part of German historians who insist that other countries were responsible for similar deeds.

I recall one day when I was searching for railroad data in an archive in Nuremberg located in a toy museum over there—a strange place for an archive. I had asked for some telltale documentation, about special trains for civilian traffic with such localities as Oppeln or Berlin in mind, and the archivist made a long-distance call and said he had an American professor here who wanted to do some research on civilian traffic during the war. He did not mention Oppeln or Berlin. I said to myself, well, he broke a rule so that I could see the material where otherwise permission would probably have been refused. Last month I returned to the archive since I happened to have been in Nuremberg. I said, "Mr. Illenseer, you know I want to thank you." He said, "Well, you know, there's one small addition about the railways that must yet be written, for they also carried millions of Germans, under bombs, from the eastern regions of the German Reich so that they would escape from the Bolshevik yoke, and I, as a child, was one of those people on one of those trains."

I talked to Jörg Friedrich, a German writer, of the protest generation of postwar Germany, who calls himself by an untranslatable phrase, "Nestbeschmutzer"—one who is willing to dirty his own nest. And one day he said after a long evening: "Do you realize how many Germans died of gas asphyxiation in World War II?" I said, "Well now, let me see, yes I know because I've got the statistics of the euthanasia program and we know there were 80,000 of these mental patients who were killed by the end of August 1941—we've got that statistic." "Oh no," he said, "that's not what I meant." "Oh? Did I miss something?" "Oh yes," he said, "you did. You see, when the bombing of Germany took place in 1943, 1944, 1945, a lot of people took refuge in air raid shelters and they would not venture out because they did not want to be killed by debris or be burned, so they died in these shelters, sitting there, asphyxiated."

Thus we see a young man groping for a mythical connection—a fate of Germans which was, curiously, in terms of cause of death, not unlike the fate of the Jews. Of course, all this is to be expected; it is perhaps necessary that we all look at the world from where we stand, from what we've experienced and what we know.

Cynthia Ozick

It goes without saying that I am not a philosopher, political scientist, historian, thinker, or knower of any sort. I write stories—a disqualifying work, a naive and chaotic sort of work, the work of willed chaos. And what I have here are some hasty and scattered notes that developed out of what you might call the "cracks" in the conference. Every conference has these cracks—periods between the scheduled panels through which leak the most remarkable unplanned moments, private conversations of great passion and interest. There have been many of these. As for the panels themselves, they strike me as having been not merely consistently illuminating, but very often on the edge of the extraordinary, and sometimes over the edge *into* the extraordinary. All this has set me wondering about what one could perhaps very coarsely term the "sociology" of this conference, or its anthropology—its emerging culture, so to speak, as it progressed. Pondering this, I have been asking myself what the makeup of such a conference will be two decades from now. What will the conversations in the cracks be like? For one thing, twenty years from now there may be no live firsthand witnesses.

As for *this* conference, the one we are just now concluding, among the Jews present there have been a handful of such witnesses, living witnesses of the depredations; there have been a handful of survivors' children; there have been children and grandchildren of the immigrants of the steerage generation; and the last group, those immigrants' children and grandchildren, have themselves inherited an understanding of what it is to live in a place where there is fear of your surroundings, fear of a populace to whom you are alien, fear of an always-hostile and dangerous environment. No Jew present is untouched by this knowledge, this memory, this sorrowful heritage of victimization, however attenuated in our constitutionally wise and pleasant land.

The Gentile participants in this conference have seemed to me, each

277

278 • Hilberg, Ozick, Appelfeld, and Friedländer

and every one, to be unique and out of the ordinary. And, in fact, I have the impression that everyone who contributed here is in some way, by virtue of having been present, out of the ordinary. So if a "sociology" of our conference should begin to be adumbrated, I believe it will be an unusual one: a moral sociology, if we dare call it that.

And this brings me to an observation—an observation, not a position—that is extremely tentative, nonabsolute, possibly naive; not digested, perhaps indigestible. It seems to me that the moral sociology—the moral fragrance, the moral aura—of this conference has again and again leaned toward, pressed toward, spots of goodness in the cruelty. These spots of goodness may be defined as a kind of healing, or mending, or perhaps even a struggle toward redemption. There has been an urge, an urgency, in the direction of redemption. Someone here turned up the phrase "redeeming meaning," and it almost begins to take hold. Those aspiring consolation-words have sought to apply themselves to the destruction of the Jews. Is there a "redeeming meaning" in the murder of the six million? For me, the Holocaust means one thing and one thing only: the destruction of one-third of the world's Jewish population. I do not see a "redeeming meaning" in a catastrophe of such unholy magnitude.

Of course, we do not want to conclude our enterprise with an absence of meaning, without at least a touch of the veil of redemption. We cannot endure it; our moral sense, the yearning for healing, for mending, does not allow us to endure it. We want to escape from the idea of closure, of an absolute dead end. We want to escape from the idea of having to quit in the bottomless muck of annihilation, with nothing else on the horizon. Let us get some good out of this, we tell ourselves, let us look for spots of goodness on the rump of evil.

Regretfully, sorrowfully, I find this view unacceptable. I find I cannot assimilate it. I find that it begins from the premises of our current world, our safe and civilized world, the world of universities and conferences, for instance. The contributors to this book live at the moment in free countries, in the kind of normality that permits us to reflect on the moral life and to take moral positions. But this premise of a moral aura—this search for spots of goodness, for redemptive meaning— seems to me to be a retroactive impulse, an anachronism. It suits what *we* are, we in the safety and decency of our current lives; it does not suit the events themselves, which are radically different from what we are.

We know what we are; we are those strivers who desire to live a moral life, desiring it so penetratingly that we will try to wrest such a vision out of the past, even retroactively.

But—regretfully, sorrowfully—it seems to me that no promise, no use, no restitution and no redemption can come out of the suffering and destruction of one-third of the Jewish people. And I ask: why is it we have been trying so passionately to make this happen, to bring a mite of good out of atrocity and murder? Is it because we are inherently good citizens? I think the answer is yes. We *are* good citizens. But there is something else, and it applies to all of us equally, Christians and Jews. We emerge from a redemptive tradition. For Jews at this season, Passover is about to recur, a very powerful model of redemption. For Christians, the Resurrection is still another powerful model of redemption. Christianity offers redemption of the spirit; Judaism gives us the opening of the Red Sea after the abyss of slavery and darkness, the opening into liberation of the spirit. This is how we have learned to think.

Yet, in thinking about the Holocaust, we have to take into ourselves a different possibility, an alien thesis: one that we have never been taught, one that goes against our moral grain, that seems overwhelmingly indigestible and repugnant. It is that *this* time there was no redemption, the Red Sea did not open, nobody walked through the parting of the waters, the waters remained high and cold and deadly and closed. Nor did the tomb of salvation open to release the spirit of redemption; the tomb of salvation remained shut and sealed. Closure. The sealed and gaseous tomb, into which the crystals of Zyklon B were poured by an ordinary hand with five fingers, a hand like yours or mine. This time, those very powerful models that are the controlling metaphors of our civilization will not be made to work.

They will not be made to work, except through some kind of opacity or mystification. I am on the side that opposes mystification. I do not understand the claim for mystification. Here is an event that had a habitation and a name; and although it leaves us, like Lear, unaccommodated, and although, like Lear, it leaves us howling on the heath, all the same we know that it *does* have a habitation and a name. We know what was done. We know where it was done. We know to whom it was done. We know by whom it was done. What we do not know—as Raul Hilberg remarked—is why it was done. Yet I am not persuaded that even the *why* of it is opaque. Don't we know what Wordsworth meant by man's inhumanity to man? Don't we know what nihilism is? Haven't we ourselves witnessed the joy of tearing down and breaking up and blotting out? Don't we know all those theories of aesthetics that support nihilism, and that are evident in our own society today more than ever, through, for instance, elitist literary analysis? You might say that Nazism was a "medical" idea: eliminate the evil bacterium, the bacillus, the microbe, the disease-bearing insect. But, even more persuasively, you might conclude that Nazism was an *aesthetic* idea: Hitler was an artist, after all, and Goebbels a novelist and playwright. Let us have a beautiful and harmonious society, said the aesthetics of Nazism; let us get rid of this ugly spot, the Jew, the smear on the surface of our glorious dream. Do we not know the meaning of aesthetic gratification?

Another way of reflecting on the *why* is to note that the Jews, vis-à-vis nihilism, stand for No: not the No of nihilism, but the No against nihilism, the No that presses for restraint. The ornamental elegance of the King James Version gives us the Ten Commandments with rather a baroque thrill to them—all those Thou Shalt Not's. But if you listen to the Commandments in Hebrew, you will hear a no-nonsense abruptness, a rapidity and a terseness. They begin with *Lo*, the Hebrew word for No. *Lo tignov*, Do not steal. *Punkt*. The Torah the Jews carry stands for No, for all the things we ordinary mortals want to do and take glee in doing. The Jews stand for the hard demands of monotheism— nobody wants monotheism. It is hard stuff—Jews do not want it either. And Jews, who are the genuine human article like everyone else, do not want restraint; the claims of Torah are as hard for Jews as they are for everyone. Harder. Because of the burden of being the people that carries monotheism into the world, monotheism with its uncompromising obligations to mercy, monotheism with its invention of conscience.

What we have been trying to do in this conference, I think, is to bring a moral umbra to that which cannot sustain or maintain or contain a moral umbra.

It was frightening to hear Saul Friedländer's summary of current historical opinion in Germany. It was more than frightening; it was astounding, it was fever-arousing. He gave us an account of intellectual nihilism; he told us the story of the negation of all normal valuation. Moral, immoral, amoral—all wiped away. These historians he described should suggest to us that we *cannot* pry redemption out of events that are in their nature not amenable to redemption. Such events can produce only their own kind. They are generative seeds that will bear fruit solely as copies of themselves, ideationally if not in action. To copy is the fundamental meaning of reproduction. Turning to Lear again: *nothing will come of nothing.* Nihilism will give birth to nihilism. The only thing that the Holocaust can give birth to is further images of itself. "Never again" is not the message we get from the Holocaust. The message we get is that the Holocaust will replicate itself. Once the restraints are down, the next time becomes easier; the next time will have a precedent and a model. What was acceptable once will be acceptable again. "Never again" is not what humanity learns from the destruction of the Jews. The PLO knows that! Replication is what the Holocaust teaches. This so-called revisionism that we have heard about—it is not revisionism in the usual sense, of course; it is simple anti-Semitism—is replication of the seed. And yet the amazement of it! We think of the imagination as a *making* force, as that which puts something in place of nothing. The "revisionists" employ imagination to put nothing in place of something. Who would have dreamed that a new sort of inventive cleverness would arise with the power to undo history? Who would have dreamed that somebody would come and say it never happened? The Swiftian fancifulness of it—that those who delight in its having happened are the very ones who say it never happened!

I see no spots of goodness.

Still, I commend to you an important essay by the novelist Norma Rosen on the subject of Holocaust metaphor. She calls it "The Second Life of Holocaust Imagery," and it appears in the April 1987 issue of *Midstream.* For a long time we would not allow what seemed like frivolous comparisons—we would protest if we heard an ordinary sub-way rider complain of being jammed into a "freight car." We would recoil from that kind of analogy: it was offensive. But Norma Rosen's point is somewhat different. Every time somebody has a feeling like that, she says, what is created is a moment of commemoration, a moment of memorial. "For a mind engraved with the Holocaust," she writes, "gas is always that gas. Shower means their shower. Ovens are those ovens. . . . Of course this does not always happen. Some days the sky is simply blue and we do not wonder how a blue sky looked to those on their way to the crematoria" (p. 58). Hers is not an argument for redemptive meaning, but rather for the universalizing sanctification of memory. Although my response to it still remains tentative and undecided, I think Norma Rosen's essay will finally convert me to its viewpoint. There *is* an appropriate universal "use," in her special sense, of the language of the Holocaust: as a way of sensitizing and enlarging us toward mercifulness. But her premise is crucial: all of this must take place in "a mind engraved with the Holocaust," in a mind committed to remembering.

My own act of memorial is expressed in the negative and for decades remained common enough. That it is a negative act of memorial is not surprising—what is there about the Holocaust that can be "positive?" It began long ago, in my parents' drugstore, in the 1930s, at the bottom of the Great Depression, when to turn away a customer was a serious loss. My parents would not sell Bayer's aspirin. It was the most popular brand; in those days, the name "Bayer's" had almost become generic, like Kleenex. People would be reluctant to accept a substitute (even though my father explained that the ingredients were identical) and would walk out and go two blocks down the street to the next pharmacy. This would happen more often than not. But my parents preferred to lose money rather than sell Bayer's, because Bayer's was a German firm. Their action was part of a widespread Jewish boycott of Germany when Nazi power was brutally taking hold; it was well before the death camps, of course. Even now, I will not buy so much as a German spoon. I will certainly never go near a Volkswagen, the very name of which is Hitler's own. Primo Levi points out that Topf, the company that obligingly made the crematorium ovens according to Nazi specifications, has (like Volkswagen, like slave-labor Krupp) never bothered to change its name; it remains shameless, apparently. Topf goes on manufacturing ovens, though nowadays, presumably, only for kitchen use.

Now what does it mean—not to be willing to buy a German spoon? What use is it? What does it demonstrate? It has no meaning economically or politically. It has no meaning at all, you might argue; and Germany is an American ally, a member of NATO. Well, it is a private memorial. I will not forget that Krupp and Volkswagen were once covered in Jewish blood, and are not now ashamed of it. If they were ashamed, they would hide or change their names. So, in my own life, I will take care to blot out those names. It is not for the Germans that I will not buy German goods—God knows it doesn't in any way touch *them!* Isn't Germany famous for having the most prosperous economy in Europe? If a Jew in New York refrains from purchasing a German clock, will that hurt the German clock company? A thousand other people will not hesitate to buy those excellent clocks. I do that company no economic harm; but it is not myself doing harm I am thinking of. It is the slaughtered I think of: the victims. Not buying a German spoon is a memorial act for its own sake; it has no power to punish anyone, nor is it meant to. If I avoid buying something marked Made in Germany, I do it for myself: to keep alive the memory of Jews marked Murdered in Germany. It is the way I remember. I remember how my parents deprived themselves of a quarter when a quarter weighed heavily. I remember Father Coughlin, the "radio priest" who preached anti-Semitism during the years my parents would not sell Bayer's aspirin. I remember my very intelligent classmate, H. W., whose parents were German immigrants, and who in 1939 (we were both eleven years old) explained to me that Hitler *"had* to put the Jews in concentration camps," because, she said with a sophistication of language that left me helpless to reply, "they are political prisoners."

Nor will I set foot in Germany or Austria, for the same reasons. And whoever despises me for my act of memorial should examine his or her conscience: why do you despise an act of memorial for the murdered? Why does that anger you? An act of memorial *is* an act of separation. When you approach Yad Vashem, the Holocaust memorial in Jerusalem, the first thing you see is a row of trees honoring the Righteous Gentiles who sheltered Jews from the Nazis. And the second thing you see, when you enter, is a sign that gives a name to the murdered: *kidush hashem*, those who sanctified the Name [of God] by their martyrdom. The word *kidush* is related to *kadosh*, which means "holy"; but it also means "separate," because holiness is what separates itself from the things and places that are unclean, that deny and despoil, that desecrate. In that spirit I want to separate myself from the soil where Jewish blood was spilled in the millions of liters. Why does that anger you? Because it does not let bygones by bygones? But who is it who does not hear, or does not want to hear, the voice of his brother cry out from the ground? Look, Abel is dead, is he not? What can be done about it now? Let bygones by bygones. Choose erasure. Wipe out memory. There are new generations now, on both sides. Let amnesia hobnob with amnesia. (Much, much, much more needs to be said on the subject of Germany and Austria today, but clearly this is not the forum for it.)

Of the idea of separation there is more to be said as well, and this again has to do with the search for a redeeming meaning. I have argued that the event itself is incapable of any hint or aura of redemptiveness— you cannot pull anything good out of the abyss. But the lost lives of the slaughtered and the maimed lives of the survivors are something else. The Holocaust happened *to* its victims. It did not happen *in* them. The victims were not the participants. The event swept over them, but they were separate from it. That is why they are "sanctified"—because they did not perform evil. Even as they were herded into the sealed and gaseous tomb, they were being separated from its meaning. They had clean hands. If it was their lungs into which the gas was poured, it was not *their* hands that did the pouring. Philip Hallie's extraordinary pre- sentation of a whole village that would not implicate itself in evil is a case in point. Not that there were spots of goodness on the rump of evil, but that goodness separated itself from desecration. And if there is one notion we need to understand more than any other, it is this principle of separation. The people for whom the Holocaust "happened" were the people who made it happen. The perpetrators *are* the Holocaust; the victims stand apart. In this distinct sense, I would deny that the Holocaust belongs to the Jews. It belongs to the history and culture of the oppressors; it is theirs. It is German universities and churches that should be holding Holocaust conferences. And no Jew need or ought to be present.

Finally, about writing fiction. In theory, I'm with Theodor Adorno's famous dictum: after Auschwitz, no more poetry. And yet, my writing has touched on the Holocaust again and again. I cannot *not* write about it. It rises up and claims my furies. All the same, I believe that the duty of our generation, so close to the events themselves, is to absorb the data, to learn what happened. I am not in favor of making fiction of the data, or of mythologizing or poeticizing it. If we each had a hundred lifetimes, there would not be enough time to assimilate the documents. I constantly violate this tenet; my brother's blood cries out from the ground, and I am drawn and driven.

Aharon Appelfeld

Saul Friedländer's attempts and efforts for years to understand the drama, the system, of evil are really admirable. But, to create a kind of balance, I want to relate some of the good experiences of my life during the Holocaust.

I came, you see, from an assimilated Jewish home, from a very assimilated Jewish town. A lot of blonde aunts, you know, wonderful, healthy, big, blonde—my uncles were thin, but the aunts were blonde, you know, German, wonderful, beautiful—a bit cold but still very beautiful. And then, suddenly, we were separated; terribly, the color separated us. The blonde aunts with the blonde children remained at home, and the other ones who were not blonde went to the camps. So, we were separated just by color. Middle-class, upper-middle-class Jews, we had been deprived of all Jewish tradition. In my home, for instance, Yiddish was forbidden to be spoken at all. The one holy language was German. And German was, you know, really more than a language for us, more than communication—it was culture, it was religion. And this was the life of middle-class Jewry in my town, Czernowitz, where I was born . . . until suddenly we were pressed into the camps. The first was the labor camp, and there, for the first time, we met the real Jews. A bit primitive, these Jews, but strong Jews, healthy Jews, altogether different from us and our regenerated Jewish-German Jews who were living somewhere on the surface of life. Here we encountered warm Jewish families, strong men, Jews with passion, with faith. Of course, this was only the first stage, the labor camp; then came the other camp, the extermination camp. But this first one was an easy kind of camp. And then to meet these religious people: perhaps my parents had seen them before, but for me it was the first time I had seen the Hebrew letters, the Torah, the attitude to the book, the affinity between these people and Jewish books. It was the first time that I heard a prayer. I had never in my life heard a prayer, never attended a synagogue. So, this was, you know, a wonderful meeting. Suddenly, in this hell, there were people who were praying, there were people who were studying, there were people who had belief. The sentiment I have for Jewish books and for Jewish learning . . . it came through these people whom I met in the camp.

Then, of course, we met other kinds of Jews, as well—for example, the new kind of Yiddish-speaking Jews who had lived all around Czernowitz, but whom we had never been allowed to meet or to talk with before. The language was a new melody. And then there were the Jewish Communists, believers of a different sort. They insisted on being called Communists, not Jews, but with all the Jewish gestures, you know, arguing, proving, disproving. So there was, from one side, the prayers; from the other side, arguments about capitalism—Soviet politics—all the secrets of Soviet politics. And then, of course, also a small group of Zionists. And here were the first Hebrew words I heard; I picked up from them probably five or six Hebrew words. They were dreamers, nonreligious people, but very devoted, dreaming all the time about Israel.

Then there was also another group, a very interesting group, the Jewish thieves; you see, we had that, too . . . Jewish thieves. I had not even imagined that these thieves existed, but there they were. So, this was my entrance, strange to say, the door by which I entered Judaism. And all these people became relatives of mine. They became my aunts and they became my sisters, my brothers. And if I think now about Jewish life or the Jewish people as a whole, I think about these people.

Saul Friedländer

I must admit that I do not much believe in closing statements; it seems to me that, at this stage, discussion would be more helpful. So, just a word or two. I have been thinking about the question of what this conference is actually about. I have read the program, of course; I have participated in the discussions, I know what questions have been asked . . . but, still, what did we want to say? And possibly the answer that we have been looking for has to do with how one can give meaning to the sentence that Raul Hilberg quoted in his opening lecture, from a daily report filed at Mariupol, October 29, 1941: "8,000 Jews were executed by the Security Service." In its terseness, this is an historical statement that defies fiction. And our whole effort, in a way, has been to grapple with that sentence. Can the historian build a structure around this . . . "8,000 Jews were executed by the Security Service"? A simple message from one administrator to the other? Can the poet do anything with this? Can the novelist?

I think that we return constantly to this issue, all the time looking for coherence, for closure, and even for a redemptive sense on the side of the victims. During this exchange, however, I have been very impressed by what Cynthia Ozick said about this; I have thought along similar lines myself for many years. There is no redemptive message in this at all. It is clear that others try now to give coherence, to shift the images of what occurred, and certainly historians such as Raul Hilberg and myself and many others have to deal with this in our professional work. But, even beyond that, to look for a meaning or a message on a more general level has failed whenever it has been attempted. I think we should try to face the fact that we have to live with this without following our natural tendency to find meaning.

You may know that in Israel an attempt was made officially to establish such meaning. When the survivors arrived and when the authorities took in what had happened in Europe, they attempted to give significance to the events by creating an official mythology. So the *Yom HaShoah Ve-Hagevurah* (Day of the Holocaust and Heroism) was not only established but was given a *payrush* (explanation), which one can read very easily as a text. The day of commemoration was set for the day of the Warsaw ghetto revolt (a few days later, in fact), an armed revolt that hardly relates either to the past as a history of catastrophe or to a Shoah. Surely that revolt is an heroic moment to be remembered, but to place the date of commemoration there does not really relate to the sheer destruction of the Shoah, because it looks for a message.

This decision itself, as you may know, was discussed many times, for even after it had been made, the message did not seem to penetrate. The Knesset came back to the issue five or six times: why does this day mean nothing to the young? Well, ultimately, even Menachem Begin tried to find a way (I do not speak of his political rhetoric now). He proposed to separate the two dates of Shoah and Gevurah by setting the Yom HaShoah on Tishah-b'Av and, by thus giving it a religious meaning, to make it consonant with Jewish history and its religious significance. The Yom HaGevurah he wanted to place on the day commemorating the fallen soldiers of the Israeli wars. But the Knesset opposed this, and Begin asked what the fuss was all about: "I just wanted to set those two dates, to link them to dates we understand, so that people can remember the events in generations to come." This was a rather strange comment because Begin seemed to be implying that what had been set up would be remembered only if it were somehow linked with significant events in Jewish history and within a Zionist view of the world. Now, this says a good deal in itself—that the attempt to establish a meaning seemed to have failed and that, therefore, a further attempt should be made to link the Shoah to other meaningful events.

Well, Begin's proposal failed, too, and for years one had the impression (and I speak here as an Israeli) that the events of the Shoah were disappearing from Israeli memory. Now, strangely enough, over the last two or three years, this past has come back into Israeli consciousness in the most vivid way, as it has almost everywhere else. There are today more books in Israel about the Shoah than about probably any event in Israel's history, certainly more than have been written about the creation of the State. Novels, theater pieces, discussions, historical books about the attitude of the Yishuv—the whole issue is coming back. But this time, I would say, it is coming back in a more mature society, one that has perhaps less self-assurance but more self-reflectiveness. There is no attempt to hide the Shoah; the desperation and the destruction are clear. There is no attempt to place it within a framework of heroism in order to give it a meaning; there is no attempt, so far as I know, to identify it as part of a great historical interpretation. There is the facing of the Catastrophe as such, not in search of something, nor even for coherence, but as a means of rediscovering the past. And I would say that possibly here, against what we naturally wish to do, we can reflect, each of us and all of us together: we can forgo the attempt to enclose the Shoah in our various worldviews; we can reconsider the hope of finding some redeeming aspect in it; and we can simply face it as it was, a catastrophe of absolutely untold magnitude.

Perhaps, too, by this act of reconversion, we can reach toward the artistic expression that we are looking for and that will undoubtedly entail irony. I was very impressed with Terrence Des Pres's discussion: it is not the comic that will be found there; it is really the most bitter irony, which is present, it seems to me, from the very beginning. By leaving behind the frameworks we have become accustomed to, perhaps we will come to that deepest ironic vision which is tragic-ironic, in the sense of that total chaos and senselessness referred to by Paul Fussell in his account of the "Great War in modern memory." It may be that, on the *individual* level, there is something redeeming here, moments of revelation of a world one had not known. But to speak in this way on a more global level—here, I concur with Cynthia Ozick that to look for a message in such events is certainly not for me. This certainly is the most difficult task we face: precisely *not* to look for redemption in these events.

Notes on Contributors

AHARON APPELFELD is the author of, among other novels, *Badenheim 1939, The Age of Wonders, Tsili,* and *In the Land of the Cattails.* He is Professor of Literature at the Ben-Gurion University of the Negev in Beersheba.

TERRENCE DES PRES, who died in November 1987, was Professor of English at Colgate University. He is the author of *The Survivor: Anatomy of Life in the Death Camps.*

LESLIE EPSTEIN is the author of five books of fiction, including the novel, *King of the Jews.* He directs the creative-writing program at Boston University.

SIDRA DEKOVEN EZRAHI is on the faculty of the Institute of Contemporary Jewry, in The Hebrew University, and author of *By Words Alone: The Holocaust in Literature.*

ELLEN S. FINE is Professor of French at Kingsborough Community College, City University of New York, and the author of *Legacy of Night: The Literary Universe of Elie Wiesel.*

SAUL FRIEDLÄNDER is Professor of History at the University of Tel Aviv and the University of California at Los Angeles. His writings include

Pius XII and the Third Reich, When Memory Comes, and *Reflections of Nazism.*

PHILIP HALLIE is William Griffin Professor of Philosophy and Humanities at Wesleyan University and the author, among other works, of *Cruelty* and *Lest Innocent Blood Be Shed.*

WILLIAM HEYEN is Professor of English and Poet in Residence at the State University of New York College at Brockport. A Guggenheim Fellow in poetry, his work includes *The Swastika Poems,* which have been republished, in an expanded version, in *Erika: Poems of the Holocaust.*

RAUL HILBERG is John G. McCullough Professor of Political Science at the University of Vermont and author of *The Destruction of the European Jews.*

IRVING HOWE is Emeritus Distinguished Professor of English at the City University of New York. He is the author, among other works, of *World of Our Fathers, Politics and the Novel,* and *The American Newness.*

EMMANUEL LE ROY LADURIE holds the chair of the History of Modern Civilization in the Collège de France and is the author, among other works, of *Montaillou, Le Carnaval de Romans,* and *L'État royal 1460– 1610.*

BEREL LANG is Professor of Philosophy and Humanistic Studies at the State University of New York at Albany and the author, among other works, of *Philosophy and the Art of Writing* and the forthcoming *Act and Idea: Aspects of the Nazi Genocide.*

LAWRENCE LANGER is Professor of English at Simmons College. His writings include *Versions of Survival* and *The Holocaust and the Literary Imagination.*

HOWARD NEEDLER is Professor of Letters at Wesleyan University. He collaborated with Norman Shapiro on the volume *Fables from Old French* and has published essays on medieval Italian and Hebrew literature.

CYNTHIA OZICK is the author, among her other writings, of the novels *The Cannibal Galaxy* and *The Messiah of Stockholm*. Her collection of essays, *Metaphor and Memory*, is forthcoming.

KENNETH SEESKIN is Professor of Philosophy and Chairman of the Department of Philosophy at Northwestern University. His writings include *Dialogue and Discovery: A Study in Socratic Method* and the forthcoming *Jewish Philosophy in a Secular Age*.

LORE SEGAL is Professor of English at the University of Ilinois at Chicago Circle and author of the novels *Other People's Houses* and *Her First American*.

GEORGE STEINER is Professor of English and Comparative Literature at the University of Geneva and Extraordinary Fellow of Churchill College, Cambridge. He is the author, among other works, of *Language and Silence*, *On Difficulty*, and *Antigones*.

JAMES E. YOUNG is Assistant Professor and Dorot Fellow in English and Hebrew and Judaic Studies, New York University, and author of the forthcoming book *Writing and Re-Writing the Holocaust: Narrative and the Consequences of Interpretation*.

Index